D1405789

WebSphere Certification Study Guide

An Introduction to Web Application Development with IBM WebSphere Studio

IBM Certified Associate Developer

WebSphere Certification Study Guide

An Introduction to Web Application Development with IBM WebSphere Studio

IBM Certified Associate Developer

Gary Craig and Peter Jakab

MC PRESS

An Introduction to Web Application Development with IBM WebSphere Studio
IBM Certified Associate Developer
Gary Craig and Peter Jakab
Published by MC Press Online, LP
IBM Press Associate Publisher: Tara B. Woodman, IBM Corporation
IBM Press Alliance Publisher: David M. Uptmor, MC Press

For information on translations and book distribution outside the United States or to arrange bulk-purchase discounts for sales promotions or premiums, please contact:
MC Press
Corporate Offices:
125 N. Woodland Trail
Lewisville, TX 75077

Sales and Customer Service:
P.O. Box 4300
Big Sandy, TX 75755-4300

First edition
First printing: August, 2003
ISBN: 1-931182-11-6

Every attempt has been made to provide correct information in this book. However, the publisher, the editors, and the authors do not guarantee the accuracy of the book and do not assume responsibility for information included in or omitted from it.

The following are trademarks or registered trademarks of International Business Machines Corporation in the United States, other countries, or both: DB2, Lotus, Tivoli, WebSphere, IBM, the IBM logo, IBM Press, iSeries, and the e-business logo.

Rational, Rational Developer Network, and ClearCase are registered trademarks of Rational Software Corporation and/or IBM Corporation in the United States, other countries, or both.

Microsoft, Windows, Windows NT, and the Windows logo are trademarks of Microsoft Corporation in the United States, other countries, or both.

Java and all Java-based trademarks are trademarks of Sun Microsystems, Inc., in the United States, other countries, or both.

Intel, Intel Inside (logos), MMX, and Pentium are trademarks of Intel Corporation in the United States, other countries, or both.

UNIX is a registered trademark of The Open Group in the United States and other countries, licensed exclusively through The Open Group.

Other company, product, and service names may be trademarks or service marks of others.

Dedications

To my loving wife, Judy, and my three terrific children, Andrew, Megan, and Taylor, for their support and the sacrifice they endured while we put this book together.

—Gary Craig

To my wife, Mabel, my daughter, Jessie, and my son, Justin. Without their support and encouragement this book would not have been written. And lastly, to Shadow, our black Lab, who always kept me company during the long days and nights writing this book.

—Peter Jakab

Acknowledgments and Thanks

Building and delivering a quality book is a team effort. We would like to acknowledge all those team members who contributed to this book.

First, we would like to thank Dave Russell and Tara Woodman for their vision of the book.

For our reviewers Murray Beaton, Carrie Finneran, Joan Haggarty, Yen Lu, Ernest Mah, and Scott Peddle, a special thanks for your time and valuable comments.

We are very much appreciative of Justin Jakab for his review of the exercises.

We would also like to thank Ashish Soni, whose contributions included both review and providing the glossary and sample questions.

Thanks to our copyeditor, Jerome Colburn, who did a terrific job, and to Susie Yates, for her coordination of production.

A special thanks to Merrikay Lee and Tara Woodman for their support throughout the project.

Each of these individuals has our gratitude and our thanks.

Also thanks to everyone at IBM who helped in one way or another, especially to Dan Berg for allowing us to include the Project Interchange WebSphere Studio plug-in.

Contents

Chapter 1   **Scope and coverage of the Certification Guide** 1
Technology and tools. 1
WebSphere Studio 2
Web application development 3
A dual overview of the guide 4
    Overview of the chapters 4
    Cross referencing certification objectives 6
Summary 8

Chapter 2   **System requirements and installation** 9
What's on the CDs 10
Minimum system requirements 10
Installing WebSphere Application Server – Express 11
Verifying the installation 13
    Verifying your Site Developer installation 14
    Verifying your Agent Controller installation. 14
    Verifying your Application Server installation. 14
Exercises 15

Chapter 3   **Overview of Eclipse, Studio Workbench, and WebSphere Studio. .** 23
The Eclipse Project. 23
    The Eclipse Platform 24
    Eclipse architecture 25
    The Eclipse Workbench 25
    Java Development Tools (JDT). 26

Tools from IBM 28
    WebSphere Studio configurations 28
    Role-based development, perspectives 30
Tools from other companies 32
Where to find out more 32
Test yourself 33
    Key terms 33
    Review questions 33

Chapter 4   **Developing a simple Java application** **35**
Java projects, Web applications, and Enterprise Applications 36
Working with perspectives 36
Creating Java projects 38
The Java perspective 41
    Creating a Java package 42
    Creating Java types 44
The Java editor 47
    Editor view 47
    Code assist 49
    Outline view 51
    Compiling Java source 54
Simple source control 57
Running non-Web-based Java programs 62
Exercise 65
Test yourself 74
    Key terms 74
    Review questions 74

Chapter 5   **Debugging techniques** **75**
Why and when to debug 76
Sending messages and tracing 76
Starting a program for debugging 77
Setting breakpoints in Java code 79
Debug perspective description 82
Debugger controls and stepping through code 87
    Step filtering 88
    Other controls 89
Viewing variables 90
    Toolbar buttons 92
Expressions view 93
Display view 95

Other types of breakpoints 97
    Conditional breakpoints 98
    Java Exception breakpoints 101
    Watchpoints 104
    Method breakpoints 105
Scrapbook 107
Hot code replace 110
Exercise 113
    Debug ConsoleTest.java 115
    Debug SimpleDebug.java 115
    Debug JavaExceptionTest.java 121
    Using the Scrapbook 124
Test yourself 125
    Key terms 125
    Review questions 125

Chapter 6   **Essential HTTP and HTML** **127**
Overview of HTTP 127
    Request 128
    Response 130
    Flow of request and response 132
Overview of common and essential HTML 133
    How to create HTML documents 133
    Essential HTML tags 137
The <FORM> HTML tag, its content, and its attributes 140
    Conclusion 142
Introduction to WebSphere Studio Page Designe 143
    Library view 145
    Outline view 147
    Attributes view 147
    Other views 148
Cascading Style Sheets 151
Exercise 152
Test yourself 163
    Key terms 163
    Review questions 163

Chapter 7   **Introduction to servlets** **165**
Servlet lifecycle 166
The Web Project wizard 167
The New Servlet wizard 170
Exploring servlet lifecycle 173
Testing the servlet lifecycle 174
Producing an HTTP response stream 178

J2EE application packaging and web.xml 179
Parameterizing servlets 183
Review 187
Exercise 187
Test yourself 188
    Key terms 188
    Review questions 188

Chapter 8   **Handling HTTP requests 189**
Introduction to the HTTP request 189
The HttpServletRequest Interface 191
Reading the HTTP input stream 194
Architecture of request processing 196
Using JavaScript to perform form validation 201
Review 203
Exercise 203
    Creating the registration Web page 203
    Creating the registration servlet 207
    Setting up the TCP/IP monitoring server 211
    Inspecting the HTTP Request 212
    Adding output parameter processing and output rendering 213
Test yourself 216
    Key terms 216
    Review questions 216

Chapter 9   **Case study 217**
Case study data model 217
Application use cases 220
    Use case: vendor registration 221
    Use case: vendor login 222
    Use case: vendor review and submission of invoice 223
Use case: Administration creation of purchase order 225

Chapter 10   **Application state with servlets 227**
Application state 228
Session lifetime 234
Session scaling 235
Review 235
Exercise 235
Test yourself 245
    Key terms 245
    Review questions 245

Chapter 11   **Model-View-Controller basics** **247**
The servlet as a controller 248
Refactoring view logic from controller servlets 250
Passing object references between servlets. 251
Review 251
Exercise 252
Creating the view servlet 252
Test yourself 255
Key terms 255
Review questions 255

Chapter 12   **Introduction to JavaServer Pages** **257**
Overview of JSP document structure 258
Runtime model and page compilation 258
JSP Syntax overview 259
Directives 259
Scripting elements 261
Building JSP pages with WebSphere Studio 266
Creating a new JSP page 266
Adding content in Design view 271
Editing in Source view 274
Testing and debugging JSP pages in WebSphere Studio 274
Review 276
Exercise 277
Test yourself 284
Key terms 284
Review questions 284

Chapter 13   **Considerations for building robust Web applications** **285**
Input data errors 286
Application-level exceptions and error pages 296
Review 299
Test yourself 299
Key terms 299
Review questions 299

Chapter 14   **JSP tag libraries** **301**
Motivation for using JSP tag libraries 302
Existing tag libraries 302
Jakarta tag libraries 303
JavaServer Pages Standard Library (JSTL) 303
Using custom tag libraries in WebSphere Studio 306
Creating your own custom action tags 312

Exercise 313
Test yourself 325
    Key terms 325
    Review questions 325

Chapter 15   **Accessing databases with JDBC** **327**
The JDBC 2.0 API 328
    JDBC 2.0 Core API .328
    Using JDBC 2.0 Core API fundamentals 329
    JDBC 2.0 Standard Extension API 331
    Data sources and connection pools 331
    TYPE mappings 334
Error processing 335
Transaction control 336
Basic broker/mapping architecture 337
The Data perspective 338
Exercise 345
Test yourself 353
    Key terms 353
    Review questions 353

Chapter 16   **Deploying applications** **355**
What deployment is 355
Remote server deployment from WebSphere Studio 357
Command line server administration 358
Classpath, classloaders, and module dependencies 359
    Classloaders in WebSphere 360
    Module dependencies and utility JAR files 360
Exercises 361
    Creating a remote server and server configuration 362
    Creating the data source 367
    Testing the application running on the remote server in
    WebSphere Studio 370
    Starting the remote server outside WebSphere Studio 374
    Testing the application running on the remote server 377
Test yourself 377
    Key terms 377
    Review questions 378

Appendix A   **End-of-chapter questions and answers** **379**

Index **409**

Scope and coverage of the Certification Guide

Chapter topics

- ❖ *Technology and tools*
- ❖ *WebSphere Studio*
- ❖ *WebSphere application development*
- ❖ *A dual overview of the guide*

Certification objectives

- ❖ *This chapter does not address any specific certification objectives*

Welcome to the Certification Study Guide for *An Introduction to Web Application Development with IBM WebSphere Studio.* This chapter will provide you with a context for the rest of the Certification Guide.

Technology and tools

Certifications are associated with roles. The role to which this Certification Guide applies is that of IBM Certified Associate Developer—WebSphere Studio, V5.0: that is, for new developers to the Java Platform 2, Enterprise Edition (J2EE). A person having this role provides application development services related to design, implementation, debugging, and deployment of J2EE Web applications. The specific technology components include servlets, JavaServer Pages (JSP), JavaBeans, HTML, and JDBC. Prerequisite to mastering these technologies is a background in application development using Java and the corresponding skills in building object-oriented software artifacts.

> **Note:** For complete descriptions of all available Certification tests from IBM, see *www.ibm.com/certify*. For sample tests see *certify.torolab.ibm.com*.

J2EE is a very large technology domain. Most of the enterprise Application Programming Interfaces (APIs) associated with J2EE are *not* required by this certification role nor covered by this certification guide.

A second focus of the certified role is the platform and tools used during the development tasks. In particular the IBM Certified Associate Developer—WebSphere Studio, V5.0 role is targeted to developers who are new adopters of WebSphere Application Development technology, namely WebSphere Studio products. Thus, the focus of this guide is to highlight the developer tasks performed using the WebSphere Studio application development platform.

WebSphere Studio

The WebSphere Studio product family is a collection of tools built on an open application development framework. This base, called the WebSphere Workbench, is a robust offering by IBM of the Eclipse framework (see *www.eclipse.org*). This framework allows application development tools to be *plugged in* in a very dynamic fashion. This allows the product to grow and evolve both with a development team and as technology changes.

WebSphere Studio (and Eclipse) provides a role-based organization to the Integrated Development Environment (IDE). There are distinct *perspectives* organized around the specific tools and views need to perform a specific task or series of tasks. Frequently these perspectives are structured around the type of artifacts that are being developed or tested, such as Java code, Web assets, XML documents, data access, J2EE components, and debugging. Developers can easily adapt and create their own perspectives to reflect the tasks that they perform and the way in which they perform them.

With functionality layered and plugged in, it is possible for IBM to provide different entry points for customers to purchase and use WebSphere Studio. That is why IBM currently ships a number of different products under the WebSphere Studio name (*www-3.ibm.com/software/info1/websphere/index.jsp?tab=products/studio*). The principal editions of interest to this audience are the following:

- WebSphere Studio Site Developer

- WebSphere Studio Application Developer

- WebSphere Studio Application Developer – Integration Edition

- WebSphere Studio Enterprise Edition

Each of these products has an increasing set of features. For this certification guide, all of the role-specific tasks we will be concerned with are supported by any of these editions. As you will come to appreciate through working with WebSphere Studio, this product family is a very powerful and productive development environment. For a more complete description of WebSphere Studio, check out Chapter 3. In addition, you can visit one of the Web resources listed at the end of Chapter 3.

This book ships with a copy of WebSphere Application Server – Express. This offering supplies a copy of WebSphere Studio Site Developer. This will be the edition that most of you will use to work through the exercises in the book. However, the look and feel and operations will be the same in any edition you choose to work with.

Web application development

So if the role we are targeting is involved in Web application development, what is a Web application? A Web application is server-side software that is Web enabled. In our case, Web applications refer to implementations that are accessed via the Web through a J2EE-compliant application server. As you will see in Chapter 7, the Web gateway component is a Java servlet. This is a server-side Java (J2EE) component that enables a Web (HTTP) request to be serviced by Java code running on an application server.

Java is a very powerful development platform (much more than a programming language). With the wide range of API (class libraries) available to a Java developer, the entire range of enterprise resources is available to be manipulated. Thus J2EE, and servlets in particular (along with various connector APIs), provide a rich foundation on which to Web-enable your enterprise.

Direct Web access to enterprise data and function is not likely to be attractive to information technology (IT) departments because of the obvious issues of security and data integrity that come into play. J2EE is particularly powerful in addressing those concerns. The scope of the Associate Developer role, and of its Certification and Certification Guide, is constrained to the entry-level aspects of J2EE technology. As with most things in life, you need to learn to walk before you can run. We aim to provide you with a solid foundation upon which you can start to train for a marathon in some distant future.

To appreciate the J2EE component model and the full enterprise APIs, you first need to understand the underpinnings. The J2EE Web components and JDBC are what provides that perfect entry platform. Many large IT shops that have been developing and deploying J2EE applications for many years develop Web components exclusively. So, although we are excluding a large part of J2EE (look at Tests 484 and 287 if you are interested in this more complete scope), you will still end up with a very powerful development model and deployment platform.

For a more concrete example, suppose you want to build a customer service site in which Web users can search through a problem resolution database. Such a set of integrated applications (services) can easily be written using the Java and J2EE technology presented in this Certification Guide.

Why combine a technology-based role with a specific set of application developer job tasks? Further, why target those job tasks to a particular development platform (WebSphere Studio)? Productivity! That is the simple answer. Any role-based certification tries to measure competency. In particular, it is concerned with measuring competency at performing specific tasks. Yes, I can write Java code using a simple text editor. But once my applications grow to any reasonable size, my ability to manage the components effectively and be able to maintain that code quickly (including adding new functionality) is greatly constrained by that tool set.

If, on the other hand, you or your organization chooses a development platform, then you can be productive in building applications using that development platform only if you are well versed in letting the tool(s) perform their assistive magic. A corollary to this concept is that it is important that you learn not to use the tool in a way that will cause you to be counterproductive—that is, don't fight the tool. What follows, then, is that being productive building a servlet or a JSP page implies being productive building these components using the targeted development platform, in our case WebSphere Studio.

Each of the chapters in this guide are targeted to arm you with the expertise to understand the technology components while mastering a subset of the capabilities of the WebSphere Studio family that support building, testing, debugging, and deploying those components.

A dual overview of the guide

There are two different ways to approach this Certification Guide. The first is considering the guide as a tutorial for building Web applications. For this purpose, the guide is organized in a logical progression of tools, technology, and techniques. The best overview is a quick survey of the chapters. The second approach is more certification centered. For the reader who is primarily preparing to take Test 285, we provide a cross reference to the Certification Test Objectives.

Overview of the chapters

Chapter 2, *System requirements and installation:* This chapter helps you install WebSphere Application Server – Express edition. On the CD (included with the book) is WebSphere Studio Site Developer. After completing this installation task you will be ready to start developing on the WebSphere Studio platform.

Chapter 3, *Overview of Eclipse, Studio Workbench, and Studio:* This is a very strong chapter that provides the reader with a good overview of WebSphere Studio in general and certain aspects of Site Developer in particular.

Chapter 4, *Developing a simple Java application:* The basis of much J2EE development in WebSphere Studio is the development of Java code assets. This chapter covers the Java development tools in WebSphere Studio.

Chapter 5, *Debugging techniques:* An integrated source code debugger is one of the most significant productivity tools in any IDE. The WebSphere Studio debugger is no exception. This chapter works at building your proficiency with debugging Java code in WebSphere Studio.

Chapter 6, *Essential HTTP and HTML:* Building Web applications involves building Web assets, e.g., HTML files and JSP files. To be effective you must have a good working knowledge of HTTP and HTML.

Chapter 7, *Introduction to servlets:* The heart of the Web application, servlets, are explored in this chapter.

Chapter 8, *Handling HTTP requests:* Most servlet processing comes down to working with the HttpServletRequest and HttpServletResponse objects. Much of the response object processing is covered in Chapter 7. Chapter 8 looks at processing incoming request parameters and having them affect business processing.

Chapter 9, *Case study:* This is an overview of the use cases associated with a simple purchase order/invoicing application used to illustrate concepts throughout the rest of the Certification Guide.

Chapter 10, *Application state with servlets:* A single servlet rarely represents an entire application. Therefore the server needs to remember the application state of a user that makes several HTTP requests in order to carry out the application behavior. This chapter looks at the HttpSession API to manage application state within the J2EE Web Container.

Chapter 11, *Model-View-Controller basics:* Application layering is an extremely important tool when building software. Web application development is no exception. Model-View-Controller (MVC) is a common framework or pattern for isolating distinct application layers and structuring your code. The result is assigning application components to the appropriate layer.

Chapter 12, *Introduction to JavaServer pages:* The chapter surveys the basics of JavaServer Pages (JSP). This is a powerful scripting technology for building dynamic presentation (View) logic.

Chapter 13, *Controller design principles:* With MVC and more involved application designs, error handling, exceptions, logging, and such issues need to be addressed in a thoughtful way. This chapter looks at several of these design principles.

Chapter 14, *JSP tag libraries:* One of the tools used to extend JSP is the use of Custom Tags. These can be used to greatly improve readability and maintainability (as well as reuse) in JSP. This chapter looks at the mechanism to define custom tags while focusing on standard tag libraries (JSTL).

Chapter 15, *Accessing databases with JDBC:* We can't do business logic without some sort of connectivity API. JDBC is a central component in building Web applications. This chapter shows how to use JDBC with J2EE data sources to access corporate data located in relational data stores.

Chapter 16, *Deploying applications:* Finally, you have built, tested, and debugged your applications (over and over) within the development environment. So now you want to deploy to WebSphere Express. This is the chapter for you.

If you are ready, go ahead and jump off to the point that seems most appropriate to you. If you are not immediately going to build code from the product on the accompanying CD, start with Chapter 3. If you already have some level of experience with basic J2EE or even WebSphere Studio, start wherever is appropriate.

Cross referencing certification objectives

Certification Test Objective	Corresponding Chapter(s)
1. WORKBENCH BASICS	
A. Create J2EE projects	Chapters 3, 7, and 12 (and others)
B. Set workbench preferences	Chapter 3
C. Work with perspectives	Chapter 3
D. Import to and export from the workbench	Chapter 3 (and various)
E. Use the Help feature to aid in development activities	Chapter 3
2. JAVA DEVELOPMENT	
A. Create Java project, packages, classes, methods	Chapters 3 and 4
B. Use outline view	Chapters 4 and 6
C. Use Java browsing view	Chapter 4
D. Use refactoring features	Chapters 3, 4, and 11

E. Use content assist function	Chapters 3, 4, and 12
F. Add and organize import declarations	Chapter 4
G. Use search function	Various
H. Use task view	Chapter 4
I. Use hierarchy view	Chapter 4
J. Use property dialogs	Various

3. WEB DEVELOPMENT

A. Create a Web project	Chapters 7 and 12
B. Create resources in appropriate J2EE locations	Chapters 7–14
C. Understand classpath and module dependencies	Chapter 16
D. Use Page Designer to add and modify HTML and JSP content, including the use of JavaScript	Chapters 6 and 12
E. Use content assist	Chapters 6 and 12
F. Work with Web Application Deployment Descriptor using web.xml editor	Chapters 7 and 13
G. Use Web Page Wizards	Chapters 6 and 12

4. RUNNING APPLICATIONS

A. Create server instance and server configuration	Chapters 7 and 8
B. Configure data sources	Chapter 15
C. Understand session manager	Chapters 10 and 16
D. Run/operate server	Chapters 7–15
E. Export J2EE applications	Chapter 16

5. DEBUGGING

A. Set breakpoints	Chapter 5
B. Step through code	Chapter 5
C. View variables (e.g., display expressions and use inspectors)	Chapter 5
D. Create and run code in Scrapbook Page	Chapter 5
E. Perform JSP debugging	Chapter 12

6. DATA

A. Create connection and load catalog into a project	Chapter 15
B. Create schema and generate DDL	Chapter 15

Summary

Throughout the book there are many examples to take you through the aspects of Web application development with WebSphere Studio. Most of the chapters end with a significant exercise that walks you through the steps of performing the key tasks covered in those chapters. We are confident that the total package will significantly improve your understanding and competency at developing, testing, debugging, and deploying Web components using WebSphere Studio.

2

System requirements and installation

Chapter topics

- ❖ *What's on the CDs*
- ❖ *Minimum system requirements*
- ❖ *Installing WebSphere Application Server – Express*
- ❖ *Verifying the installation*
- ❖ *Exercises*

Certification objectives

- ❖ *This chapter does not address any specific certification objectives*

This chapter describes the system requirements for the installation of the software required to complete the exercises in this book. It also reveals the contents of the accompanying CD and walks you through the installation of WebSphere Application Server – Express.

Important: Please be sure to read the readme.html information file on the root of the CD-ROM. It contains important last minute information that could not make it in time for printing in the book. Please read this file in its entirety before you continue.

What's on the CD

The CD that comes with this book includes the following IBM program products:

- WebSphere Application Server – Express edition, which in turn contains:
  - WebSphere Application Server Version 5
  - WebSphere Studio Site Developer Version 5
  - IBM Agent Controller Version 5

In addition, the code necessary for the samples and exercises in this book is also included. As you are about to learn, WebSphere Studio can work with multiple work-spaces, each of which contains all the projects and folders that make up an application. For teaching purposes, start-up and completed workspaces for the exercises can be found on the CD. Later you will be taught how to load a specific workspace at the start of an exercise.

Minimum system requirements

For a developer to be effective and experience good response from the development tools and servers, the minimum system configuration is as follows:

Table 2.1: Minimum hardware requirements.

Component	Minimum requirement
CPU	Pentium III running at 500 MHz
Display resolution	800X600
RAM	512 MB (768 MB recommended)
Disk space	620 MB for all components
	For tools only on one machine: 650 MB minimum for installing WebSphere Application Server – Express and additional disk space for your development resources.
	For tools and remote server on one machine: 750 MB minimum for installing WebSphere Studio Site Developer and additional disk space for your development resources.
	For remote server alone on one machine for Windows NT and Windows 2000: 100 MB minimum for installation (includes SDK). You will also require additional disk space if you download the electronic image to install WebSphere Application Server – Express.
	For remote server alone on one machine for Linux on Intel (must have this separate machine for the server if using Red Hat Linux). 100 MB minimum for installation (includes SDK). Additional disk space is required for the electronic image if you are using it to install Websphere Application Server – Express.
Space for exercises	50 MB for all workspaces

WebSphere Application Server – Express is supported in the following Windows versions:

- Windows® 2000 Server or Advanced Server with Service Pack 3 or higher, remote server component only

- Windows® 2000 Professional with Service Pack 2 or higher, WebSphere Studio tools and server components

- Windows XP Professional for the Studio tools and server components

- Windows NT® Workstation Version 4.0 with Service Pack 6a or higher, WebSphere Studio tools component including the unit test environment only

- Windows NT® Server Version 4.0 with Service Pack 6a or higher, WebSphere Studio tools and server components

WebSphere Application Server – Express is supported in the following Linux versions:

- Red Hat, Version 7.2 for the WebSphere Studio tools component, including the unit test environment only

- Red Hat, Version AS 2.1 for the remote server component only

- SuSE, Version 7.2 WebSphere Studio tools component including the unit test environment only

- SuSE, Version 7.3 remote server component only

Note: The CD in this book does not include a Linux version of WebSphere Studio.

You should also have Microsoft® Internet Explorer 5.5 with Service Pack 1 or higher, or Netscape Navigator Version 4.76. These browsers are used to test some of the exercises, and Internet Explorer is used internally by WebSphere Studio for previewing HTML and JSP pages at development time.

Installing WebSphere Application Server – Express

If you already have installed your own copy of WebSphere Studio Site Developer (or WebSphere Studio Application Developer) and WebSphere Application Server, all at version 5.X, you do not need to install the program products on the CD.

Before you install the product, check the following items:

1. In addition to the space required to install the product, you must have at least 50 MB free on your Windows system drive, and your environment variable TEMP or TMP must point to a valid temporary directory with at least 10 MB free.

2. You must *not* have the IBM HTTP server, WebSphere Application Server, Version 3.5, or any other Web server running.

3. If you have a previous copy of WebSphere Application Server – Express on your system, you should uninstall it before proceeding. As an additional safety measure, reboot after the uninstall program completes.

4. If you have a previous copy of IBM Agent Controller on your system, you should uninstall it before proceeding.

5. If you have a previous copy of WebSphere Studio Site Developer on your system you should uninstall it before proceeding.

To install WebSphere Application Server – Express from the product CD, follow these steps:

1. Insert the CD-ROM into your CD drive.

2. Log in as an administrator whose Windows user ID does not contain DBCS characters.

3. If autorun is enabled on your system, the launchpad program will automatically come up. If autorun is disabled on your system, run **launchpad.exe** from root of the CD drive.

4. The WebSphere Application Server – Express installation launcher window contains several links that you can select to browse the readme file, the *Installation Guide*, the *Getting Started Guide*, the *Migration Guide*, or the Web development interactive tour. Click **Install** to begin installing the product. Click **Exit** to close the launchpad at any time. The launchpad does not have to remain running during the product installation.

5. Follow the on-screen instructions for tasks such as specifying the target installation directory.

   ◆ A typical install will install both WebSphere Studio Site Developer and the Application Server.

   ◆ A custom install allows you to select Site Developer, Application Server, or both.

6. **Important:** Do not install into a directory whose name contains DBCS characters. Doing so may cause undesirable results, such as classpath problems in the WebSphere test environment.

7. Note that the full install takes between 10 and 30 minutes depending on your hardware configuration.

8. When WebSphere Application Server – Express is installed, click **Finish** to close the installation window.

9. If any errors are reported, refer to the indicated log file (expressInstallLog in the install destination directory) for more information.

10. You will use WebSphere Studio Site Developer to create and to deploy applications to Application Server. In addition, you will use WebSphere Studio Site Developer to administer (start, stop, change configurations) Application Server. You can start WebSphere Studio Site Developer from the **Start** → **Programs** → **IBM WebSphere Application Server – Express V5.0** menu.

Verifying the installation

After installing WebSphere Application Server – Express, you should have the following directory structure under the install path that you selected during the install (which we will refer to as <Expressinstallpath> from now on):

■ **_uninst:** three files for uninstalling Express.

■ **AppServer:**Application Server files (approximately 950 files)

■ **Express:** Miscellaneous files for databases and scripts (approximately 360 files)

■ **License:** approximately 17 license files

■ **RAC:** IBM Agent Controller files—approximately 40 files

■ **readme:** the readme, installation guide, and the Getting Started PDF

■ **SiteDeveloper:** WebSphere Studio Site Developer files (approximately 22,500 files)

■ **Tour:** Flash tutorial of using WebSphere Studio Site Developer (approximately 350 files)

If any of these directories contains a substantially different number of files, then you should suspect a problem happened during installation. Look at the **expressInstallLog.txt** file in <Expressinstallpath> to diagnose the problem.

Verifying your Site Developer installation

First look at the wssdInstallLog.txt file in the <Expressinstallpath>. Go to the bottom and check the install completion status. If the installation completed successfully, start Site Developer through the **Start → Programs → Express v5.0 → Studio Site Developer** menu item. Once Site Developer starts, follow the links on the Welcome page to load and run one of the Express examples.

If the installation did not complete successfully, look through the wssdInstallLog.txt to determine the reason. If the wssdInstallLog.txt file does not exist, then it could mean that another version of WebSphere Studio Site Developer is already on the system. Uninstall the other version and retry the installation. Another technique for determining the install problem is to run the Site Developer install directly to see whether errors are reported. You can run the Site Developer install by going to the wssd\win32 directory on the WebSphere Application Server – Express CD and clicking on **setup.exe**.

Verifying your Agent Controller installation

First look at the racInstallLog.txt file in the <Expressinstallpath>. Go to the bottom and check the install completion status. If the installation completed successfully, then check that IBM Agent Controller it is running. The IBM Agent Controller is always installed as a Windows service and is automatically started. IBM Agent Controller provides the communication channel between Site Developer and Application Server. Check the **Control Panel → Administrative Tools → Services** to see that IBM Agent Controller is listed and running. If you suspect a problem, take a look at the servicelog.log file in the <Expressinstallpath>\RAC\config directory.

If the installation did not complete successfully, look through the racInstallLog.txt to determine the reason. If the racInstallLog.txt file does not exist, then it could mean that another version of IBM Agent Controller is already on the system. Uninstall the other version and retry the installation. Another technique for determining the install problem is to run the IBM Agent Controller install directly to see whether errors are reported. You can run the IBM Agent Controller install by going to the RAC\win32 directory on the WebSphere Application Server – Express CD and clicking on **setup.exe**.

Verifying your Application Server installation

You can verify the basic operation of your Application Server installation by running the <Expressinstallpath>**Express\bin\testServer.bat** file. This batch file will step through starting and stopping the Application Server using its default configuration. Note that this batch file is used only for testing your server installation. During normal use you will use WebSphere Studio Site Developer for starting, stopping, and configuring the Application Server.

Exercises

In this exercise you install WebSphere Application Server – Express on your computer.

Before installing, please read the licensing statements for the product and make sure that you agree with its terms and conditions.

Place the CD that came with this book on you CD-ROM drive. The installation program should start on its own if your machine has AutoPlay enabled. If the Launchpad program does not start on its own after inserting the CD, explore the CD contents and double-click the file **launchpad.exe**. This will start the WebSphere Application Server – Express Launchpad program (Figure 2.1), from which you can perform several tasks, including the installation of the product.

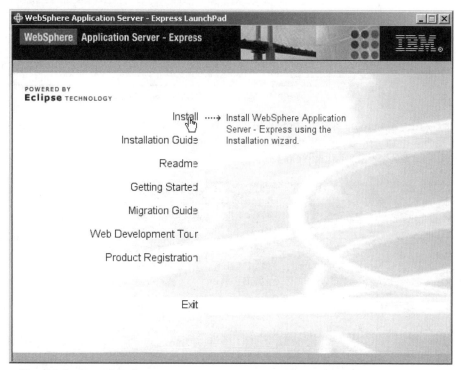

Figure 2.1: Launchpad program.

Select the **Install** option from the dialog.

The splash screen (Figure 2.2) appears for a few moments while the installer starts.

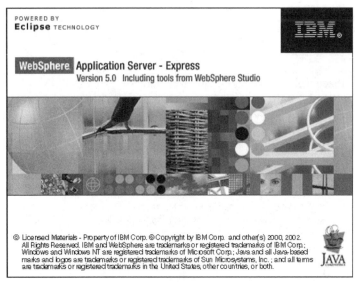

Figure 2.2: WebSphere Application Server – Express splash screen.

When the splash screen disappears, a series of dialogs will walk you through the installation of the product. The first installer dialog (Figure 2.3) welcomes you to the installation program. Click **Next** to continue.

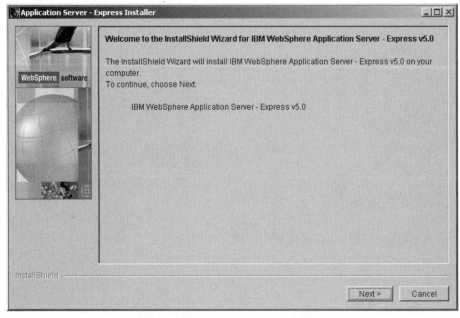

Figure 2.3: Application Server – Express Installer welcome dialog.

Please make sure you read the Software License Agreement on the next dialog (Figure 2.4). If you agree with the Terms and Conditions, indicate so by selecting the **I accept the terms in the license agreement** radio button and clicking **Next**.

If you do not accept the license agreement, the **Next** button will not become enabled, and you will need to click **Cancel** to exit the installer.

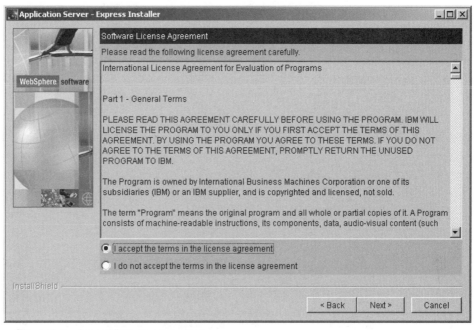

Figure 2.4: Accept license agreement.

After accepting the license agreement, click the **Typical** radio button on the next dialog panel (Figure 2.5) and then click **Next**.

Clicking Custom instead of Typical will present you with a screen where you can select which of the products contained in the CD you install.

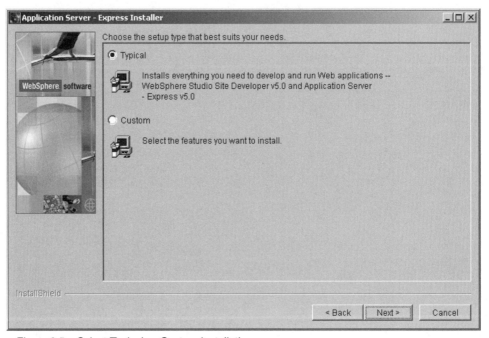

Figure 2.5: Select Typical or Custom installation.

On the next screen (Figure 2.6) you are presented with the default installation directory for the products. You may take the default or change it to the directory of your choice. We will assume that you have taken the default. Click **Next**.

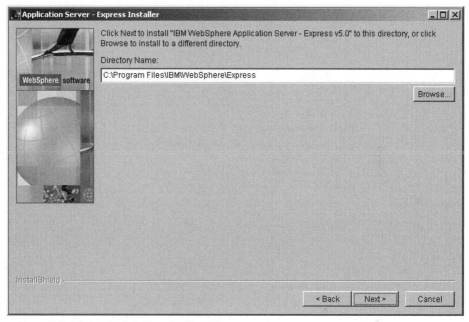

Figure 2.6: Select installation directory.

The installation confirmation dialog (Figure 2.7) shows you the products that will be installed and the amount of disk space that is needed. Click **Next**.

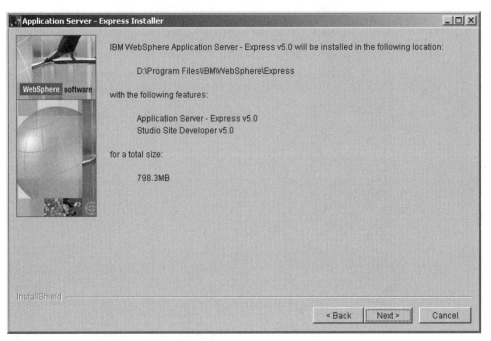

Figure 2.7: Installation confirmation dialog.

After you confirm that you wish to proceed, the next dialog (Figure 2.8) shows the progress of the installation.

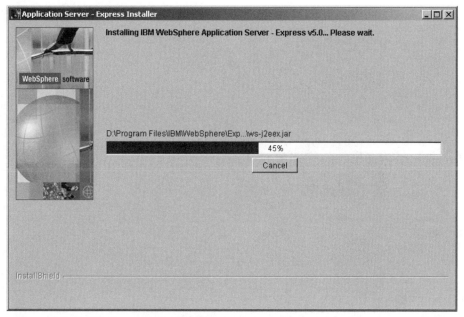

Figure 2.8: Installation progress indicator.

Depending on your machine's configuration this step may take quite a while; in fact, you may think that something is wrong when the installation for WebSphere Studio starts. Please be patient and do *not* interrupt the install at this point.

Wait until this process completes. When it does, the closing dialog appears (Figure 2.9) to inform you of the status of the completion of the installation.

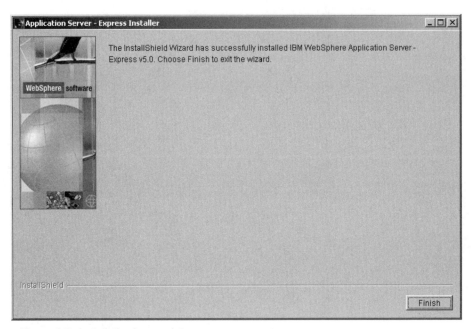

Figure 2.9: Installation is complete.

Ensure that no errors occurred, and click **Finish** to exit the installer.

During the next chapters of the book you will get a chance to verify that the installation completed successfully.

At this time you will be returned to the Launchpad. Feel free to explore the other options on its menu. You are encouraged to register the products you've just installed.

Overview of Eclipse, Studio Workbench, and WebSphere Studio

Chapter topics

- ❖ *The Eclipse project*
- ❖ *Tools from IBM*
- ❖ *Tools from other companies*
- ❖ *Resources for more information*

Certification objectives

- ❖ *Create J2EE projects*
- ❖ *Set workbench preferences*
- ❖ *Work with perspectives*
- ❖ *Import to and export from the workbench*
- ❖ *Use the Help feature to aid in development activities*
- ❖ *Create Java projects, packages, classes, and methods*
- ❖ *Use refactoring features*
- ❖ *Use content assist function*

In this chapter you will learn the differences between Eclipse, the Workbench, WebSphere Studio, and its different versions and editions.

The Eclipse Project

The Eclipse Project is an open-source software development project dedicated to providing a robust, full-featured, commercial-quality industry platform for the development of highly integrated tools. It is composed of three subprojects: Platform, JDT (Java Development Tools), and PDE (Plug-in Development Environment). The success of the

Eclipse Platform depends on how well it enables a wide range of tool builders to build best-of-breed integrated tools. But the real vision of Eclipse as an industry platform is realized only if these tools from different tool builders can be combined together by users to suit their unique requirements in ways that the tool builders never even imagined. The mission of the Eclipse Project is to adapt and evolve the Eclipse Platform and associated tools to meet the needs of the tool-building community and its users, so that the vision of Eclipse as an industry platform is realized.

The Eclipse project is an open-source project that concentrates on developing the base code for tool developers and manufacturers to use to create their own tools. The resulting product is what is normally referred to as the Workbench.

The Eclipse Platform

The Eclipse Platform is a new open-source environment for creating, integrating, and deploying application development tools for use across a broad range of computing technology. It provides a common set of services and establishes the framework, infrastructure, and interactive workbench used by project developers to build application software and related elements.

Through the Eclipse Platform, smooth integration of tools from several different vendors will be possible on Microsoft® Windows®, Linux®, and QNX developer workstations.

The Eclipse Platform provides user interface perspectives specific to different developer roles. A perspective is a predefined, yet user-configurable, set of views of tools and data that is added to the environment. The end result is an environment that offers an unprecedented level of flexibility in supporting each development role on the team. The Eclipse Platform is designed to:

- Build integrated development environments (IDEs)

- Support multiple tool providers

- Support tools used to create and manipulate any development artifacts

- Support integration of multiple Java runtime environments

- Support integration of multiple test and deployment environments

- Facilitate integration of tools and provide access to cross-platform services

- Run on Microsoft Windows and Linux operating systems

The Eclipse Platform can enable two fundamental improvements for both application developers and tool vendors during the application development process:

■ *Developers can use any plug-in tool.* In the same environment you can have a consistent user interface, code management, and testing experience. And because of this innovation, developers are not unnecessarily burdened with having to export an artifact, open a different tool, import the artifact, convert it, work with it, and then compile, test, save, and export the artifacts using yet additional tools. All development tasks can instead be performed in the same environment.

■ *Tool vendors can focus on domain-specific tool function* rather than having to maintain and support all services needed to use a tool, such as user interface and object storage. This feature makes it easier to develop a new tool and have it instantly integrated on an established platform.

Eclipse architecture

The Eclipse is a universal platform for integrating development tools. Eclipse offers a microkernel based architecture (see Figure 3.1) that is open and extensible. All functionality is supplied through plug-ins.

The platform's runtime handles the startup and discovers any installed plug-ins. Each plug-in is loaded and initialized only when the user selects its functionality from an action or menu item.

The Plug-in Development toolkit provides tools for toolmakers to create their own plug-ins.

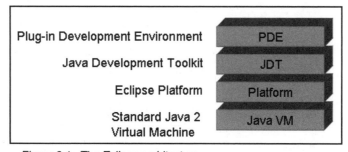

Figure 3.1: The Eclipse architecture.

The Eclipse Workbench

The Workbench provides toolmakers with an integration framework on top of which other, more sophisticated and specialized tools can be built upon.

The Eclipse Workbench is provided free of charge. It is available on the World Wide Web at *www.eclipse.org*.

The Workbench provides the user interface necessary to use the tools built on Eclipse. The Workbench presents its user interface in the way of Perspectives, Views, and Editors.

A Perspective is a collection of related views that make performing a particular task easier. For example, a Java perspective would present a user interface comprising a Java package view, a Java source editor, and a view of all outstanding errors.

Java Development Tools (JDT)

The JDT project contributes a set of plug-ins that add the capabilities of a full-featured Java IDE to the Eclipse platform. The JDT plug-ins provide application programming interfaces (APIs) so that they can themselves be further extended by other tool builders. The JDT plug-ins are categorized into the JDT Core, the JDT user interface (UI), and JDT Debug.

JDT Core

The JDT Core defines the non-UI infrastructure. It includes the following:

- An incremental Java builder

- A Java Model, which provides API for navigating the Java element tree

- Code assist and code select support

- An index-based search infrastructure that is used for searching, code assist, type hierarchy computation, and refactoring

- Evaluation support

The Java element tree defines a Java-centric view of a project. It surfaces elements such as package fragments, compilation units, binary classes, types, methods, and fields.

The JDT Core infrastructure has no built-in Sun Java Development Kit (JDK) version dependencies, as it provides the required files as part of its installation.

JDT UI

The JDT UI implements Java-specific workbench contributions:

- Packages view

- Type Hierarchy view

- Java Outline view

- Wizards for creating Java elements

- Java editor

The Java editor provides the following features:

- Keyword and syntax coloring

- Context-specific (Java, Javadoc) code assist and code select

- Method-level edit

- Margin annotations for problems, breakpoints, and search matches

- Outliner updating as editing takes place

- API help shows Javadoc specification for the selected Java element in a pop-up window

- Import assistance automatically creates and organizes import declarations

- Code formatting

The JDT UI provides refactoring support such as *Extract Method* or *Safe Rename* for Java elements that also updates references. Users can preview (and veto) individual changes stemming from a refactoring operation.

JDT searching support implements precise searches such as finding declarations of and references to packages, types, methods, and fields, scoped to the workspace, a working set, or the current selection.

JDT compare support implements a structured compare of Java compilation units, showing the changes to individual Java methods. It supports replacing individual Java elements with versions of the elements from the local history.

JDT Debug
JDT Debug implements Java debugging support and works with any JDPA-compliant target Java virtual machine (JVM). It is implemented on top of the language-independent "debug model" provided by the platform debugger.

JDT Debug provides the following debugging features:

- Launching of a JVM in either run or debug mode

- Attaching to a running JVM

- Expression evaluation in the context of a stack frame

- Scrapbook pages for interactive Java code snippet evaluation

- Dynamic class reloading where supported by JVM

Plug-in Development Environment

The PDE project provides a number of views and editors that make it easier to build plug-ins for Eclipse. Using the PDE, you can create the plug-in manifest file (plugin.xml); specify your plug-in runtime and other required plug-ins; define extension points, including their specific markup; associate XML Schema files with the extension point markup so that extensions can be validated; create extensions on other plug-in extension points, and so forth. The PDE makes integrating plug-ins easy and fun.

Plug-ins are written in Java, and the PDE provides a development and test environment to facilitate the creation of plug-ins.

The development of Eclipse plug-ins is beyond the scope of this book. If you wish to learn more about how to create plug-ins, refer to the Eclipse Web site: *www.eclipse.org*. Also, documentation and samples included with IBM WebSphere Studio products provide you with a good starting point.

Products built on top of Eclipse from IBM and others

When you download Eclipse from its Web site, you get the basic components, which are free of charge and provide the base for tool developers to construct their own specialized products. These components are the Eclipse Platform, the Java Development Toolkit, and the Plug-in Development Environment.

Currently there are several commercial products built on the Eclipse base, and more are becoming available all the time. Some of these products are stand-alone, and others are specialized plug-ins that work to provide additional, or enhanced, function to the stand-alone products. These products will be discussed in the next two sections.

Tools from IBM

IBM WebSphere Studio is available in several configurations for varied uses.

WebSphere Studio configurations

Homepage Builder

WebSphere Studio Homepage Builder is used to develop Web pages and simple Web sites. Although it is not currently implemented on the Eclipse Platform, it provides easy-to-use yet powerful tools for individual Web site developers.

Device Developer

WebSphere Studio Device Developer is used to develop embedded Java 2 Platform, Micro Edition (J2ME) applications. It is an integrated development environment for the creation and testing of applications that will be deployed on hand-held and other small devices.

Site Developer
For developing Web applications, WebSphere Site Developer provides a comprehensive, integrated suite of tools for creating, managing, and maintaining dynamic Web applications and supports the latest Web standards, including Java-based technology, JavaServer Pages (JSP) components, HTML, DHTML, XML, and Web services.

Application Developer
For developing end-to-end Java 2 Platform, Enterprise Edition (J2EE) applications, WebSphere Application Developer is award-winning J2EE development environment has integrated support for Java-based technology, Web, XML, Web services, and Enterprise JavaBean (EJB) components.

Application Developer, Integration Edition
WebSphere Application Developer, Integration Edition, consists of WebSphere Application Developer plus powerful graphical tools to build custom application adapters: flow-based tools that visually define the sequence and flow of information between application artifacts such as adapters, EJB components, Web services, or other flows. Wizards are used to build and deploy complex Web services from adapters, EJB components, flows, and other Web services.

Enterprise Developer
For developing end-to-end enterprise applications, WebSphere Studio Enterprise Developer offers a complete set of tools covering all aspects of development, from Web page creation, to Web services, to J2EE development, to enterprise connectors, to COBOL and PL/I development and maintenance, and to component generation using Enterprise Generation Language.

Asset Analyzer
WebSphere Studio Asset Analyzer is a tool that provides rapid inventory, understanding, and impact analysis of enterprise applications in order to simplify the integration of existing applications into an e-business environment.

In this book we will concentrate on the details of how the Site Developer and Application Developer versions of WebSphere Studio can be used to develop Web applications.

Differences between IBM WebSphere Studio editions
The main difference between IBM WebSphere Studio Site Developer and Application Developer configurations is that in addition to all the function available in Site Developer, Application Developer also includes an EJB development and test environment.

The look and feel of both configurations is exactly the same. Only the added function is what makes the difference.

Role-based development, perspectives

The WebSphere Studio family of tools embraces role-based development. There are many roles required to complete a Web application. Many people with different skills and roles contribute to the design, development, testing, debugging, and deployment of a Web application.

Someone in your organization may play the role of Web developer, Page Designer, J2EE developer, Database Administrator, and so forth. Some individuals may play multiple roles, while other roles will be shared by multiple individuals.

IBM, through WebSphere Studio, provides tools for all these roles. All roles use a common tool and have access to all of the assets that make up the Web application. However, each role has different needs and requires a different way to look and work with these assets.

Roles are represented in WebSphere Studio products by perspectives. A perspective is a collection of views and editors to satisfy the needs of a particular role. For example, the Java perspective of the Application Developer edition of WebSphere Studio presents views and editors to the Java developer role.

As you can see in Figure 3.2, the default Java perspective is made up of four views:

1. The Package Explorer view and the Hierarchy view are stacked on the left-hand side.

2. The Java editor view is in the middle.

3. The Outline view is on the right.

4. The Tasks view occupies most of the bottom of the window.

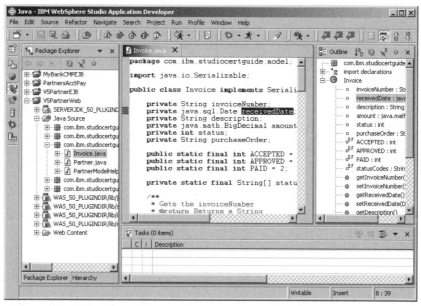

Figure 3.2: Java perspective.

The following are some of the other perspectives found in WebSphere Studio products:

- J2EE
- Servers
- Web
- Data
- Debug
- Profiling
- XML

We will work with many of these perspectives on this book, while others will go unmentioned. When we first encounter a perspective, we will explain its function and suggest to you when it would be advantageous to use a particular perspective over another. Many perspectives share the same views, so the same function can be accomplished without having to jump perspectives. Also, you can customize an existing perspective to suit the needs of your role, or just how you like to work. These new perspectives can be saved under their own name and used when necessary. The editor's view is shared by all perspectives, so that you can access any open file from every open perspective.

You can rearrange the views on a perspective by dragging and dropping to a new location. Views can also be maximized by double-clicking their title bars. Double-click the title bar a second time to restore their original size and position. It is possible to rearrange a perspective to the point where it is not useful anymore. Perspectives are easily restored to their pristine state by selecting **Window** → **Reset Perspective** from the main menu bar.

Tools from other companies

Several of the members of the Eclipse Consortium have built, or are in the process of building, other tools using Eclipse. A partial list follows:

- Rational® XDE™ Professional v2002: Java™ Platform
- Rational® Clearcase® Plug-in for Eclipse: Windows
- Instantiations CodePro Studio V1.1
- Parasoft Jtest 4.5a
- Versant enJin 2.2.3
- Merant PVCS Version Manager 6.8
- Serena ChangeMan DS
- Starbase StarTeam Studio Integration Version 1.0
- Telelogic Technologies North America, Telelogic CM Synergy 6.2

Where to find out more

To obtain additional information on Eclipse, or to get the latest Eclipse drivers, visit *www.eclipse.org*.

To obtain more information on IBM Application Development products, visit *www.ibm.com/software/ad*.

For technical information, interesting articles, product downloads, product updates, and fixes, become a member of the IBM WebSphere Developer Domain community at *www7b.boulder.ibm.com/wsdd/*.

For information on products from other companies developed using Eclipse, see their individual Web sites. Links to most can be found at *www.eclipse.org/org/index.html*.

Test yourself

Key terms

open source

Eclipse Platform

Eclipse Workbench

plug-ins

perspective

views

Editor

Java virtual machine (JVM)

J2EE

Review questions

1. What is the Eclipse?

2. What is the Eclipse Project?

3. What are the three main subprojects of the Eclipse Project?

4. What is the Eclipse Platform? What are its main features?

5. What is the Eclipse Workbench?

6. What are plug-ins? How do they make Eclipse a great IDE?

7. List a few features provided by the Java editor.

8. How do I find out about future releases of the Eclipse Platform and IBM WebSphere Studio?

9. What is a perspective is a collection of?
   a. Views
   b. Editors
   c. Outline
   d. Tools

10. What features does the Java editor provide?

Developing a simple Java application

Chapter topics

- ❖ *Java projects, Web applications, and Enterprise Applications*
- ❖ *Working with perspectives*
- ❖ *Creating Java projects*
- ❖ *The Java perspective*
- ❖ *Creating a Java package*
- ❖ *Creating Java types*
- ❖ *The Java editor*
- ❖ *Simple source control*
- ❖ *Running non-Web-based Java programs*

Certification objectives

- ❖ *Create Java projects, packages, classes, and methods*
- ❖ *Use outline view*
- ❖ *Use Java browsing view*
- ❖ *Use refactoring features*
- ❖ *Use content assist function*
- ❖ *Add and organize import declarations*
- ❖ *Use task view*
- ❖ *Use hierarchy view*

In this chapter you will start to use WebSphere Studio. You will develop a simple "Hello World" type Java application. The purpose of this chapter is to become familiar with the tool before we proceed to more complex topics.

We will cover the Java perspective in detail, including how to create basic Java constructs such as projects, packages, classes, and methods. We will also look at how WebSphere Studio makes it easy to be very productive when writing Java code.

You will also learn how to run a simple Java application from the WebSphere Studio IDE and then how to export and run it as a stand-alone Java application outside the development environment.

Java projects, Web applications, and Enterprise Applications

If you are creating Java utility classes or stand-alone Java applications, you can start creating the packages and classes for the application under a Java Project. Java projects are not directly associated with a J2EE Enterprise Application, although an archive file (JAR) constructed from a Java project can be used to provide utility classes required by one or more Enterprise Applications. In turn these Enterprise Applications can contain any combination of Application Client Projects, Web Projects, and EJB Projects.

By contrast, Application Client Projects, Web Projects, and EJB Projects have to be associated with an Enterprise Application when created in WebSphere Studio. WebSphere Studio ensures that any of these components are created in the correct structure, with the correct deployment descriptors as prescribed by the J2EE specification. More information about J2EE can be found on the Javasoft website at *www.javasoft.com*. WebSphere Studio supports both the 1.2 and 1.3 version of the J2EE specification.

Later in this book, when we cover Web applications, we will discuss in more detail some aspects of how the J2EE specification is applied and enforced by WebSphere Studio. In this chapter, we will just concentrate in learning the basic steps to creating a very simple, stand-alone Java application.

Working with perspectives

As mentioned in the previous chapter, WebSphere Studio is a role-based development tool. Roles are supported by perspectives, each of which combines various panes, views, and editors to facilitate the development tasks associated with its particular role. For developing Java applications, the most convenient perspective to use is the Java perspective.

Several perspectives can be opened in WebSphere Studio. Only one perspective is visible at any one time. This allows you to switch to a perspective that best fits the role you are performing at the time. It is not uncommon to have multiple perspectives open while working in WebSphere Studio.

WebSphere Studio remembers which perspectives were open when you last closed the workbench. These same perspectives appear the next time WebSphere Studio is started up, with the last visible perspective shown in the foreground.

Open perspectives are indicated as icons on the vertical toolbar on the left-hand side of the WebSphere Studio window. This toolbar is also called the shortcut bar, and it is used not only to indicate which perspectives are open and available, but also to switch quickly between them (Figure 4.1).

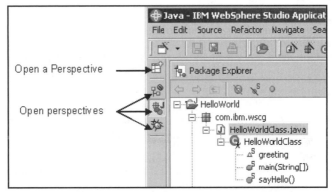

Figure 4.1: Perspectives open and available on workbench.

Another way to open a perspective is to select **Window** → **Open Perspective** from the main menu bar. If the perspective you are looking for is not visible on the list, select **Other**. This brings up a dialog listing all available perspectives (Figure 4.2). Select the one you wish to add to the workbench and click **OK**.

Figure 4.2: Available perspectives.

The Select Perspective dialog shows all predefined perspectives and any perspectives that you have customized and saved.

We will look at customizing perspectives in the next chapter, where you will customize the Debug perspective for debugging Java programs.

Creating Java projects

In WebSphere Studio, packages and classes cannot be created without associating them with a Java project. Java projects have no equivalent construct outside the tool; they are merely an organizational artifact to keep related packages and their classes in one logical place.

Under a Java project, you create packages and types (classes and interfaces), which make up the application. Another use of a Java project is to group a collection of classes that will provide utilities, or common function, to an Enterprise Application. Java projects can be exported as libraries in Java Archive (JAR) files and included in the classpath of other applications, so that the classes therein can be used.

Creating a Java project is a very simple action in WebSphere Studio. Like most tasks in WebSphere Studio, creating programming elements can be done in more than one way.

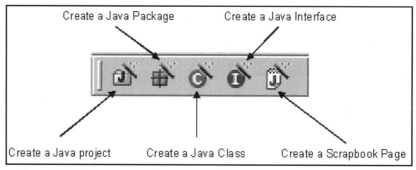

Figure 4.3: Java programming element toolbar icons.

For example you may click the toolbar icon shown in Figure 4.3, or you choose **File** → **New** → **Other** → **Java** → **Java Project** from the main menu bar. As you can see from Figure 4.4, the New dialog presents you with all the choices for creating new programming elements in WebSphere Studio.

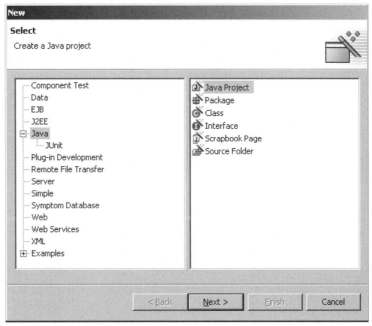

Figure 4.4: New dialog.

Regardless of which method you decide to use to get to the process of creating the new Java project, the next dialog you see is the one shown in Figure 4.5, where you define the name of the project and where the files, which will make up the project, will be stored on the file system. Most of the time there is no reason to change the default directory, but you can if you have to.

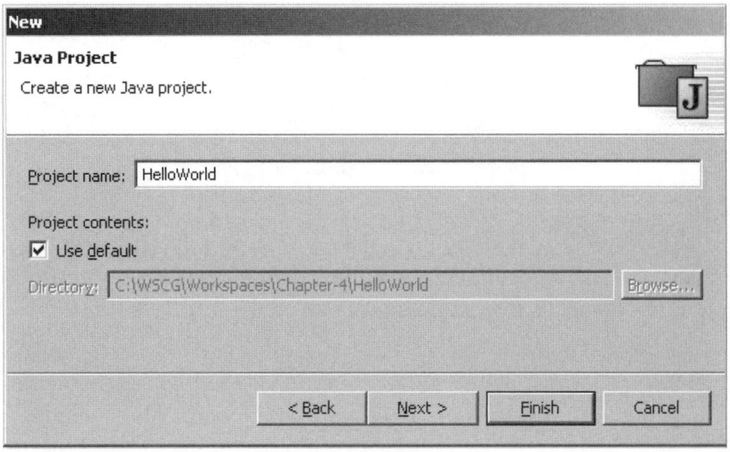

Figure 4.5: New Java Project dialog.

At this point, after entering the name of the project, you may click **Finish** or **Next**. Clicking Next presents another dialog, shown in Figure 4.6, where you can add libraries your project will require. The required JRE library, rt.jar, is added to the project by the wizard. On this dialog you can define additional libraries, and other projects in the workspace, to be included in this project's build path. You may also change the order in which these additional libraries and projects are searched to resolve references in your project. Other settings are available, such as modifying the source location as well as specifying entries to be exported to other dependent projects.

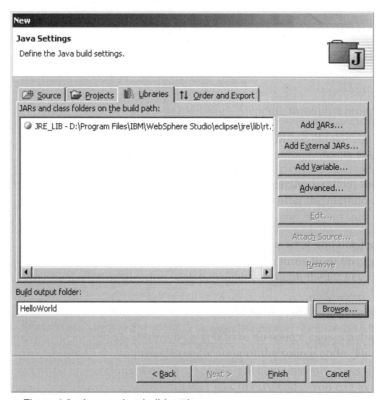

Figure 4.6: Java project build settings.

After you have defined the values for the new Java project, click **Finish**. Clicking Finish causes the wizard to complete the creation of the new Java project. You may open the Java perspective to see what was created by the wizard.

The Java perspective

The Java perspective (Figure 4.7) is, under most circumstances, the best place to work with Java language programming elements.

This perspective is made up of several panes and views that make it easy to perform tasks related to Java programming. In this section we will examine the perspective in some detail. In general, the best way to learn is to experiment with a real project. In the Exercises portion of this chapter you will build a simple Java application and will test it both inside WebSphere Studio and outside as a stand-alone application.

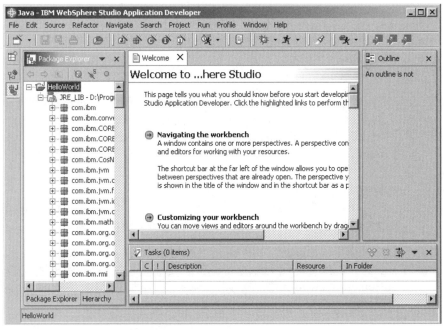

Figure 4.7: The Java perspective.

After you create a new Java project in a new workspace, WebSphere Studio opens the Java perspective. On the leftmost pane you see two stacked views: the Package Explorer view and the Hierarchy view. You may switch between views by clicking their respective tab.

The Package Explorer view shows all packages existing under each project. Packages can be expanded by clicking the plus (**+**) icon besides the name of the package. Under the package name you will find the Java types in the package. Classes and interfaces can also be expanded by clicking the plus (**+**) icon besides their names. When Java types are expanded, you see the methods defined in them. You also see the package and import declarations and any variables defined.

The Hierarchy view will show a type's inheritance chain. To activate this view you first select a type on the Package Explorer and then select **Open → Type Hierarchy** from the selected type's context menu.

The large area in the middle of the window is the editor view. Different editors, depending on the type of the file being viewed, are shown in this area. The Java editor is one of these specialized editors. Some of the other editors available in WebSphere Studio are the XML editor, the HTML/JSP Editor, and the Deployment Descriptor editor. We will cover many of these editors in this book.

The rightmost view in this perspective is the Outline view. When a Java type is open in the editor, its hierarchical outline is displayed here. This view can be used to navigate quickly to different parts of the type. There are other functions available here, such as refactoring the class by extracting code into new methods, renaming packages, and changing method signatures. We will examine what's available in this view in more detail, in different parts of the book when it becomes appropriate to use these capabilities.

The Tasks view is mainly used to display any errors and warnings that exist in the workspace, such as syntax errors or unresolved references. Each entry displays a description and location further identifying the problem. Double-clicking on an error opens the file in question and positions the cursor on the appropriate line and column containing the error.

Creating a Java package

Now that you have a Java project on your workspace, you can create one or more Java packages to contain the types for your application.

Creating a package is very easy, and again, there is more than one way to do this. You may use the toolbar button as shown on Figure4.3, or select **File → New → Package** from the main menu bar, or select **New → Package** from the Java project's context menu (Figure 4.8).

Figure 4.8: Creating a new package.

A dialog appears, prompting you for a new package name. As you know, a convention for naming packages is to use your company's URL backwards and follow it with a descriptive word related to what the package will hold. Package names are, by convention, entered in all lowercase letters. The dialog is shown in Figure 4.9.

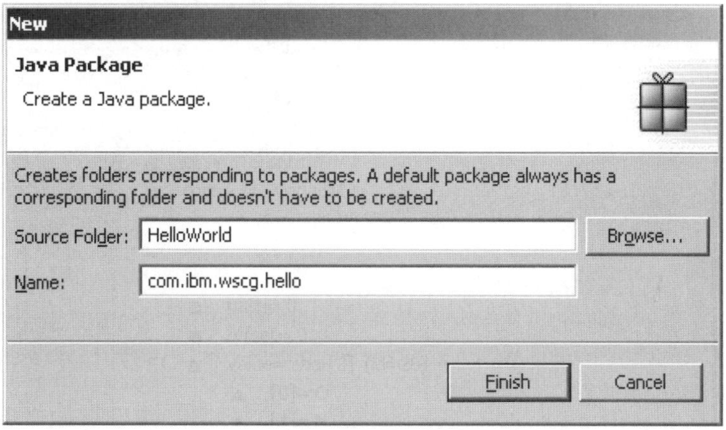

New

Java Package
Create a Java package.

Creates folders corresponding to packages. A default package always has a corresponding folder and doesn't have to be created.

Source Folder: HelloWorld   Browse...

Name: com.ibm.wscg.hello

Finish   Cancel

Figure 4.9: Naming a new package.

Now that the package is created, you can proceed to create the Java types that are to be contained in the package.

Creating Java types

In this book, when we refer to Java types, we mean Java classes and interfaces. These are treated the same way in many parts of the WebSphere Studio product. When the topic covers both in the same way we will use the word *type*.

The easiest way to create a Java type is to select the package of the type and click the Create a Java Class or Create a Java Interface toolbar buttons as shown in Figure 4.3. Of course you can also use the main menu choice **File → New → Class** (or **File → New → Interface**) or by selecting **New → Class** (or **New → Interface**) from the Java project's context menu (see Figure 4.10). The New Java Class or New Java Interface wizard appears, as described in the following two subsections.

Figure 4.10: Creating a new class.

The New Java Class wizard

The New Java Class wizard (Figure 4.11) enables you to define the class. You will not be able to proceed and create the class unless you have provided a class name; all other values are optional.

Figure 4.11: Defining new class attributes.

The following attributes can be defined using the New Java class wizard:

1. Source Folder: Generally this has the same name as the Java project the package is under, but it can be another Java source folder in the workspace.

2. Package: The class can be created in any package in the workspace. If a package was selected when the wizard was started, that package's name is entered automatically here. It can also be a new package name;, in which case WebSphere Studio will create it.

3. Enclosing type: This check box allows you to create this class as a nested class. If you check it, you also need to provide the name of the enclosing type.

4. Modifiers: These check boxes and radio buttons enable you to set any class modifiers such as public, final, abstract, or default.

5. Superclass: You can specify the superclass by typing its name, or click the Browse button to produce a list of all classes in the workspace from which to select.

6. Interfaces: Click the Add button to produce a list of interfaces in the workspace, from which you can select to add to the list of interfaces that your new class must implement.

7. public static void main(String[] args): If this is a stand-alone class, click this check box to have a main() method generated.

8. Constructors from superclass: Click this check box to have the wizard generate constructor code matching those of the superclass.

9. Inherited abstract methods: If you are implementing an interface, click this check box to have the wizard generate stubs for the methods defined on the interface.

The New Java Interface wizard

The New Interface wizard provides a dialog (Figure 4.12), similar to that of the New Java Class wizard, in which to define the attributes of an interface.

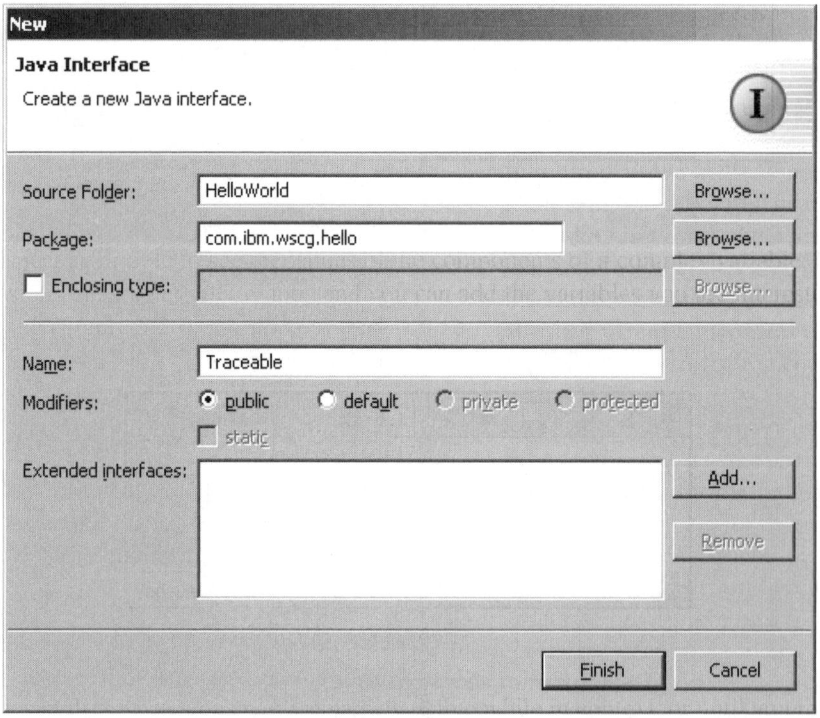

Figure 4.12: Creating a new interface.

Both class and interface names, by convention, start with an uppercase letter. For multiple-word names, start each word in uppercase; for example, HelloWorldClass.

The Java editor

After you create a new type, the Java editor will open for the type. Using this editor, you add the methods and other elements to create a functioning class.

The Java editor has several interesting features that make it a very good and productive editor when used in the Workbench. Let's take a look at some of those features.

Editor view

The editor view is where you enter and modify the Java code for the class you are creating. On the surface it looks like many other editors you may have used in the past (Figure 4.13). In fact, this editor provides you with many productivity aids to assist you while you develop code in Java.

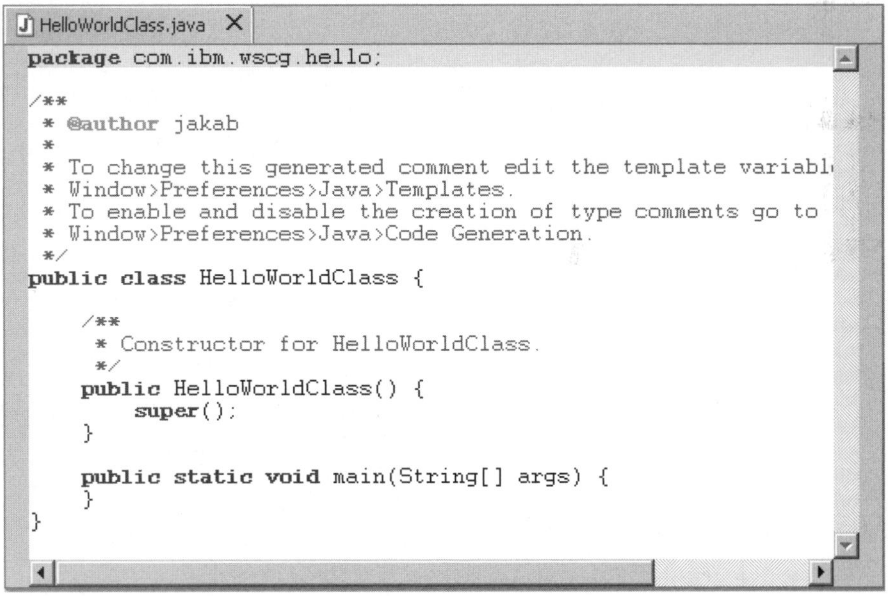

```
HelloWorldClass.java  X
package com.ibm.wscg.hello;

/**
 * @author jakab
 *
 * To change this generated comment edit the template variabl
 * Window>Preferences>Java>Templates.
 * To enable and disable the creation of type comments go to
 * Window>Preferences>Java>Code Generation.
 */
public class HelloWorldClass {

    /**
     * Constructor for HelloWorldClass.
     */
    public HelloWorldClass() {
        super();
    }

    public static void main(String[] args) {
    }
}
```

Figure 4.13: New class in Java editor.

One of the first things you will notice in the editor is that the elements of the program are color coded. As you type code in the class, you will notice that indentation is automatic, producing a cleaner-looking program. If the code becomes untidy (mainly because you have cut and pasted from another class or moved things around), you can always tell the editor to format the code. Formatting is accomplished by selecting **Format** from the context menu of the editor or by pressing the **Ctrl+Shift+F** key combination. Formatting rules can be defined in the preferences dialog under **Java → Code Formatter** (Figure 4.14).

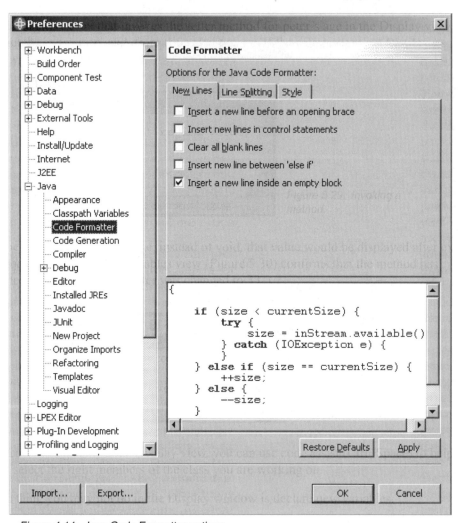

Figure 4.14: Java Code Formatter options.

If you work on a Team, you may want to agree on an acceptable format for the code that is produced by the Team. Using the formatter will produce code of a consistent style.

Another element that you can customize, to conform to your coding standards, are the comments that are inserted when a type is created; see the code at the top of the window in Figure 4.13: New class in Java editor. The format and contents of these type comments are controlled by a template called typecomment. The template can be modified from the

Java → Templates dialog by selecting **typecomment** and clicking **Edit**. This gives an opportunity to customize the text of the class comment and to insert variables such as the user and the date into the text of the comment. Variables take the form $\{var\}$; for example, $\{date\}$ inserts the current date in the comment.

The creation of Java comments based on the typecomment template can be controlled by a setting on the **Window → Preferences → Java → Code Generation** dialog.

Code assist

Some of the templates used with the Java editor have a feature called code assist (also known as Content Assist). Code assist completes a line of code for you based on what you have already typed on that line. For example, if you are working on a method and the next element to code is a while statement, you could type the word **while** and press **Ctrl+space**. This key combination activates code assist. Based on what word is located to the left of the cursor, code assist determines what are acceptable completion elements. In the case of a *while* keyword the completion choices are to iterate with an enumerator or to iterate with an iterator. These choices are presented to you on pop-up windows, from which you can select using your mouse pointer, or arrow keys (Figure 4.15).

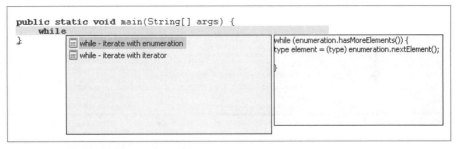

Figure 4.15: While loop code assist.

Selecting one of the options causes the code defined by the *while* template to be inserted into the source code at the cursor, as shown in Figure 4.16.

```
public static void main(String[] args) {
        while (enumeration.hasMoreElements()) {
                type element = (type) enumeration.nextElement();

        }
    }
```

Figure 4.16: While loop code inserted by code assist.

Many templates are already predefined for most of the Java constructs. More can be added from the **Window → Preferences → Java → Templates** dialog.

Extra Credit: Open the **Preferences** dialog and examine the various options available under the Code Formatter, Code Generation, and Templates sections.

Code assist can also be used to insert other programming elements in the code. For example, after a variable has been defined, and at a place where you need to use the variable you can enter the first few letters of the variable name, press **Ctrl+Space**, and a dialog offering suggestions of available terms will be presented to you. From this list you can select the variable.

Another variation works with variable names that represent complex types. Typing the variable name followed by a period and **Ctrl+Space** brings up a list of available methods for the type represented by the variable name. This is extremely useful, because you don't have to remember method names. While the dialog with the suggestions is shown, you can enter the first few letters of the method name to narrow down the number of options available by eliminating the entries that don't contain the letters you typed. A second window shows the Javadoc for the element selected (Figure 4.17).

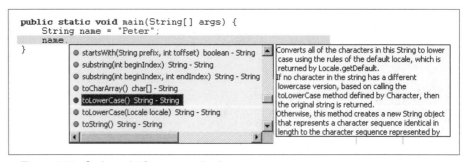

Figure 4.17: Code assist for type methods.

Additional settings that control code assist can be found on **Window → Preferences → Java → Editor → Code Assist** (Figure 4.18).

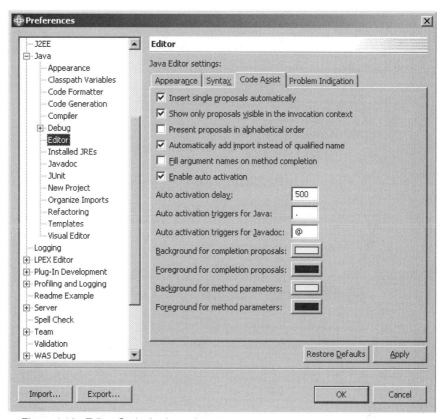

Figure 4.18: Editor Code Assist options.

One of the interesting options is to propose method names automatically after a period following a class or interface name is typed. The activation delay is customizable and set to 500 milliseconds as the default value. A similar trigger exists for Javadoc when you enter an ampersand.

Outline view

The Java editor is coupled to the Outline view. The outline view displays an organized component view of the file opened in the editor. Depending on the file type, the Outline view will display different things. For example, if an HTML or XML file is open, the Outline view shows a containment hierarchy of the elements on the file. This makes it very easy to navigate to the different parts of the file; for example, to go to a cell of a table that is contained within another table.

For Java files, the Outline view (Figure 4.19) displays the package and import statements, type definition, global type variables, and methods. Selecting any of these components in the Outline view causes the Java editor to position the cursor on the selected element on the source file.

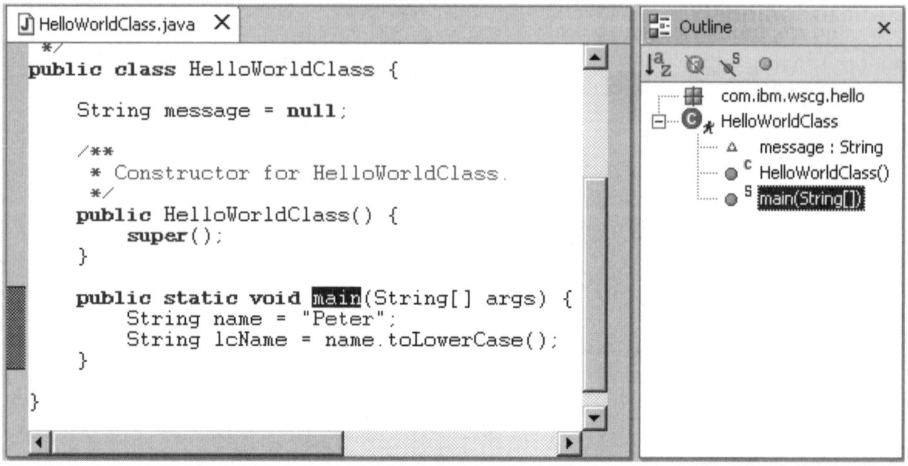

Figure 4.19: Outline view in sync with Java editor.

Notice the small icons at the left of the variable and method names, such as the C next to "HelloWorldClass()". These are used to give you a visual clue that further describes the details of the element at which you are looking. There are many of these visual clues throughout the WebSphere Studio product. Figure 4.20 shows some of the ones used on the Outline and Project Explorer views.

△	default field (package visible)	c	constructor	
		A	abstract member	
▫	private field	F	final member	
◇	protected field	S	static member	
○	public field	◎	synchronized member	
		✳	type with public static void main(String[] args)	
▲	default method (package visible)			
■	private method	▵	implements method from interface	
◈	protected method	▴	overrides method from super class	
●	public method			

Figure 4.20: Outline view icons.

Several filters can be applied to the Outline view to sort or reduce what is shown. The filters are activated by clicking one or more of the four toolbar icons below the title bar of the view, shown in Figure 4.21.

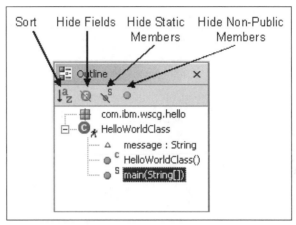

Figure 4.21: Outline view filters.

Be careful when using these filters. You may filter something out one minute and wonder where all your static methods went the next. If you think you have lost some of the members of the type, deselect all the filters first, and take a second look.

Note: The Package Explorer view offers much of the same features of the Outline view. The main difference is that the Package Explorer shows all of the elements in all the Projects currently loaded in the workspace, whereas the Outline view shows the details of only the currently selected file in the Editor view.

There is another filter that affects what you see in the Editor view depending on what you select on the Outline view. This filter is represented in the main toolbar icon named Show Source of Selected Element Only (Figure 4.22).

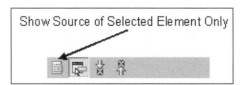

Figure 4.22: Button to show only the
element selected in Outline view.

This icon is enabled only when the focus is on the Editor or Outline views. The purpose of this filter, as its name implies, is to show in the Editor view only the element that is selected on the Outline (or Package Explorer) view, as in Figure 4.23.

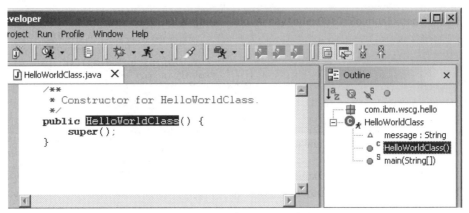

Figure 4.23: Showing only the constructor of the selected class.

Show Source of Selected Element Only is a convenience feature that allows focusing on the particular element, such as a method of a class, by seeing only the code that belongs to that method in the Editor view. If you wish to see the contents of the whole file, deselect this filter. Note that selecting the class name, while this filter is applied, displays the complete class and its methods, but not the package or import statements.

Compiling Java source

In WebSphere Studio the Java editor is tied to the compiler. The default setting is to compile whenever a Java source file is saved. You can save by selecting **File → Save** from the main menu or by pressing the **Ctrl+S** key combination.

Consider the following code segment:

```java
public static void main(String[] args) {
    String name = "Peter";
    String lcName = name.tolowerCase();
}
```

There is a String called name, which is initialized to a value of "Peter". The next line declares another String, lcName, to hold the value the lowercase value of name. The error is that the method to convert a String to lowercase has been entered incorrectly as "tolowerCase" when it should have been entered as "toLowerCase". Saving this method, obviously, produces an error. Error and warning messages can be seen in several views:

■ An entry for each error is created in the Tasks view. Double-clicking on the task opens the appropriate editor, depending on file type, and positions the cursor pointing at the error, as shown in Figure 4.24.

Figure 4.24: Tasks view with error.

Sometimes an error description is very long and cannot be completely displayed in the space available on the Tasks view. To see a full description, click on the task and read the error description on the information line at the bottom of the WebSphere Studio window (Figure 4.25).

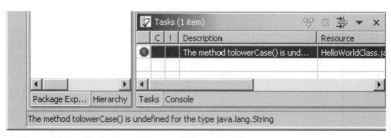

Figure 4.25: Task description on information line.

■ Errors are also indicated in the Package Explorer and the Outline views with red circles containing a white X (Figure 4.26). An error indicated at the class level means that either a method in the class has an error, or that the class definition itself has an error. Errors are also reported in package and import statements.

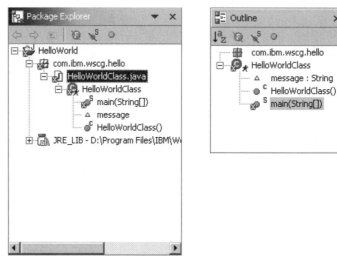

Figure 4.26: Errors indicated in Package Explorer and Outline views.

Warnings are reported in a similar manner, but instead of the red circle, a yellow triangle with a black exclamation point inside is displayed.

■ The marker bar of the Editor view, the dark vertical bar on the left edge of the editor, can display several icons, or markers, depending on the situation. Errors and warnings appear aligned with the line of code containing the error. Placing the mouse pointer over top of a marker displays the description associated with the marker.

In some cases you will see a marker that looks like a light bulb on top of the error marker; this is the quick fix marker, shown in Figure 4.27. This indicates that WebSphere Studio has a suggestion on how to fix the error. Clicking the marker produces a list of possible solutions to the problem. Selecting one of the proposed suggestions will repair the code and remove the quick fix marker, but the error marker remains until you save the method.

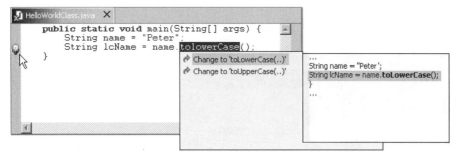

Figure 4.27: Proposing a suggestion.

The quick fix marker can also appear by itself, without the error marker. In that case WebSphere Studio has detected a condition where it can offer some help. Clicking on the marker will provide you with suggestions that will prevent an error later on.

Simple source control

Even without any Source Control Management (SCM) program configured, WebSphere Studio keeps track of your changes to the source and other files in the Workbench.

This simple source control mechanism is called the Local History. The Workbench features Compare with, Replace with, and Restore from Local History functions.

The compare and replace functions allow you to see the differences and, in the case of the replace function, to regress to a different version of a file.

The Restore function allows you to recover an element of a file that you have previously deleted, for example a method or a variable definition.

These functions are available from the context menu of the file in the Project Explorer and Outline views, as shown in Figure 4.28.

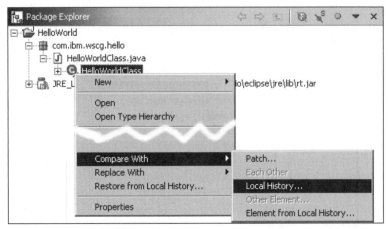

Figure 4.28: Local history functions.

In Figure 4.29 you see the dialog used to compare the current version in the workspace with another version held in the Local History.

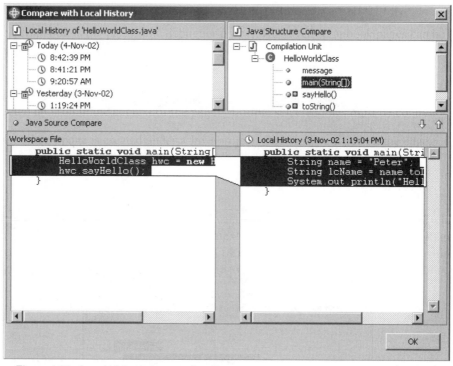

Figure 4.29: Local history compare function.

The top left pane shows all of the available versions, sorted by date. The top right pane shows the compilation unit (a class in this case). What is compared is determined by what is selected in this pane. You can compare the complete class or a single method or element.

The bottom left pane shows the currently loaded element, and the right bottom pane displays the version selected in the right top pane. In the example you see the comparison between the main() methods.

The Replace function is similar to the Compare function. You can, however, select another version and use it to replace the currently loaded version. This is an extremely useful function.

If you know that you would like to replace the current version with the previous version of a file, you can simply select **Replace With → Previous from Local History** from the context menu of the file. The Replace from Local History window appears as shown in Figure 4.30.

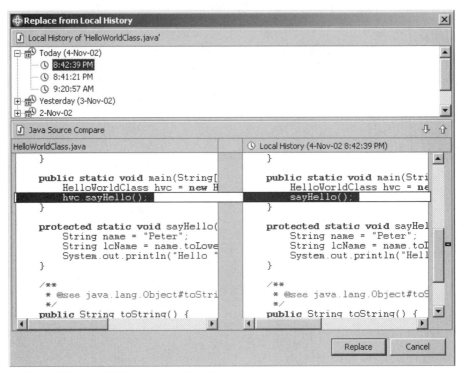

Figure 4.30: Local history replace function.

The arrows on the right-hand side of the Java Source Compare pane allow you to travel to the next and previous differences in the file. Clicking **Replace** moves code from the right to the left pane, replacing the existing file.

The last function available from the local history is the ability to recover deleted elements of a file, or the complete deleted file by selecting the containing package name.

Selecting a class file and clicking **Restore from Local History. . .** from its context menu (Figure 4.31) brings up a dialog (Figure 4.32) in which you can see the deleted elements of a class and choose which ones to bring back into the current version on the workbench.

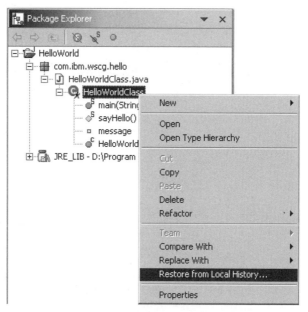

Figure 4.31: Selecting to restore from local history.

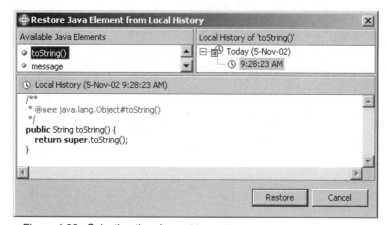

Figure 4.32: Selecting the element to restore.

As you can imagine, keeping a local history of all your changes takes up room on your hard drive. WebSphere Studio allows you to configure how long you keep history files, how many changes per file to keep in the history, and how much space on your hard drive to use. These settings, shown in Figure 4.33, can be reached from **Window → Preferences → Workbench → Local History**.

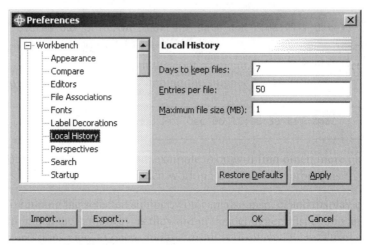

Figure 4.33: Local history settings.

The local history changes are kept in metadata, separate from the actual files in the project. The files under the project folder, in the file system, contain the current version of the files in the Workspace.

Running non-Web-based Java programs

Running a Java program in WebSphere Studio is a very simple task. Since the Java files are compiled every time they are saved, there is no need for an extra compilation step. Even when the program is to be debugged, there is no need for any special compilation step. We will look at debugging and the Debug perspective in the next chapter.

To run a Java program all you need to do is select the .java or .class file in the Package Explorer and click the Run icon, shown in Figure 4.34.

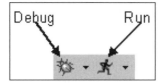

Figure 4.34: Run toolbar icon.

The first time you run a Java program, you will need to define what kind of environment the program needs. To select the correct Launcher for your application, click the arrow beside the Run toolbar button, then select **Run . . .** from the context menu. The Launcher

Configurations dialog appears. Select **Java Application** from the Launch Configurations list and click the **New** button.

For a stand-alone Java program, select the name of the class under Java Application (Figure 4.35). In this dialog you can also supply arguments to be passed to the main() method, which JRE to use or whether to adjust the classpath.

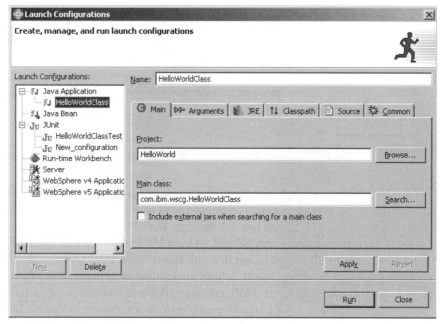

Figure 4.35: Launch Configurations dialog.

Consider the simple program listed in Figure 4.36:

```java
public class HelloWorldClass {

    public HelloWorldClass() {
        super();
    }

    public static void main(String[] args) {
        HelloWorldClass hwc = new HelloWorldClass();
        hwc.sayHello();
    }

    protected static void sayHello() {
        String name = "Peter";
        String lcName = name.toLowerCase();
        System.out.println("Hello " + lcName);
    }

}
```

Figure 4.36: Source for the hello program.

Clicking **Run . . .** in the Launch Configurations dialog starts the JVM and runs the program. The main() method gets called, and the program runs to completion.

The output of the program appears on the Console view. In the Java perspective the Console view (Figure 4.37) can be found on the bottom pane of the main window, sharing space with the Tasks view.

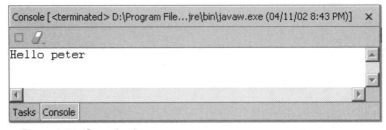

Figure 4.37: Console view.

Web applications require a different setup, in which a server is configured to provide the proper runtime environment. Components of J2EE Web Applications are made up of many components such as servlets, JSP pages, HTML pages, and EJBs. These components need to run in special containers as defined in the J2EE specification. The WebSphere Test Environment provides this environment. In later chapters you will learn how to run, test, and debug Web applications.

Exercise

In this section you will get to practice the principles of operating in the WebSphere Studio development environment presented in this chapter.

You should be able to complete this exercise after reading the chapter. You may have to refer to the details of the chapter. Be confident that after a little practice you will be able to create projects, packages, and classes without even thinking. You will be able to add logic through methods in your classes and run and test the completed program.

In this exercise you will write an extremely simple Java program to display a greeting on the console.

In all the exercises in this book where we give you a task to complete, this task will be a numbered step. If you feel confident that you can complete the task without looking at the details, go ahead and complete the step. To help you when you need a little more detail in completing more complex steps, there will be substeps under the numbered steps to complete the task. For example:

1. Start WebSphere Studio with a new workspace in the **C:\WSCG\work-spaces\Chapter-4** directory.
   a. Open a Windows Explorer window.
   b. Navigate to the **C:\WSCG\workspaces\Chapter-4** directory.
   c. Drag and drop this directory onto the **WebSphere Studio** icon on your Windows desktop.

If you need help completing step 1, then you would proceed and complete steps a through c. Note that if you complete step 1, then there is no need to complete the substeps.

Let's begin.

Most labs in this book will start with either an empty workspace or with a workspace containing a startup set of files. A desktop icon can be set up to receive a dropped workspace folder and start WebSphere Studio loading that workspace.

1. Create a Windows desktop shortcut pointing to the WebSphere Studio executable file.
   a. Right-click anywhere you see an empty space on the Windows desktop.
   b. From the context menu, select **New → Shortcut**.
   c. On the Create Shortcut dialog, click **Browse** and navigate to the **C:\Program Files\IBM\WebSphere\Express\SiteDeveloper** directory.
   d. Select the **wasexpress.exe** file and click **OK**.
   e. Click **Next**.

    f. Enter **WebSphere Studio** for the name of the shortcut.

    g. Click F**inish**.

You should now have a shortcut to WebSphere Studio on your desktop.

2. Modify the shortcut you just created with the -data flag so that it will accept a dropped workspace folder.

    a. Right click on the **WebSphere Studio** shortcut.

    b. Select **Properties** from the context menu.

    c. Click the **Shortcut** tab.

    d. Locate the **Target** entry field.

    e. At the end of the line, type a space character and enter **-data** right after it, as shown in Figure 4.38.

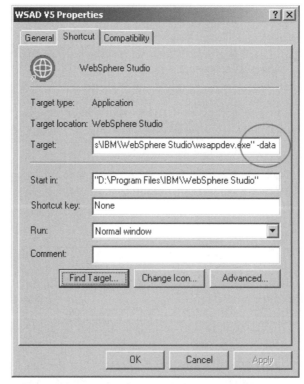

Figure 4.38: Adding the -data switch to the target of the shortcut.

    f. Click **OK**.

Note: WebSphere Studio can also be started from the command line with the **-data** flag to startup and load the workspace folder following the flag. For example: C:\ Program Files\IBM\WebSphere\Express\SiteDeveloper\wasexpress.exe -data *myworkspace*.

Of course you may also start WebSphere Studio by clicking the icon the program installer created under the **Start → Programs → IBM WebSphere Application Server – Express v5.0 → Studio Site Developer**. Starting WebSphere Studio this way presents a dialog box where you can type the location and name of the workspace you want to load. You will use this method in some of the exercises.

3. Start WebSphere Studio with the new workspace in the C:\WSCG\workspaces\Chapter-4 directory.

   a. Open a Windows Explorer window.

   b. Navigate to the **C:\WSCG\workspaces\Startup\Chapter-4** directory.

   c. Drag and drop the Chapter-4 directory onto the WebSphere Studio icon on your Windows desktop.

4. After the WebSphere Studio window opens, switch to the Java perspective.

5. Create a new Java project. Name it **Greetings**.

   a. Switch to the Java perspective.

   b. Select **New → Project** from the context menu of the Package Explorer.

   c. Select **Java → Java Project** on the New project dialog.

   d. Click **Next**.

   e. Enter **Greetings** as the project name.

   f. Click **Finish**.

   g. Verify that a new Java Project called Greetings exists on the Package Explorer

6. Create a new Java package under the Greetings project. Name it **com.ibm.wscg.greet**.

   a. On the Java perspective, select the **Greetings** Java project. From its context menu, select **New → Package**. You can also create a new package by clicking the **Create a Java Package** toolbar button.

   b. Enter **com.ibm.wscg.greet** in the Name field of the New Java Package dialog.

   c. Click **Finish**.

   d. Verify that a new Java package called com.ibm.wscg.greet exists under the Greetings Java project on the Package Explorer.

7. Create a new Java class under the com.ibm.wscg.greet package. Name it **Greeter**.

a. Select the **com.ibm.wscg.greet** package.

b. Click the **Create a Java Class** toolbar button. You can also create a new class by selecting the package and then selecting **New** → **Class** from its context menu.

c. Ensure you have the correct source folder and package names.

d. Name the class **Greeter**.

e. Set the class to extend **java.lang.Object**.

f. Ensure that the check box to create the main() method is checked.

g. Click **Finish**.

h. Verify that a new class called Greeter exists under the com.ibm.wscg.greet package.

8. Double-click the new class to open it in the Editor view.

9. Add a String class variable. Name it **personName**. Initialize it to your name.

a. After the class declaration enter:

```
private String personName = "Peter";
```

10. Add code in the main() method to instantiate a Greeter object; extract the first command line argument and, if that argument exists, assign its value to the personName variable; next call the greetThem() method, passing personName as a parameter. Try to use code assist and any quick fixes offered to make your job easier. Figure 4.39 shows a possible solution.

```
public class Greeter {
    private String personName = "Peter";
    public static void main(String[] args) {
        Greeter greeter = new Greeter();
        if (args.length > 0)
            greeter.personName = args[0];
        greeter.greetThem(greeter.personName);

    }
}
```

Figure 4.39: Possible code solution for Greeter class.

When typing code in a Java file, you can format the text, according to the rules set in **Window ‡ Preferences** → **Java** → **Code Formatter**, by pressing **Ctrl+Shift+f** or by selecting **Format** from the Java editor's context menu.

11. If you took advantage of the quick fix offered, WebSphere Studio will already have created the method greetThem(). If not, create a private method called **greetThem()**. It should take a **String** as a parameter. Name the parameter **personName**.

```
private void greetThem(String personName) {
}
```

12. Add code to the greetThem() method to display a greeting on the console using the parameter passed.

```
private void greetThem(String personName) {
        System.out.println("Hello " + personName);
    }
```

13. Save the file by pressing **Ctrl+S** or selecting **File** → **Save Greeter.java**.

14. Run the program first without setting the command line argument. Observe the Console view for the output.

    a. Click the **Run** toolbar icon and create a new **Java Application** launch configuration.

    b. Point to the class you just created.

    c. Click **Run**.

15. Set a command line argument to someone else's name and rerun the program. Observe the Console view for the output.

Hint: Use the **Launch Configurations** dialog to enter the command line parameters.

16. Next, you export a JAR file containing your program and run it outside the Web-Sphere Studio environment.

This part of the exercise assumes that you have JDK 1.3 or above properly installed and configured on your machine.

---

a. Select the Greeting Java project. From its context menu select **Export**.

b. Select **JAR File** from the export format choices, as shown in Figure 4.40. Click **Next**.

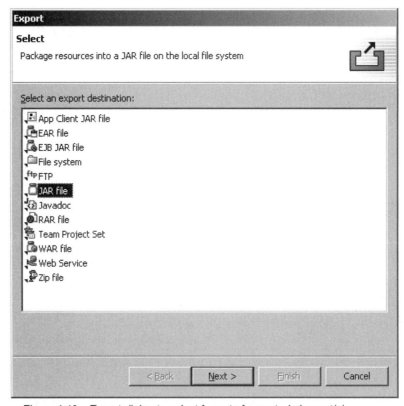

Figure 4.40: Export dialog to select format of exported element(s).

c. Ensure that the Greetings project is selected. Enter **C:\WSCG\JarsAndWars \greeting.jar** for the JAR file name, as shown in Figure 4.41. Click **Next** twice.

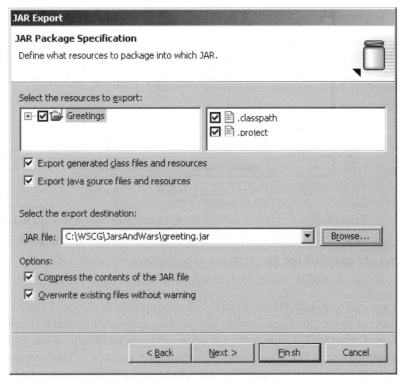

Figure 4.41: Selecting what to include in the JAR file.

d. If you intend to run the program from a class in the JAR file, you need to designate one of the classes in the JAR file as the one being the entry point into the application (the class containing the main() method). Click the **Browse** button next to the **Main class** entry field and select **com.ibm.wscg.greet. Greeter** from the list, as shown in Figure 4.42. Click **OK**. Click **Finish**.

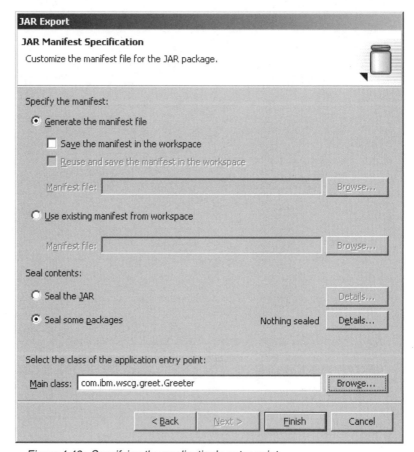

Figure 4.42: Specifying the application's entry point.

e. Open a command prompt window. Switch to the **C:\WSCG\JarsAndWars** directory. This is the directory you exported the JAR file to.

f. Enter command lines to execute the Greeter program without and with a command line argument.

```
java -jar greeting.jar
java -jar greeting.jar Gary
```

g. The console output should look like Figure 4.43.

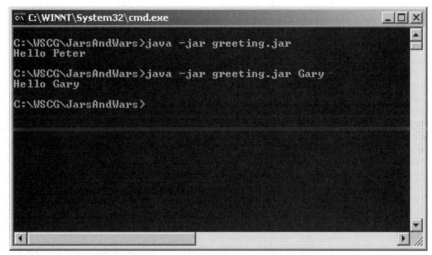

Figure 4.43: Running the program outside WebSphere Studio.

If you don't have a separate JDK installed, you can still run the completed exercise using the JRE that was installed with WebSphere Studio. Just switch to the C:\Program Files\IBM\WebSphere\Express\AppServer\java\jre\bin directory and, on the command line fully qualify the name of the JAR file:

java -jar C:\WSCG\JarsAndWars\greeting.jar

This completes this exercise.

Test yourself

Key terms

Java perspective	*JRE (Java Runtime Environment)*
Java projects	*editors*
Web application	*Outline view*
Enterprise Application	*code assist*
J2EE (Java 2 Enterprise Edition)	*templates*
JAR (Java archive)	*filters*
Task view	*Javadoc*
source control	*Package Explorer*
Debug perspective	

Review questions

1. How does WebSphere Studio support role-based development?

2. How do you view the list of available perspectives?

3. What is a Java project, and how do you create one in WebSphere Studio?

4. What are the various components of the Java perspective?

5. What is code assist, and how can you activate it in the editor?

6. What is the Outline view?

7. How do you compile a program in WebSphere Studio?

8. Briefly describe the source control available in WebSphere Studio.

9. How do you execute a simple Java program (non-Web-based) in WebSphere Studio?

10. How are errors handled in WebSphere Studio?

5

Debugging techniques

Chapter topics

- ❖ *Why and when to debug*
- ❖ *Sending messages and tracing*
- ❖ *Starting a program for debugging*
- ❖ *Setting breakpoints in Java code*
- ❖ *Debug perspective description*
- ❖ *Debugger controls and stepping through code*
- ❖ *Viewing variables*
- ❖ *Expressions view*
- ❖ *Display view*
- ❖ *Other types of breakpoints*
- ❖ *Scrapbook*
- ❖ *Hot code replace*

Certification objectives

- ❖ *Set debugging checkpoints*
- ❖ *Step through code*
- ❖ *View variables*
- ❖ *Create and run code in Scrapbook Page*

In this chapter we examine the basic debugging techniques required to find logic problems in your programs. Unfortunately, we all make mistakes in our programs. These mistakes cause applications not to perform as designed. The programs are syntactically correct, they compile, but at runtime they either throw unexpected exceptions or produce incorrect results.

WebSphere Studio has an excellent built-in source debugger. The Debug perspective provides you with all the views necessary to figure out quickly what has gone wrong. Even though you will learn to how to debug some simple Java programs, the techniques you learn here will serve you well to debug complex Web applications involving servlets, JSP pages, and even EJBs in distributed, multitier architecture applications.

Why and when to debug

We are all human, and unfortunately we make mistakes. Some of the mistakes we make are caught by the Java compiler when we save a file after making a change or adding new code. These problems are the easy ones to fix. Harder problems occur when our program compiles and even runs, but the results are not what we expect. Perhaps a wrong value shows up, a database does not get updated as expected, or the program mysteriously *abends* (*ab*normally *end*s). These are the times when having a good debugger is priceless.

Programmers commonly inherit other programmers' code for the purpose of maintenance or for further improvements. Using the debugger to examine a program will assist you in understanding how the program flows and to become familiar with it.

Fortunately, there is an excellent debugger built into WebSphere Studio. To use it you don't really have to do anything special to your program. All you really do is run the offending program under the control of the debugger.

Sending messages and tracing

Although we have an excellent debugger in WebSphere Studio, it does not preclude the use of other debugging techniques you may have used in the past. For example, if you have a C or C++ background, you are very familiar with setting up a program to send messages to the console using printf() statements to communicate status or variable values from the program to the console.

The equivalent function in Java is provided by the System.out.print() and System.out.println() statements. These, like printf() in C++, produce output that appears in the console at runtime. These methods are very versatile in that they can take any type of parameters and send their values to the console. For example, consider the following code snippet:

```
int age = 3;
String name  = "Shadow";
System.out.println("My dog " + name + " is " + age + " years old.");
```

This code would produce the following message on the console when the lines are executed:

> My dog Shadow is 3 years old.

If a nonprimitive object is used as a parameter, its toString() method is called and the results are displayed on the console. This is one of the reasons why, when creating your own classes, you should always implement the toString() method.

The Console view (Figure 5.1) is available in nearly every perspective. Usually it can be found near the bottom of the WebSphere Studio window, stacked in the same pane as the Tasks view. However, it can be placed in any perspective and any pane, because WebSphere Studio is fully customizable.

Note: You can add a view that is not currently visible to any perspective using the **Windows** → **Show View** menu item.

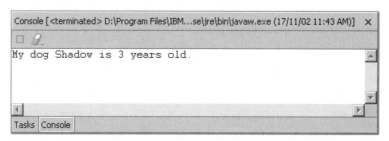

Figure 5.1: Console view.

Starting a program for debugging

In the previous chapter you learned how to run a Java program. To debug a program while in the J2EE, Java, or Debug perspective, all you need to do is click on the Debug button instead of the Run button (Figure 5.2).

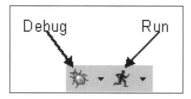

Figure 5.2: Debug and Run toolbar icons.

The first time you debug a Java program, you need to define what kind of runtime environment the program needs. If no special parameters or setup is required, you may select **Debug As** → **Java Application** (Figure 5.3).

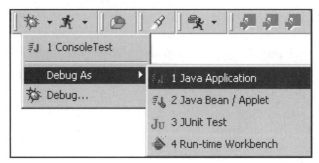

Figure 5.3: Debug as... menu option.

If you need to customize the launcher to provide command-line arguments, select a different JRE, or other parameters, select **Debug. . .** from the menu. The result is the Launch Configurations dialog for the debugger (Figure 5.4). This dialog provides the same function as the Launch Configurations dialog used in the previous chapter to run a Java program. The only difference is that this launcher will run the program in a debug-enabled Java virtual machine and the Debug perspective will be opened to enable you to debug the program.

Note: As you keep defining launchers for the debugger, the definitions are saved and appear on the drop-down list for the debugger launcher. After a while you may have many entries in this list that you no longer need. To remove them from the menu, select **Window** → **Preferences** → **Debug** → **Launch History**, select the entries to remove from the Recent Debug Launches list, and click **Remove**.

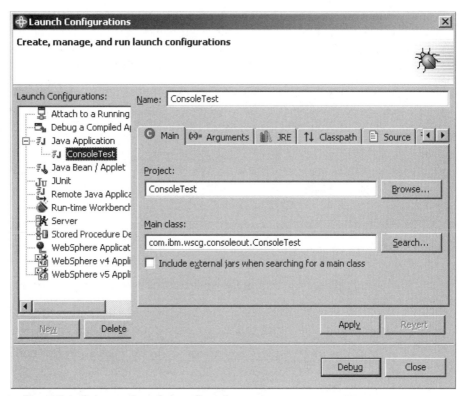

Figure 5.4: Debugger launcher configuration.

After completing the dialog with the required values, click **Debug** to launch and debug the program.

If no breakpoints have been set, the program will run to completion or until a runtime error occurs. The idea is to set breakpoints in the code where you suspect the problem is being caused, or just before it. Once the breakpoint is reached, single-step and examine variables as the program executes under the control of the debugger, recognize and fix the error, retest, and continue to completion.

The next section will show you how to set breakpoints in your code so that the debugger will suspend execution of the program and give you a chance to find out what is wrong.

Setting breakpoints in Java code

Breakpoints can be set on any line of live Java code (not on comment lines). Breakpoints cause the debugger to suspend the execution of a Java program before the code line at the breakpoint, is executed.

While execution is suspended, the debugger takes control and provides access to various components of the program, such as the values of variables and the current state of the call stack. It also provides you with fine-grained ways to control the execution of the program, such as the ability to step through the program.

Line breakpoints are set from the Java editor view. While viewing a Java file, place the mouse pointer so that it is situated on top of the marker bar and aligned with the line of code where you want to apply the breakpoint.

Note: The marker bar is the dark vertical bar located along the left side margin of the Java editor view.

You now have two choices:

1. Double-click to toggle between setting and resetting a breakpoint.

2. Right-click and from the context menu select **Add Breakpoint**.

If a breakpoint already exists, the context menu displays other choices: Remove Breakpoint, Disable Breakpoint, and Breakpoint Properties.

Breakpoints first appear as blue circles on the marker bar (Figure 5.5).

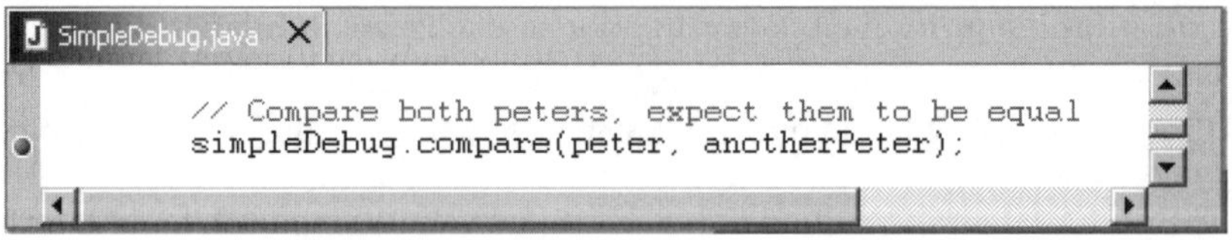

Figure 5.5: Set breakpoint.

Once the class is loaded and the breakpoint is installed in the virtual machine, the plain blue circle changes to a blue circle with a check mark (Figure 5.6).

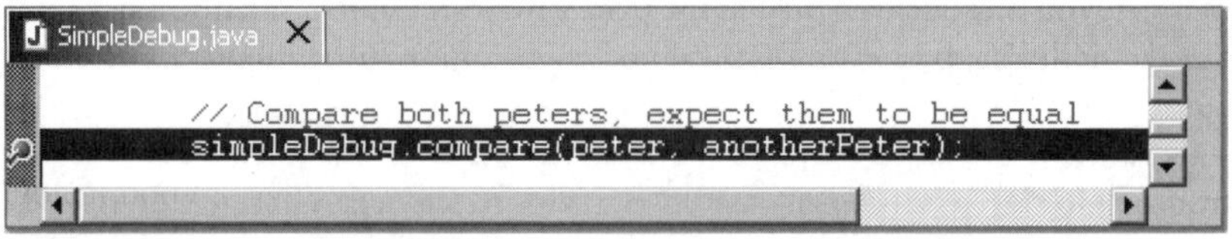

Figure 5.6: Loaded breakpoint.

Disabled breakpoints appear as a white circle on the marker bar (Figure 5.7).

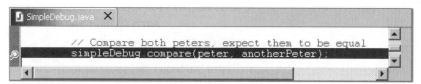

Figure 5.7:   Disabled breakpoint.

Normally the program will run until an enabled breakpoint is reached, at which point the execution of the program is suspended and the Debug perspective is opened.

You could view the individual breakpoints by opening the source files that contain them and looking for blue circles on the marker bar. Although this method can be useful for visualizing quickly where the program will stop next in the current Java file, it is not a practical way to see all breakpoints. To view which breakpoints are set in your code in all files loaded in the workspace—some of which may not be opened in the Java editor at the moment—you use the Breakpoints view.

The Breakpoints view (Figure 5.8) is located, by default, on the upper right-hand pane of the Debug perspective. This space is shared by other views that will be covered later in this chapter.

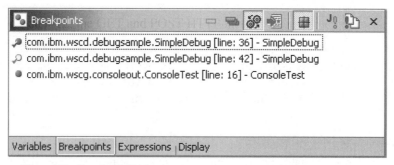

Figure 5.8:   Breakpoints view.

From this view you can see and control all the breakpoints currently set in the work-space. In Figure 5.8 you can see a loaded breakpoint, a loaded but disabled breakpoint, and a set but not yet loaded breakpoint. You can also double-click on a breakpoint in the view to find that line in the source code. The file will be opened and scrolled to that point.

Breakpoints can be manipulated from this view through the context menu of each of the breakpoints, shown in Figure 5.9.

Figure 5.9: Breakpoint context menu.

Some interesting, and self-explanatory, options on this menu are Enable, Disable, Remove, Remove All, and Go to File. Other very interesting, but not so intuitive, options include Add Java Exception Breakpoint, Hit Count, and Properties. We will look at these options in greater detail in the section "Other types of breakpoints" later in this chapter.

Debug perspective description

Once an enabled breakpoint is reached, execution is suspended and WebSphere Studio opens the Debug perspective.

Note: Which perspective opens when a breakpoint is encountered is determined by a preferences choice. If for some reason you would like to debug in a different perspective, you can change this default by selecting **Window** → **Preferences** → **Debug** → **Default perspective for Debug**.

The Debug perspective presents you with a preconfigured window (Figure 5.10), comprising multiple panes and views specifically designed to aid you in determining what is wrong with your code.

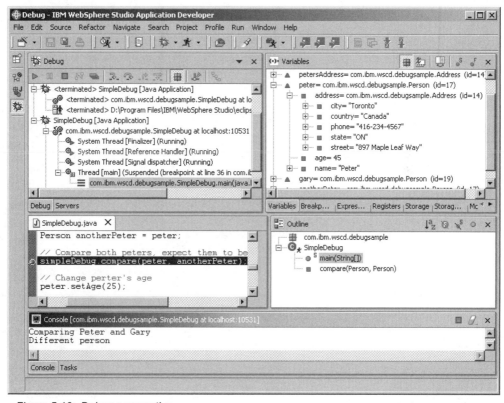

Figure 5.10: Debug perspective.

Figure 5.10 shows you a very busy perspective. In fact, in "real life" this is a very usable and useful perspective. Let's take a quick tour of the different views that make it up.

The bottom pane contains the stacked Console and Tasks views. Their functions are the same as in the Java perspective.

Note: The Console view will display any debugging messages from your program, generated by System.out.println() statements, as it executes under the control of the debugger. Error messages will also be displayed on the console.

The upper left-hand pane is shared by two views: the Debug view and the Servers view. The Servers view is used to manipulate any servers that may be running and are under the control of WebSphere Studio. This view will be explained later in the book when we cover running and debugging Web applications.

The Debug view is where you see the processes and threads currently running. Any terminated processes are also displayed here. Terminated processes can be removed from the view by selecting **Remove All Terminated** from the view's context menu (Figure 5.11). From this context menu you have control over the running, suspended, and terminated processes.

When you run a program under the debugger (selecting one of the Debug options to run), the Debug perspective opens. The Debug view (Figure 5.12) will highlight the process and thread where program execution suspended.

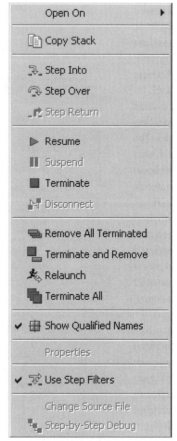

Figure 5.11: Debug view context menu.

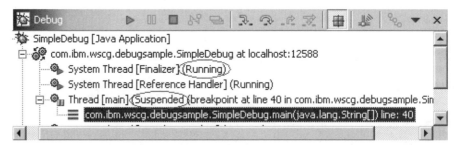

Figure 5.12: Debug view, stack frames.

Looking at Figure 5.12, notice that there is one process, SimpleDebug, and the class that is running has several threads. Not necessarily all of the threads are programmer created; some are system threads. Two threads are running and one thread is suspended. The green triangle icon overlay indicates a running thread, and the two-vertical-bar icon indicates a suspended, or paused, thread.

The Editor view (Figure 5.13) contains the source file being debugged, and the next line that will be executed is highlighted. The editor view is synchronized with the stack frame that is selected in the Debug view.

```
SimpleDebug.java  X
        Person anotherPeter = peter;

        // Compare both peters, expect them to be equal
        simpleDebug.compare(peter, anotherPeter);

        // Change perter's age
        peter.setAge(25);
```

Figure 5.13: Editor view at breakpoint.

The Outline view (Figure 5.14) is synchronized with the current selection on the Stack view. At the same time, any element selected on the Outline view selects the same element in the source editor view.

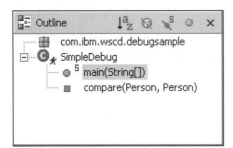

Figure 5.14: Outline view at breakpoint.

Both the Outline and editor views were described in detail in the previous chapter. They behave in exactly the same way in the Debug perspective as they do in the Java perspective. However, while code is suspended at a breakpoint, some additional functionality is available in the Editor pane.

■ Letting the mouse pointer hover over a variable name will display information about the variable. The variable's type and current value are displayed on a pop-up window. Complex objects display their object ID.

■ A Java expression can be selected and evaluated directly from the editor pane. The results of the expression can be displayed (Figure 5.15) or inspected. We will cover the difference between these two methods of looking at variable values later in this chapter.

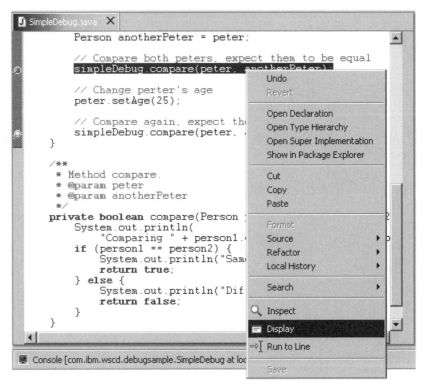

Figure 5.15: Displaying an expression.

The results of inspecting or displaying an expression are displayed in the Display view. The Display view (Figure 5.16) is located on the top right hand side of the window of the Debug perspective.

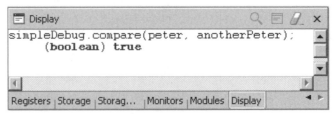

Figure 5.16: Evaluation results in Display view.

The pane containing the Display view is shared by a number of other views. Some of these views are not necessary for debugging Java programs; in fact, they have an active role only in debugging applications written in languages that are compiled to native machine code, such as C or C++. If you work only with Java, you may want to remove some of these views from the pane. This will give more room for the tabs of the views that you do need and unclutter the pane.

The following views can safely be removed from the pane because they are not used with Java applications:

- Registers

- Storage

- Storage Mapping

- Monitors

- Modules

To remove these views, simply select the corresponding tab and click the X icon to close the view. WebSphere Studio will remember your choices. Should you ever want to bring any of these views back, select **Window → Show View** and, from the context menu, select the view you want to add.

If you removed the views just mentioned, make sure that you still have the following views. They are needed, and used frequently, during the debugging of your Java applications.

- Variables

- Breakpoints

- Expressions

- Display

Later in this chapter we will explorer these remaining four views in quite a bit of detail.

Debugger controls and stepping through code

Earlier, we mentioned that while an application is suspended and under the control of the debugger, you have some fine-grained ways of controlling the execution of the program.

One technique involves setting a breakpoint to suspend the application just before the program fails, then single-stepping through the program, paying extra attention to the flow of the program and examining variables as the program slowly advances toward the failure point.

Stepping and thread controls are provided via toolbar buttons and function keys as shown in Figure 5.17.

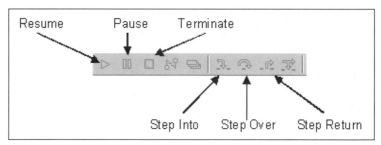

Figure 5.17: Debug toolbar buttons.

There are three different controls to use while single-stepping through a program:

- If the next step to be executed is a method call, *Step Into* will take you inside the method being called. This function is also available through the F5 key.

- *Step Over* will not take you inside a step that calls a method; rather, the method call is executed and you are returned to the next step after the method call. This function is also available through the F6 key.

- If you have stepped into a method call, you have seen what you needed to see, and you want to get quickly to the line of code that returns from this method, select *Step Return*. This function is also available through the F7 key.

Step filtering

Stepping into the code of a method for which you have no source causes a dialog to appear that gives you a chance to provide the location of the source code. This situation can happen when you are working with library code that contains only class files. This is a common occurrence when you step into Java class library code. You can avoid falling into this situation, which interrupts your train of thought and is inconvenient, by setting up step filters. Any packages, or classes, in the filter list will not cause the debugger to prompt you for source when stepping into binary only libraries. The debugger will not step into packages or classes that are defined as step filters.

To set up stepping filters, select **Window → Preference → Java → Debug → Step Filtering**. Notice that a number of well-known binary packages are already precon-figured as the default (Figure 5.18).

Step filtering can be toggled on and off from the context menu of the Debug view.

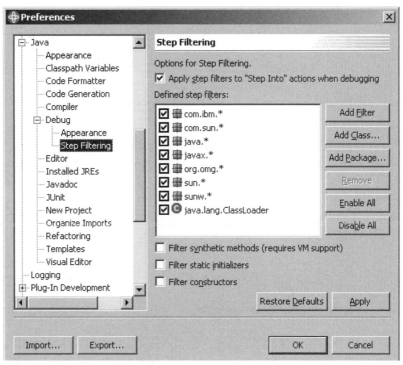

Figure 5.18: Debug step filtering.

Other controls

In addition to the stepping controls just mentioned, the Debug toolbar contains three other controls for managing the processes and threads.

- The Resume function is used to start a suspended thread. This can be used after you have finished debugging a section of code and would like to continue quickly to next breakpoint or to execute the program to completion if there are no further breakpoints. This function is also available through the F8 key.

- The Pause function is used to suspend a currently running thread. After you select a running thread and click Pause, the thread will suspend at the next step.

- The Terminate function is used to kill a thread. You may want to do this to exit an endless loop or a hang condition or to terminate an application abruptly.

Another way to move quickly through the code is to use the Run to Line action, which is available on the context menu of the Java editor view while in the Debug perspective (see Figure 5.15). This action allows you place the cursor on a line of code and run to that line. The program executes from its current position until the instruction at the cursor is reached, at which point execution is suspended. Any breakpoints encountered during execution of the Run to Line action are honored.

Viewing variables

Once the program is suspended at a breakpoint and you have stepped through it, you may notice that the flow of the program is incorrect. For example, an *if* statement you expected to execute didn't, or the output you expected from some operation is incorrect. At that point you are a long way from determining what is causing the program to fail. All you need to do is examine some variables and determine whether they hold an incorrect value.

There are several ways to examine the values of the variables in a suspended program. For simple variables, especially if you only need a glimpse of their values, you may place the mouse pointer and hover it on top of the variable name (no clicking required) in the Java editor view. A text box will open and display information about the variable, including its current value, as shown in Figure 5.19.

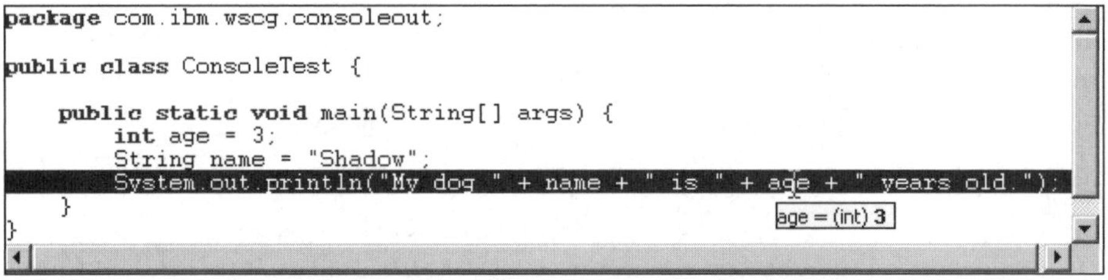

```
package com.ibm.wscg.consoleout;

public class ConsoleTest {

    public static void main(String[] args) {
        int age = 3;
        String name = "Shadow";
        System.out.println("My dog " + name + " is " + age + " years old.");
    }
}
```
age = (int) 3

Figure 5.19: Primitive variable under cursor.

This method works well for primitive and String variables. For complex variables, all it displays is the object ID and its type, which, although useful, does not provide you with the variable's value. If there is any Javadoc comment associated with the type under the cursor, it is displayed as well (Figure 5.20).

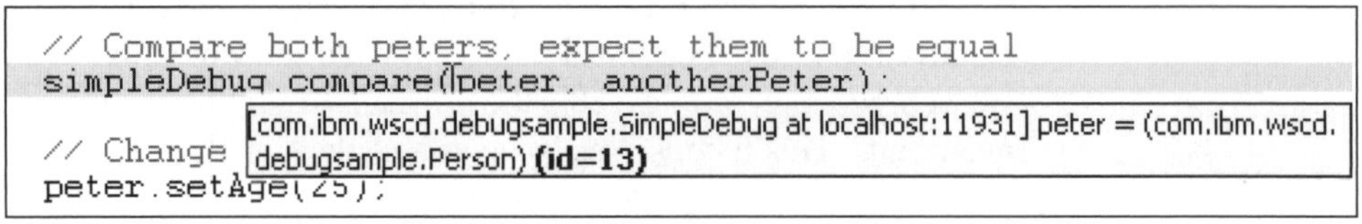

```
// Compare both peters, expect them to be equal
simpleDebug.compare(peter, anotherPeter);
                    [com.ibm.wscd.debugsample.SimpleDebug at localhost:11931] peter = (com.ibm.wscd.
    // Change    debugsample.Person) (id=13)
peter.setAge(25);
```

Figure 5.20: Complex variable under cursor.

To display complex variables, or if you want the value of the variable to be visible after you move the cursor away, use the Variables view.

The Variables view (Figure 5.21) is located, by default, in the upper right-hand corner of the window. Its pane is shared by other views that we will cover later in the chapter.

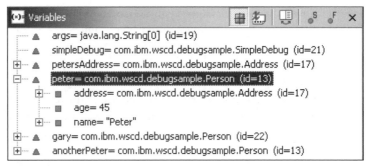

Figure 5.21: Variables view.

From the Variables view you may also change the value of a variable. To do this you select the variable and, from its context menu, select **Change Variable Value**. For complex variables, you need to select a specific element of the variable, for example peter.age.

The Variables view displays all the variables currently in scope.

As you can see on Figure 5.21, the variable called peter is of type com.ibm.debugsample.Person. The variable has been expanded to show the components that make it up: address, age, and name. Primitive types and Strings have their values displayed directly. Complex variables may contain other variables of interest and can be expanded by clicking the plus (+) sign to the left of their names. Clicking on the plus sign further expands the type, allowing you to drill down and see their individual components (Figure 5.22).

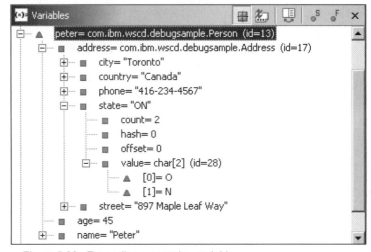

Figure 5.22: Expanding a complex variable.

Now you can see that Person has an Address, and that address is made up of several other components: city, country, phone, state, and street. Further, the value for the String state is ON, and its components are count, hash, offset and a char[].

Toolbar buttons

The Variables view has several toolbar buttons, shown in Figure 5.23, that allow you to change the amount of information you see displayed. These toolbar button functions are also available through the view's context menu.

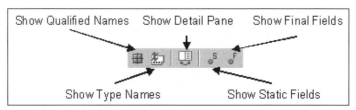

Figure 5.23: Variables view toolbar buttons.

The graphic in Figure 5.22 displays variables with the Show Qualified Names button selected. As you can see, the variable peter is represented as

```
peter= com.ibm.wscd.debugsample.Person   (id=13)
```

The type of the variable peter is shown fully qualified. If the button had not been selected, you would see

```
peter= Person   (id=13)
```

The type of the variable peter is no longer fully qualified.

The Show Type Names button causes the type of the variable to appear preceding the variable name. The variable peter would be represented as

```
Person peter= Person   (id=17)
```

The Show Detail Pane button gives you a split-screen view. Selecting a variable on the top pane displays its value on the bottom pane (Figure 5.24).

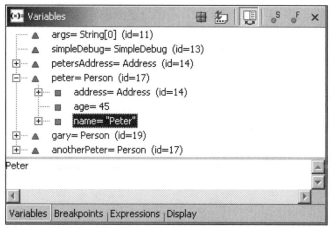

Figure 5.24: Variable value on detail pane.

The next two buttons are filters. They control whether static and final variables are displayed on the Variables view. Be aware that deselecting these filters causes members of that type not to be shown on the view.

Expressions view

The Expressions view is where variables being inspected are displayed. You can inspect any variable in scope while the application is in suspended state, for example while stopped at a breakpoint or while single-stepping through code.

To inspect a variable, select its name from the Java editor, and from its context menu select Inspect (see Figure 5.25). You can also follow these same steps from the Variables view.

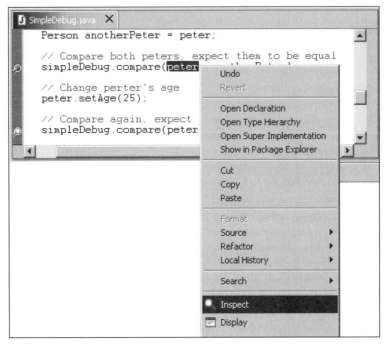

Figure 5.25: Inspect variable context menu.

You Inspect a variable to see the values of the components of a complex variable. The Expressions view is initially empty, and you can add the variables you are interested in inspecting (Figure 5.26).

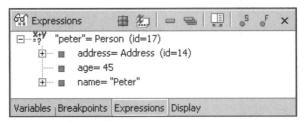

Figure 5.26: Expressions view.

Variables in the Expressions view remain available while in context, or until you remove them using the appropriate toolbar buttons as shown in Figure 5.27.

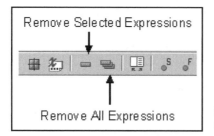

Figure 5.27: Expressions
view toolbar buttons.

The rest of the toolbar buttons provide functions consistent with those already explained in the Variables view.

Display view

The Display view provides you with a way to evaluate any valid Java expression. This is a very powerful feature of WebSphere Studio. Similar in function to a Scrapbook page, which we will discuss later in the chapter, the Display view gives you a window into the running Java virtual machine, which can be accessed while an application is suspended by the debugger.

As an example, you may evaluate a very simple expression like 5 + 7, as shown in Figure 5.28:

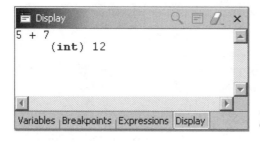

Figure 5.28: Simple
expression evaluation.

To evaluate an expression, follow these steps:

- Enter the expression in the Display view.

- Highlight the expression by swiping the mouse over it.

- From the context menu of the selection, select **Display**.

The evaluated result is displayed under the expression.

Code executed in the Display view runs in the context of the current stack frame. All variables in scope are available. Complex variables, representing instances of classes, can have their methods invoked. This can be very useful, as you can invoke methods that are not part of the program.

For example, to change the age of the Person represented by the variable peter, you could enter an expression that invokes the setter method for peter's age in the Display view, select the expression, and, from the context menu of the selection, select **Display**, as shown in Figure 5.29.

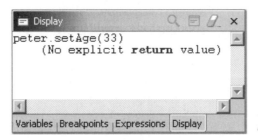

Figure 5.29: Invoking a method.

If the method returned a value, instead of void, that value would be displayed after execution. Switching to the Variables view (Figure 5.30) confirms that the method has indeed run and the age of peter was changed to 33.

Figure 5.30: Value of variable after method invocation.

When entering code in the Display view, you can use code assist (Ctrl+Space) to help you select the right members of the class you are working on.

One thing you may not do in the Display window is declare new variables.

The toolbar buttons on the Display view (Figure 5.31) give you shortcuts to the some of the items on the context menu.

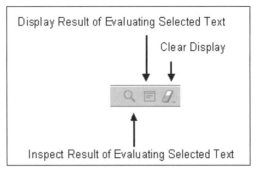

Figure 5.31: Display view toolbar buttons.

Other types of breakpoints

So far you have seen the use of simple line breakpoints to suspend program execution at a predetermined line of code. These types of breakpoints, when enabled, will always suspend the program when they are reached.

There are circumstances when you do not wish to suspend the program every time the breakpoint is reached, or you may want to suspend execution when an exception is encountered. WebSphere Studio provides you with facilities to do just that.

In addition to line breakpoints, the following breakpoints are available:

- Conditional breakpoints
  - ◆ Hit count
  - ◆ Logic condition
- Java Exception breakpoints
- Variable watchpoint breakpoints
- Method breakpoints
  - ◆ Entry
  - ◆ Exit

Let's briefly describe the characteristics of each of them.

Conditional breakpoints

Conditions can be set against a line breakpoint. Start by setting a breakpoint as described earlier in the chapter. From the breakpoint's properties you can enter a hit count or a logic condition. To get to a breakpoint's properties, you select **Properties** from its context menu on the Breakpoints view or select **Breakpoint Properties** from the context menu of the breakpoint itself on the marker bar of the Java editor, as shown in Figure 5.32.

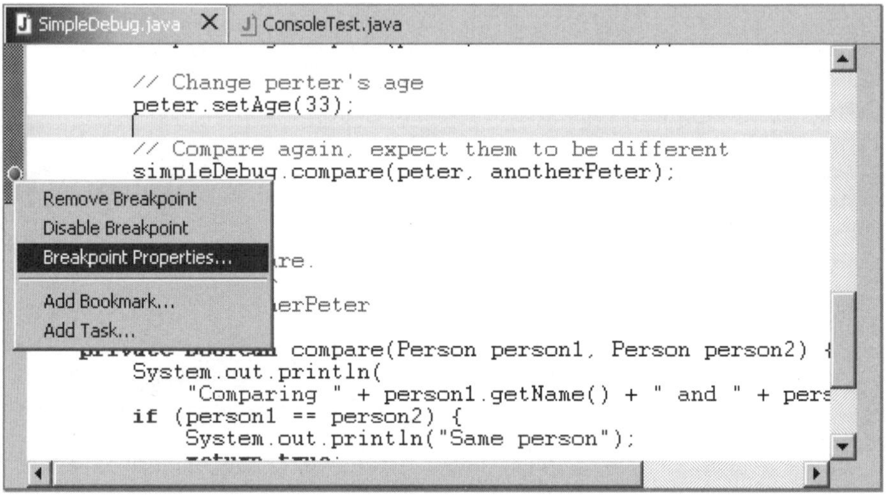

Figure 5.32: Opening breakpoint's properties.

In the breakpoint's Properties dialog, you can use check boxes to select whether to Enable Hit Count, Enable Condition, or both (Figure 5.33).

Enabling the hit count allows you to enter a number in the Hit Count field. This is the number of times the statement will be executed before the debugger will cause the application to suspend. This is especially useful, for example, inside of a loop where you are interested in seeing what happens after a certain number of iterations.

When the hit count is reached, execution suspends, and the breakpoint becomes disabled. At this point you may proceed debugging. You can also re-enable the breakpoint and Resume execution; in that case the count starts again, and execution suspends when the hit count is reached again.

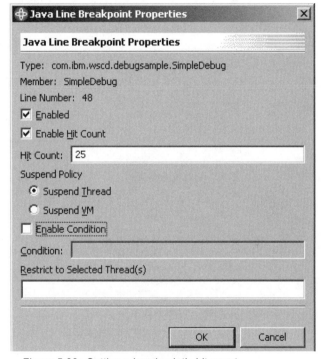

Figure 5.33: Setting a breakpoint's hit count.

A logic-based conditional breakpoint causes suspension of execution when a particular condition is true. Selecting Enable Condition in the Java Line Breakpoint Properties dialog allows you to enter an expression in the Condition field, as in Figure 5.34. This Condition can be any expression that evaluates to true or false. When the debugger reaches the breakpoint, the expression is evaluated. Execution is suspended if the condition is true, otherwise it continues.

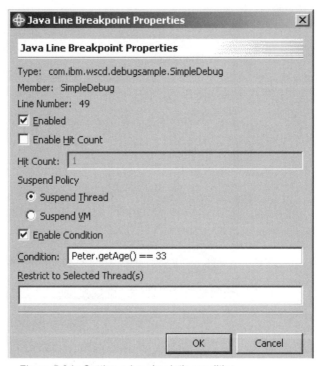

Figure 5.34: Setting a breakpoint's condition.

In this case the *intent* is to stop at the breakpoint only if the getAge() method of the Person object instance, peter, is 33 years old. As you can see, the name of the variable peter was entered erroneously with an uppercase initial. The Condition entry field does not do any syntax checking, and code assist is not available, so you could make a mistake and be allowed to click OK without a warning. However, at runtime, you will get an error dialog (Figure 5.35) when the breakpoint is first reached.

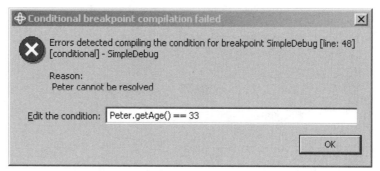

Figure 5.35: Syntax error on condition.

At this point you can correct the error right on the dialog and continue.

Note: Hit Count and Condition can be enabled at the same time, giving you even greater flexibility. Also, conditional breakpoints have a question mark overlaying the blue ball breakpoint icon on the marker bar.

Other options on the Java Line Breakpoint Properties dialog allow you to select whether the complete JVM, or only the thread on which the breakpoint is reached, suspends. Normally you would want only the one thread to suspend, but there may be cases in which you want nothing else executing while you are suspended. You may also choose which thread to monitor for breakpoint conditions. Normally you monitor all threads, so no restrictions are applied.

Java Exception breakpoints

Sometimes a Java Exception will be thrown during the execution of your program. If the exception is not caught, the program will abend without providing you with an opportunity to report the problem or to attempt recovery. In these cases a good course of action is to set a Java Exception breakpoint.

A Java Exception breakpoint will suspend execution when the exception is thrown. In many cases, examining the stack frame will help you determine the conditions that led to the exception being thrown.

For example, consider the code listed in Figure 5.36.

```java
public class JavaExceptionTest {

    public static void main(String[] args) {
        //This is for testing a java.lang.ArrayIndexOutOfBoundsException
        int array[] = { 0, 1, 2, 3, 4, 5 };
        for (int i = 0; i < 30; i++) {
            System.out.println(
            "Value in array at index: " + i + " is " + array[i]);
        }
    }
}
```

Figure 5.36: Code containing a logic error leading to an exception.

As you can see, this code will throw a java.lang.ArrayIndexOutOfBoundsException exception at runtime, because the index of the array is incremented beyond the size of the array. If a program that throws this exception contains many methods that manipulate arrays, looking for this kind of error in each method may be very tedious, and it would be much easier if we could have the debugger stop when the exception occurs and show us the code that is actually causing the problem.

To let the debugger suspend execution when the exception occurs, you set a Java Exception breakpoint. To set a Java Exception breakpoint, select **Add Java Exception Breakpoint** from the Breakpoints view context menu (see Figure 5.9) or click the Add Java Exception Breakpoint button on the Breakpoints view toolbar (Figure 5.37).

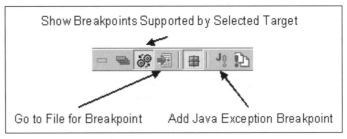

Figure 5.37: Breakpoints view toolbar buttons.

There are two other toolbar buttons shown in Figure 5.37 that we have not covered:

- ■ *Go to File for Breakpoint*: Clicking this button switches the Java editor view to the file and line number where the currently selected breakpoint is set. This action can also be triggered by double-clicking on the breakpoint in the Breakpoints view.

- ■ *Show Breakpoints Supported by Selected Target*: This action allows you to toggle between a display of all set breakpoints and only those breakpoints that are supported by the debug target; that is, for the program being debugged. Otherwise, breakpoints for the entire workspace are shown, by default.

At the bottom of the Add Java Exception Breakpoint dialog (Figure 5.38), use the check boxes to specify how you want execution to suspend at locations where the exception is thrown.

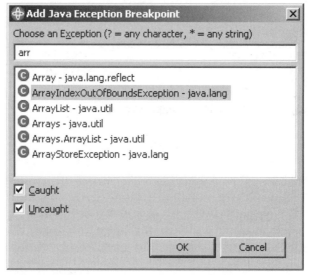

Figure 5.38: Selecting a Java Exception to set a breakpoint on it.

- ■ Choose **Caught** if you want execution to suspend at locations where the exception is thrown but caught.

- ■ Choose **Uncaught** if you want execution to suspend at locations where the exception is uncaught.

With Java Exception breakpoints there is no indication on the marker bar of the Editor view that a breakpoint exists, because this type of breakpoint is associated with the process and not a particular line of code. Java Exception breakpoints are listed, and can be modified or removed, in the Breakpoints view.

As you can see in Figure 5.39, the console output shows the array being accessed by the index, and all goes well until the count reaches five. The next attempt to access the array, with an index value of 6, causes the exception, and the debugger suspends execution. You can clearly see the problem and can easily fix it.

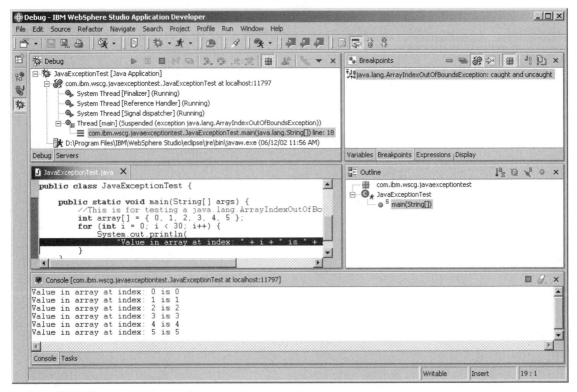

Figure 5.39: Suspended at exception.

Watchpoints

Watchpoints, another very powerful debugger feature, enable you to suspend execution of the application when a selected variable is accessed or modified. This is particularly useful for detecting unauthorized or unpredicted access to a variable. Perhaps some thread or method call is changing the value of a variable, making its value inaccurate at the time you need to access it.

To set a watchpoint, you select the variable in the Variables or Expressions views and, from the context menu, select **Add/Remove Watchpoint**. Note that execution of the program must be suspended before you can select this option, and that the variable in question must already be displayed in the views mentioned.

Complex variables can have only members selected, such as the age field on the Person class.

Watchpoints are listed only in the Breakpoints view. From their context menu the following manipulations are available:

- Hit Count
- Modification
- Access
- Enable
- Disable

Note: These same attributes can also be accessed through the breakpoint's properties dialog for a watchpoint.

Method breakpoints

Method breakpoints can be applied only to binary files. In the case of Java applications they can be applied to .class files. If the corresponding source is available for the class file, then you can step through the code and debug normally once the breakpoint is encountered.

Method breakpoints will suspend execution upon entering or exiting a method call. In the case of an entry method breakpoint, execution is suspended before any code is executed in the class. An exit method breakpoint will suspend execution at the method's closing brace.

To apply a method breakpoint, you first open a class file. From its Outline view, select the method you want to add the breakpoint to, and from its context menu select **Add/Remove Method Breakpoint** as shown in Figure 5.40.

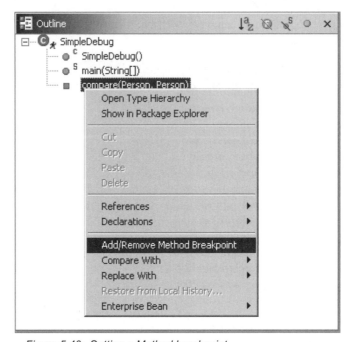

Figure 5.40: Setting a Method breakpoint.

Method breakpoints are listed only in the Breakpoints view. From their context menu the following manipulations are available:

- Hit Count

- Entry

- Exit

- Enable

- Disable

Note: These same attributes can also be accessed through the breakpoint's properties dialog.

Scrapbook

The Scrapbook is not part of the debugger proper. However, scrapbook pages can be used to try new code and figure things out before committing the code to a Java class.

Scrapbook pages are very similar in function to the Display view in the debugger. Code snippets can be entered and run in isolation. Single or multiple lines of code can be selected and run in the context of the page. Multiple selected lines must be contiguous.

A Scrapbook page is created under a Java project. Code is then typed on the page, selected, and executed. The results can be displayed in the console, using System.out.println() or similar methods. Also, expressions can be evaluated and their execution results displayed or inspected.

To create a Scrapbook page while in the Java perspective, first select the project in which you want to contain the page. From its context menu, select **New** → **Scrapbook Page** (Figure 5.41), or from the main menu select **File** → **New** → **Scrapbook Page**. A third way is to click the Create a Scrapbook Page toolbar icon on the Java perspective.

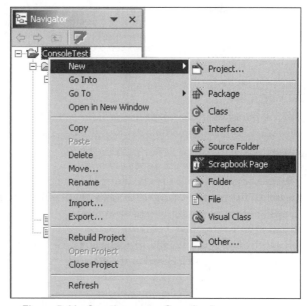

Figure 5.41: Creating a new Scrapbook page.

The Create Java Scrapbook Page dialog (Figure 5.42) opens, enabling you to name the page. Any name conforming to Java naming conventions will do.

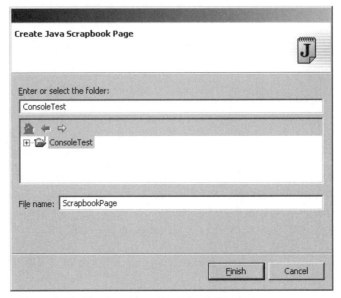

Figure 5.42: Naming a Java Scrapbook Page.

The wizard will add the *jpage* extension to the name you provide. Next, the Scrapbook page opens in the editor.

The first thing you will probably want to do is to set the import statements so that you don't have to fully qualify the names of the types you will use in the code snippet. Imports can be set at the class or package level.

To open the Java Snippet Imports dialog (Figure 5.43), select **Set Imports** from the context menu of the Scrapbook page, or click the Set the Import Declarations for Running Code toolbar button on the Java perspective.

Figure 5.43: Java Snippet Imports dialog.

After you click **Add Type . . .** , the Add Type as Import dialog (Figure 5.44) opens. In this dialog you select the type you need and click **OK** to add it. Note that in this dialog you may start typing the first few letters of the type you are looking for to narrow down the list of types displayed.

Do not type the package name in the entry field; only the name of the actual type is required. If the name you select exists in more than one package, you will need to select the package as well before clicking OK.

After selecting all the required types, or packages, click **OK** to return to the Scrapbook page editor.

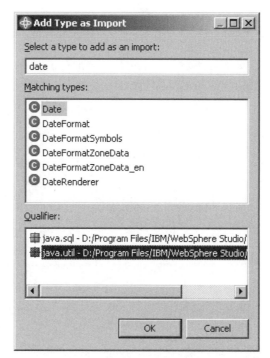

Figure 5.44: Add Type Import to Scrapbook page.

Note that no import statements show up on the Scrapbook page editor. Reopen the Java Snippet Imports dialog at any time to view the available classes for the scrapbook page.

On the Scrapbook page you may enter any Java code you wish to experiment with. Consider the following code:

```
Date date = new Date();
System.out.println(" Current date and time: " + date);
```

Select the two lines of code and, from the context menu, select **Run Snippet**. On the Console view, examine the result of running the snippet:

```
Current date and time: Fri Dec 06 15:36:39 EST 2002
```

This is, of course, an overly simplistic example. You will find other, more challenging, opportunities to use the Scrapbook when working on your own programs.

In addition to running the selected snippet, you can also inspect and display expressions. These work in much the same way as they did in the debugger. Inspecting an expression causes an Expressions view to open, and the result is displayed there. Displaying the results of an expression places the returned value of the expression to the right on the same line as the expression.

If an expression you evaluate causes a runtime exception, the exception will be reported in the Scrapbook page editor.

As usual, the actions available on the context menu are also available on the toolbar of the Java perspective, as shown in Figure 5.45.

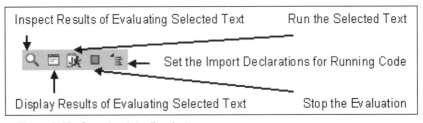

Figure 5.45: Scrapbook toolbar buttons.

Hot code replace

If you are successful in finding the problem on your code using the debugger, you will certainly want to change the offending line or expression. You can do so directly in the Java editor view from the Debug perspective. After changing the code, you save the file.

This capability, called hot code replace or hot method replace, is a feature of the JVM that allows a changed class to be loaded on the fly without restarting the JVM. If hot code replace is not supported by the current JVM, the error message shown in Figure 5.46 will come up.

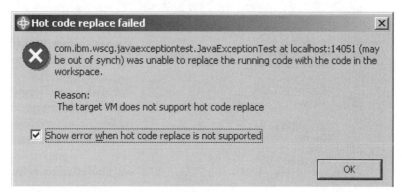

Figure 5.46: Hot code replace warning.

The reason why the warning in Figure 5.46 appears is that the JVM in the Java Runtime Environment (JRE), which runs your programs, does not support hot code replace. Hot code replace is supported by JVM versions 1.4 and higher. JVM 1.3, is the version specified by J2EE 1.3, and is the JVM used by WebSphere Application Server Version 5.x. If you are developing Web applications that will run in this application server, you cannot change the JVM running in WebSphere Studio. If you are building a stand-alone Java application, however, you can define another JVM, at version 1.4 or higher, and use it to run and debug your programs in WebSphere Studio. Doing so will automatically enable the debugger to allow you save Java classes and immediately load the changed class into the JVM. Any changes you made in the debugger will be immediately available without restarting the application.

You can obtain the latest JRE from *www.javasoft.com*. After downloading the JRE, run its setup program to install it in the directory of your choice.

To use the new JRE in WebSphere Studio, select **Windows** → **Preference** → **Java** → **Installed JREs**. The Installed Java Runtime Environments page of the Preferences dialog comes up, as shown in Figure 5.47.

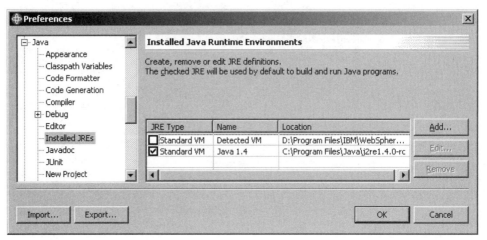

Figure 5.47: Selecting JRE to run.

On the Installed JREs page of the Preferences dialog, click **Add**. In the Add JRE dialog (Figure 5.48), point the JRE home directory field to the directory where you installed the JRE.

Click **OK** to add the JRE. Then, back on the Preferences page, select the checkbox under **JRE Type** besides the just-installed JRE; this will make it the default JRE that will be used when running Java applications. Click **OK**.

You can now change code in the debugger and save the class. It will be immediately available to the rest of the program, and you will not get the warning in Figure 5.46.

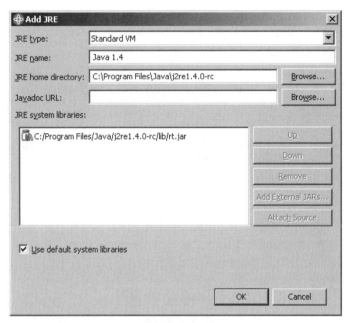

Figure 5.48: Point to desired JRE on file system.

Remember that you can effectively change JREs only for stand-alone applications. Also, make sure that whichever JRE/JVM is used for testing is the same version as the one used in production.

Exercise

In this section you will get to practice the principles of debugging using the WebSphere Studio development environment you read about in this chapter.

You should be able to complete this exercise after reading the chapter .and you may have to refer back to it for details. In this exercise you will use several code snippets provided to you in the Chapter 5 workspace.

Make sure that you have configured a shortcut to WebSphere Studio on your desktop and that it has been configured to accept workspace drops. This was explained in the last chapter.

1. Start WebSphere Studio with the workspace for Chapter 5.
   a. Using Windows Explorer, navigate to the **C:\WSCG\Workspaces\Startup\Chapter-5** directory.
   b. Select the directory and drag and drop it on top of the WebSphere Studio shortcut on your desktop.
   c. Wait until WebSphere Studio starts and loads the workspace.
2. Verify that the workspace has loaded correctly.
   a. If not already there, switch to the Java perspective.
   b. Confirm that the projects, shown in Figure 5.49, are present in the Package Explorer view.

Figure 5.49: Workspace loaded.
C:\WSCG\Workspaces\Chapter8

This workspace contains the code that was discussed in this chapter. You will now use it to gain experience working with the debugger.

Debug ConsoleTest.java

1. Select and open **ConsoleTest.java** in the Java editor.

2. Take a look at the very simple code listed in Figure 5.50. This is just an example of how you can use messages sent to the console to see the value of variables at runtime.

```
public class ConsoleTest {
    public static void main(String[] args) {
        int age = 3;
        String name = "Shadow";
        System.out.println("My dog " + name + " is " + age + " years old.");
    }
}
```

Figure 5.50: ConsoleTest.java.

3. Run the program in the debugger.

    a. Select **ConsoleTest.java**.

    b. Click the arrow next to the Debug toolbar button.

    c. From the drop-down list select **Debug As → Java Application**.

    Note that the program runs to completion and the output displays on the Console view.

4. Set a line breakpoint on the line of code that displays the output, just after the name variable is assigned its value.

5. Debug the program again.

6. What happened? Why?

7. On the Variables view take a look at the String called name. What is its value?

8. While on the Variables view, change the value of name to the name of your dog. If you don't have a dog, use the name Snoopy.

9. Click **Resume**. What printed on the console? Did the change to the variable take?

Debug SimpleDebug.java

1. The package com.ibm.wscg.debugsample contains three classes: Address, Person, and SimpleDebug.

2. Take a few minutes to examine these very simple classes, starting with Address and Person. These are JavaBeans; they are mainly used to hold the attributes

describing them. There is a simple containment relationship in which Person has an Address.

3. The SimpleDebug class has a main() method, listed in Figure 5.51.The main method does the following:

    a. Creates and initializes an Address object

    b. Creates two Person objects using the constructor that takes a name, age, and address parameters: the peter object, constructed using the Address object created on the first step, and the Person instance named gary, created using a new address

    c. Compares peter and gary

    d. Manipulates and compares different Person objects

```java
public static void main(String[] args) {

    // Create instance
    SimpleDebug simpleDebug = new SimpleDebug();

    // Create address and initialize
    Address petersAddress = new Address();
    petersAddress.setCity("Toronto");
    petersAddress.setCountry("Canada");
    petersAddress.setPhone("416-234-4567");
    petersAddress.setState("ON");
    petersAddress.setStreet("897 Maple Leaf Way");


    // Create persons
    Person peter = new Person("Peter", 45,petersAddress);
    Person gary = new Person("Gary", 36, new Address());

    // Compare peter and gary, expect them not to be equal
    simpleDebug.compare(peter, gary);

// Create another peter
    Person anotherPeter = peter;

    // Compare both peters, expect them to be equal
    simpleDebug.compare(peter, anotherPeter);
// Change anotherPeter's age
    anotherPeter.setAge(33);

    // Compare again, expect them to be different
    simpleDebug.compare(peter, anotherPeter);
}
```

Figure 5.51: The main method of the SimpleDebug class.

4. The compare() method (see Figure 5.52) prints the names of both persons being compared to the console. Then it compares both persons, printing an appropriate message. It returns true if both persons are equal, false if not.

```
private boolean compare(Person person1, Person person2) {
    System.out.println(
        "Comparing " + person1.getName() + " and " + person2.getName());
    if (person1 == person2) {
        System.out.println("Same person");
        return true;
    }else {
        System.out.println("Different person");
        return false;
    }
}
```

Figure 5.52: The compare method.

Well, this code has some problems, mainly that the comparison between the two classes is inadequate. But if the code wasn't flawed, we wouldn't be debugging it, would we?

You will use this code to become more familiar with the debugger. Refer to the text of the chapter if you get stuck performing the following steps. Also, feel free to go beyond these listed steps, and experiment and explore on your own.

5. Place the following line breakpoints:
   a. The line where petersAddress is instantiated
   b. The line where the compare() method is called with peter and gary as parameters.
   c. The second line of the compare() method, after the method declaration

6. Debug the program.

7. Once the debugger suspends execution at the first breakpoint, select the Variables view. Notice that petersAddress is not displayed. That is because a breakpoint causes the debugger to suspend *before* the code on the line is executed; therefore petersAddress does not yet exist.

8. Click **Step over**.

9. Now you see petersAddress. Expand it and see the members of this class. Notice that all the members of Address are null, which is their initialized value.

10. Continue single-stepping and observe how the members of Address are assigned their proper values by the program.

11. Click **Resume** to reach the next breakpoint quickly. This time click **Step into**. You are now in the first line of the compare method.

12. Continue to advance the execution of the program, verify variable values, and observe console output until you feel comfortable with the basic operation of the debugger.

13. Obviously the comparison between the peter and gary Person objects returns false. Although similar in many respects, Peter and Gary are two different people.

14. Back in main(), the program now creates another Person called anotherPeter and initially uses peter to create the new object with similar attributes. Hmm; it looks as though this program was written by a new Java programmer.

```
// Create another peter
Person anotherPeter = peter;
```

15. As the program continues, peter and anotherPeter are compared. The result is true, because at this point they are the same. After all, one was created from the other.

16. It turns out that anotherPeter is younger than the original peter. The code changes the age of anotherPeter.

```
// Change anotherPeter's age
anotherPeter.setAge(33);
```

17. Surely now the two peters are different now; let's compare them.

```
// Compare again, expect them to be different
simpleDebug.compare(peter, anotherPeter);
```

18. The result of the compare() method is true. They are still considered the same. How can that be?

19. Something is wrong. peter and anotherPeter should be different after the change in anotherPeter's age, shouldn't they? From the Breakpoints view, disable or remove the existing breakpoints. Place a new breakpoint on the last line of main(), where both peters are compared for the second time.

20. Terminate the current process, and restart debugging. This time execution will suspend at a point just before the peter and anotherPeter Person object instances are compared.

21. On the Variable view examine both peter and anotherPeter, as shown in Figure 5.53. What are the differences and similarities?

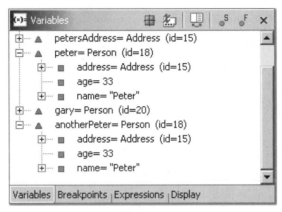

Figure 5.53: Comparing peter and anotherPeter.

22. What do you notice that would, to the untrained eye, seem strange?

    a. What are the ages? They are both the same. Why?

    b. Why when the age was changed in anotherPeter, did both ages change?

    c. What are the objects' Ids? They are both the same. Why?

    As you can see, both objects have the same object ID, therefore they are the same object. When you change a value in one object, they both change because both peter and anotherPeter are referencing the same object. That is the bug. The assignment, `Person anotherPeter = peter,` did not create another Person object instance; instead, it created a new reference to the existing instance of Person called peter.

    Here is another way you could have found that both peter and anotherPeter referenced the same object. After noticing that both ages had changed, you might suspect some part of the program was changing its value. If you set a watchpoint on the age attribute of peter, the debugger will suspend whenever anything modifies or accesses this field.

23. From the Variables view, add a Watchpoint on the peter.age attribute. Remove all other breakpoints. Rerun the program in the debugger.

24. Unexpectedly the debugger stops when loading the Person class into the JVM and initializes the age field to its default value. Now that you think about it, that is OK, age was being accessed and modified.

25. Click **Resume**. Next the debugger stops at the constructor for Person, again with good reason.

26. Click **Resume**. Every time the debugger stops, look on the call stack in the Debug view and find out which part of the program caused the modification of the age attribute.

Figure 5.54 shows the stack frame right after the watchpoint suspended the program. Note that the first stack frame is selected and the corresponding code is displayed in the Java editor view.

As expected, you are in the setAge() method of the Person class. Your watchpoint is monitoring modifications to the age field.

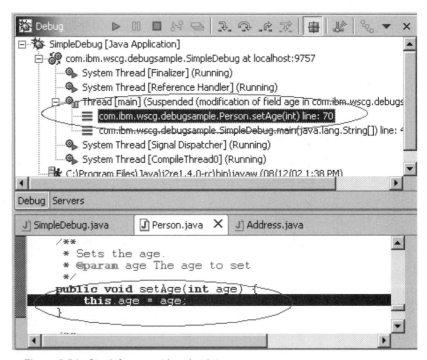

Figure 5.54: Stack frames at breakpoint.

In Figure 5.55, the second stack frame is selected. This is the previous stack frame, the one that called the setAge() method. Look at the corresponding code in the Java editor view. Here you see that setAge() is being called on the anotherPeter instance. Yet the watchpoint is monitoring the age field of the peter instance. This is another indication that something is wrong. Indeed, both peter and anotherPeter refer to the same instance of Person.

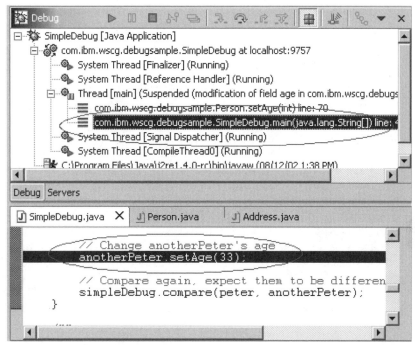

Figure 5.55: Calling stack frame.

Debug JavaExceptionTest.java

The JavaExceptionTest class is another very simple class for experimenting with conditional, hit count, and Java Exception breakpoints.

Consider the code listed in Figure 5.56:

```java
public static void main(String[] args) {
    //This is for testing a java.lang.ArrayIndexOutOfBoundsException
breakpoint
    int array[] = { 0, 1, 2, 3, 4, 5 };
    count(array, array.length);
    count(array, array.length + 5);

}

public static void count(int[] array, int c) {
    for (int i = 0; i < c; i++) {
        System.out.println(
            "Value in array at index: " + i + " is " + array[i]);
    }
}
```

Figure 5.56: JavaExceptionTest main method.

The method main() creates and initializes an int array of six elements. Then it calls the count() method twice. The count method iterates through the array and prints the contents of each element. The number of times the loop executes is determined by the second parameter.

The first call to count() uses the length of the array to control the number of iterations in the loop. The second call, purposely, uses a count larger than the capacity of the array. This will force a java.lang.ArrayIndexOutOfBoundsException exception to be thrown when the value of the index of the array exceeds its capacity.

By default, the debugger is configured to suspend execution of a program whenever an uncaught exception occurs. This is a fine default because it will prevent the program from abending and giving you a stack dump, which might be hard to decipher.

If you wish to use Java Exceptions breakpoints with a finer granularity, you should uncheck this default by selecting **Window → Preferences → Java → Debug** and unselecting **Suspend execution on uncaught exceptions** (as shown in Figure 5.57).

1. Ensure that your workspace does not have the preference to Suspend execution on uncaught exceptions selected. Now you can set more finely grained Java Exception breakpoints, as explained earlier in the chapter.

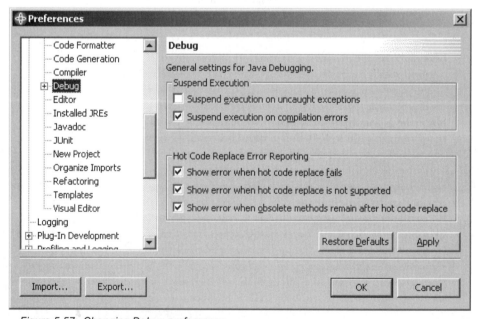

Figure 5.57: Changing Debug preferences.

2. Run the program once and observe the console output, listed in Figure 5.58. The first call to count() executes fine (see the first group of six values). The second call to count() reaches a count of six and, trying to access the seventh element of the array, throws the exception, and the program ends.

```
Value in array at index: 0 is 0
Value in array at index: 1 is 1
Value in array at index: 2 is 2
Value in array at index: 3 is 3
Value in array at index: 4 is 4
Value in array at index: 5 is 5
Value in array at index: 0 is 0
Value in array at index: 1 is 1
Value in array at index: 2 is 2
Value in array at index: 3 is 3
Value in array at index: 4 is 4
Value in array at index: 5 is 5
java.lang.ArrayIndexOutOfBoundsException at
com.ibm.wscg.javaexceptiontest.JavaExceptionTest.count(JavaExceptionTest.java23)
at com.ibm.wscg.javaexceptiontest.JavaExceptionTest.main(JavaExceptionTest.java:7)
Exception in thread "main"
```

Figure 5.58: Console output for JavaExceptionTest class.

3. To get a better grasp of what caused the exception, set a Java Exception breakpoint for caught and uncaught exceptions of type java.lang.ArrayIndexOutOfBoundsException. Consult the text of this chapter if you need to.

4. Restart the program under the control of the debugger.

5. What observations can you make:
   a. What is the value of the variable c, controlling the maximum iterations?
   b. What is the current value of the array index, i?
   c. Was any output produced?
   d. Selecting the previous stack frame, can you determine where count() was called from, and with which parameters?
   e. Why is there no exception showing on the console?

6. As extra credits, practice the following:
   a. Remove or disable the Java Exception breakpoint.
   b. Having determined that the index of the array should never exceed five, set a conditional breakpoint on the line printing the value of the array. The breakpoint should suspend execution when the value of *i* is equal to, or exceeds, 6. Run through the code again and see how that works.

   c. As an alternative to the conditional breakpoint, set a line breakpoint with a hit count. Cause execution to suspend before the exception is thrown.

   d. Finally, fix the count() method so that it cannot index past the length of the array.

Using the Scrapbook

In this exercise you create a Scrapbook page and experiment entering code and running code snippets, displaying and evaluating expressions.

1. Create a new Scrapbook page. Select the Debug Test folder, from its context menu select **New → Scrapbook Page**, call the page **MyScrapbookPage**.

2. Enter the following code:

```
Date date = new Date();
System.out.println(" Current date and time: " + date);
```

3. Select both lines of code and click the Run the Selected Code button from the toolbar.

4. You will get errors, because the page does not have the correct imports associated with it. From the scrapbook page's editor view, bring up the context menu and select **Set Imports** and the add java.util.Date type.

5. Run the code again. This time it should run, and the output should be displayed on the console.

6. Now you are on your way. Experiment with the SimpleDateFormat class to change the way the date displays. Experiment with the code to produce the following output.

```
Current date and time: Sunday Dec 8, 2002 at 04:01 PM, EST
```

7. Consult the Java.text.SimpleDateFormat class documentation for details.

Figure 5.59 shows a possible solution. This will work after you set imports for the java.util.Date and java.text.SimpleDateFormat classes.

```
//Play with time and date
Date date = new Date();

SimpleDateFormat df = new java.text.SimpleDateFormat("EEEEEEEE MMM d,
yyyy 'at' hh:mm a, z");

String formattedDate = df.format(date);


System.out.println(" Current date and time: " + formattedDate);
```

Figure 5.59: Possible solution to date format problem.

Test yourself

Key terms

tracing

breakpoint

debugger

Debug perspective

process

thread

step filtering

Variables view

Expressions view

Display view

Scrapbook

conditional breakpoint

Java Exception breakpoint

watchpoint

method breakpoints

Review questions

1. Why and when to debug?

2. What are some traditional techniques of debugging?

3. How do you debug a program in WebSphere Studio? What is the goal behind debugging?

4. How do you set a breakpoint in the Java editor?

5. What operations can you perform on breakpoints?

6. What are the three controls available to the developer while single-stepping through the Java program?

7. What is step filtering? How can I set up step filtering?

8. How can you view the value of variables in the Debug perspective?

9. What is the Display view?

10. Name two techniques for controlling breakpoints.

Essential HTTP and HTML

Chapter topics

- ❖ *Overview of HTTP*
- ❖ *Overview of common and essential HTML*
- ❖ *Introduction to WebSphere Studio Page Designer*

Certification objectives

- ❖ *Use outline views*
- ❖ *Use Page Designer*
- ❖ *Use content assist*
- ❖ *Use Web Page wizards*

In this chapter we cover the minimum amount of HyperText Markup Language (HTML) that you need to know to successfully understand the examples and exercises on this book. It should also be sufficient to answer the questions on the certification exam that have HTML content.

Before we talk about HTML, we will introduce the HyperText Transfer Protocol (HTTP), HTTP is the primary transfer protocol of the Web.

Overview of HTTP

HTTP is fully defined by the W3C organization. For a complete description of HTTP see *www.w3.org/Protocols*. Refer to that site if you are interested in a deeper understanding of HTTP. There are also a multitude of good books published on the subject.

Web traffic between clients and servers of HTML pages uses HTTP. HTTP is a very fast and simple protocol. TCP/IP is the transport protocol for HTTP.

HTTP is not a secure protocol. A variant of HTTP, HTTPS, provides means to establish a secure connection between a browser and the server through the use of the Secure Sockets Layer (SSL).

The mechanism used by HTTP is one of request and response. The client makes, or sends, a request to the server, and the server receives the request, determines whether the request can be fulfilled, and creates an appropriate response, which is sent back to the client. HTTP maintains no continuity when multiple requests between client and server take place. HTTP has no concept of state. This presents unique problems in Web applications that depend on a user going through multiple pages (multiple requests) to complete a transaction. We will see how to deal with this problem later in the book.

Request

The simplest request starts as a Universal Resource Locator (URL) entered on the address line of a Web browser. The URL takes the following form:

http://www.ibm.com:8080/index.html?action=open

The above URL can be broken down into five distinct parts:

- The protocol (*http*)

- The target server (*www.ibm.com*)

- Optional port number (*8080*; the default port is 80)

- The desired document (*index.html*)

- Optional query string (*action=open*; there may be multiple *name=value* pairs, separated by the & character)

Pressing the Enter key after entering a URL creates a request, which is sent to the server. The three major components of the request are

- Method

- Headers

- Object body

Methods

There are number of defined methods in HTTP. The most common ones used in Web applications are GET and POST.

The GET method requests a document from the server, such as an HTML page. Provided the requested document exists, it is returned as the body of the response and rendered by the client. If the document does not exist, an error header is returned on the response indicating a 404 (Not Found) error.

In the context of Web applications the POST method is used to invoke a resource in the server to take care of the request. These are usually resources that process more complex requests than just returning a document. They typically involve performing a service for the client, for example:

- Authenticating a user (login)

- Retrieving a set of properties particular to the authenticated user

- Communicating to other back-end resources to perform a lookup of merchandise or complete a purchase

In the case of multitier Web applications, which run in an application server such as WebSphere Application Server, the resource referred to in the URL is very often a servlet. A servlet is a Java program that runs completely on the server. Servlets will be covered in detail in a later chapter.

It is possible to send fairly large amounts of data in a POST request. Typically, data entered on an HTML form is sent along with the request and can be queried and extracted by the servlet named in the request.

As you will later see, the GET and POST HTTP methods map to the doGet() and doPost() servlet methods.

Other HTTP methods include:

- OPTIONS

- HEAD

- PUT

- DELETE

- TRACE

- CONNECT

Request header

The request header is created by the client software, for example the Web browser. The contents of the headers are available to the server to interrogate and act accordingly. Headers are made up of a field name and its associated value.

The User-Agent header field provides the server with information about the software program used by the client. For example, the server can determine which browser and version the client is using, and adjust the generated output so that the output will be best formatted for a particular browser type. This becomes very important when Web applications deal with multiple devices such as personal computers, Web-enabled phones, and other portable devices.

The Referer field allows the client to specify, for the server's benefit, the address (Uniform Resource Identifier (URI)) of the document from which the URI in the request was obtained.

Other header fields are the following:

- Accept
- Accept-Encoding
- Accept-Language
- Authorization
- From
- Host
- If-Modified-Since

Response

After receiving and interpreting a request message, a server responds with an HTTP response message.

The response is made up of several components:

- Status line
- Headers
- Message body

Status line

The status line is made up of three parts: the HTTP version, the status code, and the reason phrase.

The first digit of the status code defines the class of response. The last two digits do not have any categorization role, aside from differentiating one code from another within a category. Following the status code is a short description called the reason phrase.

There are five values for the first digit of the status code:

- 1xx: *Informational*—request received, continuing process

- 2xx: *Success*—the action was successfully received, understood, and accepted

- 3xx: *Redirection*—further action must be taken in order to complete the request

- 4xx: *Client Error*—the request contains bad syntax or cannot be fulfilled

- 5xx: *Server Error*—the server failed to fulfill an apparently valid request

Here are some frequently encountered status codes with their reason phrases:

- 200: Success

- 202: Accepted

- 400: Bad request

- 403: Forbidden

- 404: Not found

- 500: Internal server error

- 503: Service unavailable

Response header

Response headers are used to control and describe the information sent with the response. Some of the most commonly used headers used in the response are

- Cache-control

- Date

- Pragma

These headers are used to control how the information is to be handled by servers along the way to the browser. For example, the Cache-Control and Pragma headers can be set to indicate to servers not to cache the document in the response. This is especially useful when the server is delivering dynamically generated documents to the browser, where the content of these documents is different every time it is sent. Caching and delivering cached documents later would present an old copy, with incorrect information, to the user.

Message body

The message body contains, in most cases, the HTML document satisfying the request. These can be static HTML pages or a dynamically created page with information particular to the user who made the request.

Dynamically generated pages are usually created by the servlets and JavaServer Pages (JSP) in a Web application.

Flow of request and response

In general, a request starts at the client side. Either a URL is entered on the address line of the browser, or a hyperlink is clicked (generating a GET method request), or a Submit button is clicked on an HTML form (generating a POST method request).

For the simplest GET request of a document from a Web server (shown in Figure 6.1), the document's URL is entered on the browser. The request header is built by the browser, and the request is sent to the Web server. The Web server examines the request, uses its mapping mechanism to determine whether the requested document exists on the file system, and, if so, prepares a response header and includes the requested document in the body of the response. The response is sent back to the requester's URL. The browser parses the response and, if capable, renders the document.

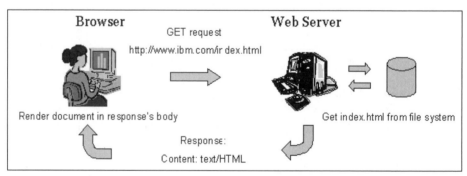

Figure 6.1: Simple GET request.

Rendering the document may result in additional GET requests going out to the same or different servers, for example to retrieve additional graphics or include parts of other URLs contained in the originally requested document.

A POST request, shown in Figure 6.2, is usually the result of clicking a Submit button on an HTML form. The request includes the form's data. Part of the HTML form definition includes a field called ACTION; this field contains the URL of a program that the server will run to service the request. In the case of Java Web applications, this program is a servlet. The servlet has access to objects that represent the HTTP request and response. Form data is available in the request object. The server running the servlet will load it and run the code in the servlet to process the request. The servlet processes the request and has access to back-end resources and computing capabilities to handle the request (in our example, registration of a new user to the system). Then the servlet generates the appropriate response depending on the success of failure of the operation. The output is sent back to the browser as part of the body of the response.

We will cover how servlets operate, in great detail, later in this book.

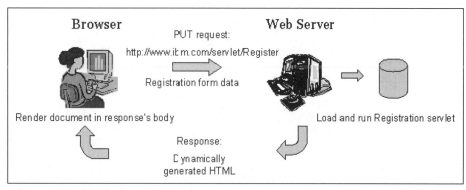

Figure 6.2: POST request processing.

Overview of common and essential HTML

HTML is a markup language used to design the layout of Web pages. It can also be used to compose other types of documents as well, such as presentations. In the majority of cases HTML documents will be displayed to the user in a Web browser such as Microsoft Internet Explorer, Netscape Navigator, Mozilla, or Opera. Web browsers parse and render the HTML tags as appropriate.

The complete specifications for the HTML markup language can be found at *www.w3.org/MarkUp/html-spec*. Countless publications exist that describe HTML in great detail with many examples. The purpose of this book is not to cover HTML in depth but only to cover the essential amount of information to enable you to understand the examples and exercises in the book and to aid you in the few questions in the Certification exam that may require basic HTML knowledge to answer correctly.

How to create HTML documents

HTML documents are basically text documents. Any text editor can be used to compose these documents. However, using a text editor requires that you visualize the layout and formatting of the page, because these editors do not render the document. A simple HTML page can look pretty cryptic to the uneducated eye.

As you can see, even the simple page listed in Figure 6.3 presents a challenge to visualize.

```
<HTML>
<HEAD>
<TITLE>JK Partner Invoice Submission Home</TITLE>
</HEAD>
<BODY>
<TABLE border="0" width="100%">
<TBODY>
<TR>

<TD bgcolor="#155927" align="center" valign="bottom"><IMG border="0"

src="images/JKBanner2.gif" width="640" height="68"></TD>
</TR>
<TR>
<TD>
<h1>Business Partner Invoice Submission Service</h1>
<p><br />
<a href="jsp/Login.jsp">Login</a>
<br />
<a href="jsp/registration.jsp">Register (add new vendor)</a>
<br />
Submit an Invoice -- login first<a href="jsp/createPO.jsp">
<br />
Add PO (admin)</a></p>
</TD>
</TR>
</TBODY>
</TABLE>
</BODY>
</HTML>
```

Figure 6.3: HTML page.

- What are the colors used?

- How is the text arranged? Does it align properly?

- What do the fonts look like?

- How about the image? What does it look like?

For these and many other reasons, creating HTML pages using a text editor is just not convenient or productive. There are many tools that provide a WYSIWYG (what you see is what you get) editor to create HTML pages. Because HTML pages are meant to be seen formatted, it is very important that they are composed using these editors, where the pages can be composed visually.

WebSphere Studio provides a very good HTML editor, Page Designer. It can be used for both HTML and JSP pages. As you will learn soon, JSP pages are composed in a very similar way to HTML pages; the difference is that HTML pages contain only static content. JSP pages can contain both static and dynamically generated pages.

The Page Designer editor is made up of three different views:

- Design

- Source

- Preview

The Design view is where you compose the pages using the WYSIWYG paradigm. You mainly select widgets from a list, or menus, and place them on the page. You can also type directly on to the page and rearrange the components visually. Changes made are immediately reflected in what you see in this view.

The Source view allows you both to see the generated code resulting from your activities in the Design view and to enter, or modify, HTML or JSP code directly.

Any changes made in either view are reflected in the other.

The Preview view allows you to see how the rendered page will look on an Internet Explorer browser. Be aware that dynamic elements in JSP pages will not be rendered here, because the page is just being shown by the browser and not actually composed on the server.

The HTML page listed in Figure 6.3, when viewed in the Preview view of the HTML editor in WebSphere Studio, looks like Figure 6.4:

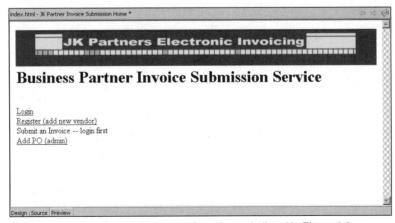

Figure 6.4: Rendered HTML page from the code listed in Figure 6.3.

The page shown in Figures 6.3 and 6.4 was created in the Design view of the HTML editor in WebSphere Studio, where it appears as shown in Figure 6.5. As you can see, the
Design and Preview views display a very similar representation of the page, which is
exactly what you want. As you design, you will get a very good idea of what the page
will look like in the browser. To get an exact rendering, all you need to do is switch to the
Preview view.

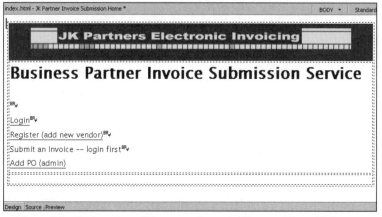

Figure 6.5: Design view of the page shown in Figures 6.3 and 6.4.

HTML tags

As you can see in the code of the Web page in the previous section (Figure 6.3), an HTML
page is composed of a number of tags. Each tag has a particular syntax associated.

All HTML tags are enclosed between less-than and greater-than signs, for example,
<H1>. End tags have a forward slash character "/" following the less-than sign: </H1>.
Tags are not case sensitive; they can be all lowercase, all uppercase, or mixed case.

```
<h1>Business Partner Invoice Submission Service</h1>
```

Note: Some elements have only a start tag without an end tag. For example, to
create a line break, use the <BR> tag. Additionally, the end tags of some other
elements, such as Paragraph (</P>), List Item (</LI>), Definition Term (</DT>),
and Definition Description (</DD>) elements, may be omitted.

Documents must be well formed. End tags must appear in the reverse order of appear-
ance to the corresponding start tags, as shown in Figure 6.6.

```
<HTML>
<HEAD>
<TITLE>JK Partner Invoice Submission Home</TITLE>
</HEAD>
<BODY>
...
</BODY>
</HTML>
```

Figure 6.6: Nested tags with end tags in reverse order as the corresponding start tags.

Some HTML tags accept *attributes* to define their function further, or to provide additional information to the rendering engine. In the listing in Figure 6.3, for example, the <TABLE> tag was further defined with border and width attributes, and the <TD> tag was defined with attributes for background color (bgcolor) and horizontal and vertical alignment (align, valign). The HTML specification defines which attributes are valid for what tags.

Essential HTML tags

To identify information as an HTML document conforming to the HTML specification, each document must start with a document type declaration. The declaration indicates the level of HTML used, and the Document Type Definition (DTD) used to validate the document:

```
<!DOCTYPE HTML PUBLIC "-//W3C//DTD HTML 4.01 Transitional//EN">
```

Table 6.1 lists the minimum number of tags and attributes you should be familiar with to read and understand most HTML documents.

Table 6.1: Essential HTML tags.

HTML Tag	Notes
<HTML>	Beginning of document
<HEAD>	Start of header section
<TITLE>	Places title on title bar of browser
<P>	Paragraph; following text starts in a new line
 	Line break; can be used to provide extra spaces between paragraphs
<OL> </OL>	Begin and end ordered list (numbered list)
<UL> </UL>	Begin and end unordered list (bullet list)
<LI>	List item; either ordered or unordered
<[OL] [UL] COMPACT>	A compact list, less space between list items, saves space on the page
<! >	Comments must be of this form: <!--Comment lines are ignored -->
<Hx>	Headings; the "x" is replaced by a number from 1 through 6. Each heading level has different emphasis and font size. Headings can be aligned: <h2 align="center">This is centered</h2>
<EM>	Emphasis; text between tags is darker
<IMG>	Image, must provide source URL: <IMG SRC="images/logo.jpg" WIDTH="340" HEIGHT="255" ALT="IBM Corp.">
<CENTER>	Center following elements on page
<A>	Anchor hyperlink; transfer user to page defined in HREF, text is shown in hyperlink emphasis, can also include an image as a link: <A HREF="login.html">Click here to login</A> <A HREF="login.html"><IMG SRC="login.jpg"></A>
<TABLE>	Beginning of a table; other tags between the begin and end tags for the table are required to actually create a functional table
<TH>	Table header row
<TR>	Table row; this tag creates a row in a table
<TD>	This tag goes between <TR> tags; each <TD> tag represents a cell (one row, one column) of the table. (See the following example.)

Figure 6.7 lists the source for a sample HTML table:

```
<TABLE ALIGN="CENTER" BORDER CELLSPACING="0" CELLPADDING="0" width="296">

<CAPTION><B>Soccer teams standings</B></CAPTION>
<TH>Team</TH>
<TH>Place</TH>
<TR>
<TD><B>Raleigh Demons</B></TD>
<TD align="center"><B>1</B></TD>
</TR>
<TR>
<TD><B>Toronto Badgers</B></TD>
<TD align="center"><B>2</B></TD>
</TR>
<TR">
<TD><B>Ottawa Kings</B></TD>
<TD align="center"><B>3</B></TD>
</TR>
</TABLE>
```

Figure 6.7: Code for HTML table.

Notice that the <TABLE> tag is further defined with alignment, padding, and border attributes. You also see the <TD> tag with an alignment attribute. The results of rendering the table on a browser are shown in Figure 6.8:

Soccer teams standings	
Team	**Place**
Raleigh Demons	1
Toronto Badgers	2
Ottawa Kings	3

Figure 6.8: Rendered table from the HTML code shown in Figure 6.7.

As you can see, a number of extra attributes can be used in a table to control its size, border, alignment, and other characteristics.

The <FORM> HTML tag, its content, and its attributes

One tag deserves its own section because it is used so frequently in enterprise Web applications: the <FORM> tag.

Like most tags, <FORM> has a beginning and an ending tag. The attributes between these tags define how HTML forms behave.

HTML forms are the most common way to collect information from the user. This information is later retrieved in an application and acted upon to fulfill the request for a service from the application.

Examples of the uses of forms include

- Registration forms

- Login user ids and passwords

- Making selections

- Collecting preferences

Forms include a variety of widgets that provide the graphical user interface (GUI) for a particular page of the application. Some examples of these widgets are

- Text area

- Text field

- Radio buttons

- Check boxes

- List boxes

- Drop-down menus

- Submit and Reset buttons

Usually these widgets are placed in table cells to facilitate their alignment. The form is rendered by the browser; the user enters the required information and eventually clicks the Submit button.

Let's look at the simple form shown in Figure 6.9, which could be used to log into a Web application. Figure 6.10 lists the HTML source for just the <FORM> tag part of the page.

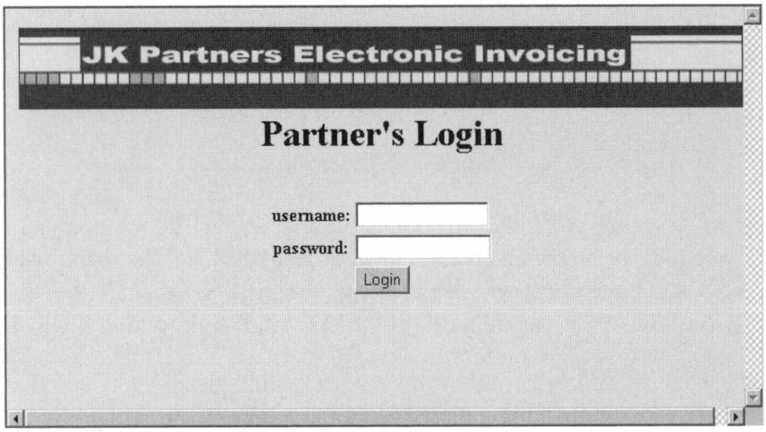

Figure 6.9: Login form for an application.

```
<FORM action="/partners/LoginServlet" method="post">
<CENTER>
<TABLE border="0">
<TBODY>
<TR>
<TH>username:</TH>

<TD><INPUT type="text" name="username" size="16" maxlength="16"></TD>

</TR>
<TR>
<TH>password:</TH>

<TD><INPUT type="password" name="password" size="16" maxlength="16"></TD>

</TR>
<TR>

<TD colspan="2" align="center"><INPUT type="submit" name="login" value="Login"></TD>

</TR>
</TBODY>
</TABLE>
</CENTER>
</FORM>
```

Figure 6.10: Code for <form> tag on the Web page shown in Figure 6.9.

The ACTION attribute of the <FORM> tag defines which program will be loaded when the server processes the request. The program may be a CGI script; in the case of Web applications created in Java, it will be a servlet. For the rest of this book we will assume that ACTION attributes point to a servlet in a Web application. In this case the servlet specified is the LoginServlet, which is part of the JK Partners application.

Note: The JK Partners application is used through the book as a simple case study to derive examples from.

The second attribute, METHOD, defines the HTTP method that will be used in the request header. This method can be GET or POST. As mentioned previously, the methods in the request will determine which method gets called in the servlet, either doGet() or doPost(). In the majority of the cases the method in a <FORM> tag is POST.

The rest of this form contains a table, with some headers and two rows. Each row contains a cell containing an INPUT field where the user can type text. Attributes of the INPUT field further define the physical length of the text field and the maximum number of characters each field will accept. Also notice that the type attribute of the text field used to enter the password is PASSWORD rather than TEXT. This type of text field hides the keyboard input.

Finally there is another INPUT field of type SUBMIT. This displays as a button that, when clicked, causes an HTTP request, of the type specified by the METHOD parameter of the FORM tag, to be sent to the URL specified in the ACTION parameter of the FORM tag, containing the information the user typed in.

As is common in forms, there is an INPUT field of type RESET. This is displayed as a button that, when clicked, blanks out any data present on the form.

The data entered on the form should be validated, if possible, by the browser before the request is sent to the server. This eliminates a trip to the server just to ensure that all data is correct, within limits and all required fields present. Usually validation is done by including JavaScript functions on the form. An addition parameter, ONSUBMIT, is added to the form to call a JavaScript function when the Submit button is clicked. This will be covered later on in this book.

Conclusion

There are a multitude of tags not covered in this chapter, and some are important to know. You cannot learn all the HTML tags by reading a book. You will discover and learn more and more tags as you need them.

It is beyond the scope of this book to present an all-inclusive treatise on HTML. For more information on other HTML tags or on attributes to further define the tags covered here, consult the W3C organization at the URL given at the beginning of this chapter. There are also numerous free, online tutorials on the Internet that can help you find the tag you need and to learn more about this very interesting topic.

Introduction to WebSphere Studio Page Designer

WebSphere Studio has a very powerful easy-to-use, WYSIWYG HTML and JSP page editor called Page Designer.

Using Page Designer you can create complex HTML and JSP pages very simply. Most of the time you can just drag and drop components, or select elements from menus. Page Designer is very intuitive to use once you have had a quick orientation to familiarize yourself with the functions available. In this chapter we will deal only with HTML pages. Creating JSP pages with Page Designer will be covered later in the book.

The Page Designer editor opens when you edit an existing HTML file or when you create a new HTML file through the wizards. The editor comprises three views:

- Design

- Source

- Preview

These views are selectable through tabs at the bottom edge of the editor pane.

The Design area is where you create and compose the page through menus or drag and drop. Very complex pages can be composed visually. Creating tables within tables becomes child's play. Adding an image or text to a cell in a table and converting it to a hyperlink is no harder.

The Source view shows the HTML source for the document. If you wish, you can enter HTML code in this view. Whatever changes you make will be reflected on the Design view and vice versa.

The Design and Source views of Page Designer are synchronized. Selecting something on one view and switching to the other will maintain the cursor position at the same place. This is a good feature when you compose in the Design view and want to locate the generated HTML code quickly in the Source view.

The Preview view is really an Internet Explorer browser window that renders the page. This rendering is very accurate, but be aware that different browsers under different operating systems may display the same page with slight variations. It is important to test your pages in as many browser types as possible.

The Web perspective in WebSphere Studio is designed to provide you with the tools you need to work with Web applications, including HTML pages. In Figure 6.11 you see the login page shown in Figures 6.3 through 6.5 opened in Page Designer.

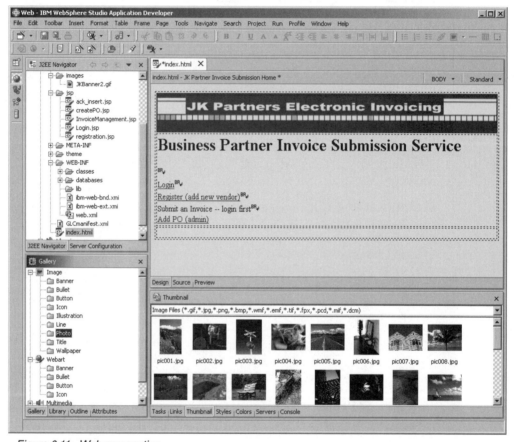

Figure 6.11: Web perspective.

Notice that when an HTML page is open, an additional toolbar is added to the WebSphere Studio window. This toolbar can be used to quickly select fonts and align-ment and to add form elements, tables, lists, and other page elements. Some additional items on the menu bar are present only when an HTML or JSP file has the focus on the editor pane. Some of these menu items are

- Insert
- Format
- Table

- Frame

- Page

The large area on the upper-right corner is the editor pane. Currently, it is occupied by the Page Designer editor opened on an HTML document. You can see the tabs that represent the three editor views mentioned above: Design, Source, and Preview.

The top left pane shows the J2EE Navigator view; from here you can travel through the workspace and find the files you need to work on.

The bottom left pane is shared by multiple views, which are selectable by clicking their tags. Currently showing is the Gallery view. It displays several folders containing useful images you may want to include in your pages. This view is synchronized with the Thumbnail view on the bottom right pane. From the Thumbnail view you can drag and drop images on to the page.

The other views on the bottom left pane and the Web perspective-specific views tabbed below the editor are described next.

Library view

The Library view (Figure 6.12) can be used to select and insert a JavaScript or JSP code snippet on the page. You select the function from the list, then drag and drop it on to the page at the position where you want the code to appear.

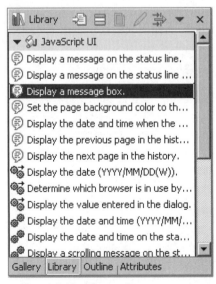

Figure 6.12: Library view.

Depending on the function you select, you may get an additional dialog to confirm or further customize the generated code when you drop it on the page. A message box, for example, requires the message text. The dialog shown in Figure 6.13 opens to capture that information.

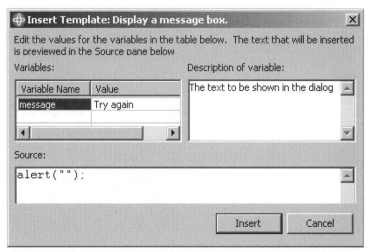

Figure 6.13: Providing additional information for a library template.

The resulting generated code for inserting the message box is shown in Figure 6.14. It will be placed right after the cursor. You can drop library code into a page in both the Details and the Source views. However, for accuracy it is recommended you position the cursor at the point you wish the code inserted in the Source view.

```
<SCRIPT type="text/javascript">
<!--
alert("Try again");
//-->
</SCRIPT>
```

Figure 6.14: Generated code for inserting a message box.

Outline view

The Outline view (Figure 6.15) shows the hierarchical composition of the page and can be used to navigate quickly to a part of the page as well as to see its overall structure.

The Outline view is synchronized with both the Design and the Source views of the Page Designer editor. Selecting an element on the outline will select the corresponding element on the editor. This is very useful for quickly locating elements on busy pages

Clicking the plus sign on an element in the Outline view causes that element to expand and reveal additional information.

A very powerful feature, one to be used with caution, is the ability to drag and drop HTML elements in the Outline view. This capability can be used to move a table row with all its contents to another position in the table, to move paragraphs around, and so forth. Remember that if rearranging the layout of the page after dragging and dropping elements does not produce the desired effect, you can select **Edit → Undo** (or press **Ctrl+Z**) to undo the move.

Attributes view

The Attributes view (Figure 6.16) shows the attributes of the currently selected element on the page. Selecting an element on either the Design or the Source view of the editor will cause the element's attributes to be shown.

This view is also used to edit the values for the parameters of the selected element. You can also select an element on the Outline view, switch to the Attributes view, and customize the element.

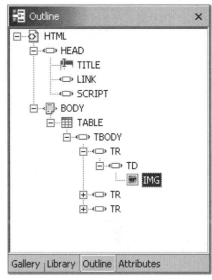

Figure 6.15: Outline view.

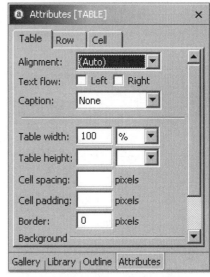

Figure 6.16: Attributes view, table selected.

Other views

The bottom right-hand pane also contains multiple stacked views; some of these views have already been discussed, or will be discussed later in the book. For designing and creating Web pages, the following views apply:

Links view

The Links view (Figure 6.17) shows which pages have links pointing to the current page and also pages that the current page references with a link.

This view is synchronized to the J2EE Navigator view. Whichever file is selected on the navigator becomes the current page. The Links view is not synchronized with the editor view.

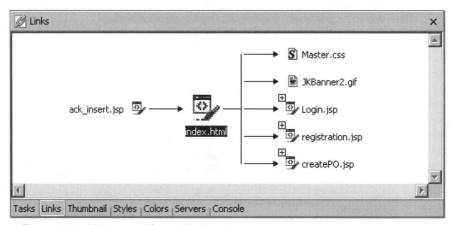

Figure 6.17: Links to and from index.html.

The current page is displayed on the middle of the diagram; to the left are pages that reference (or have links) to this page. To the right are pages that this page references.

The plus signs shown next to some of the other pages can be used to see links that those pages reference.

This view is very useful for finding inter-page references on the Web site.

Thumbnail view

The Thumbnail view (Figure 6.18) view shows a small rendition of the graphics in the folder selected in the Gallery view or in a folder in the J2EE Navigator view.

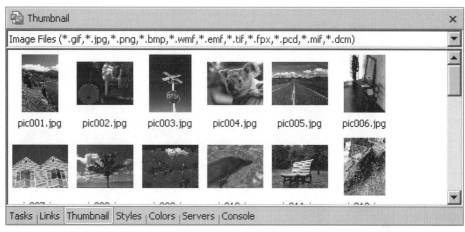

Figure 6.18: Thumbnail view.

The Thumbnail view is usually used with folders that contain graphic files, but it will also render sound files and HTML or JSP pages.

Note: If you do not wish to see HTML pages rendered in the Thumbnail view, you may turn that feature off by selecting **Windows** → **Preferences** → **Web Tools** → **Thumbnail**.

Thumbnails can be selected from the view and dragged and dropped onto an HTML page. Images can be dropped more accurately onto the Design view of Page Designer.

Styles view

The Styles view (Figure 6.19) shows the styles defined on the Cascading Style Sheet (CSS) associated with the page. More information on CSS is presented in a later section of this chapter.

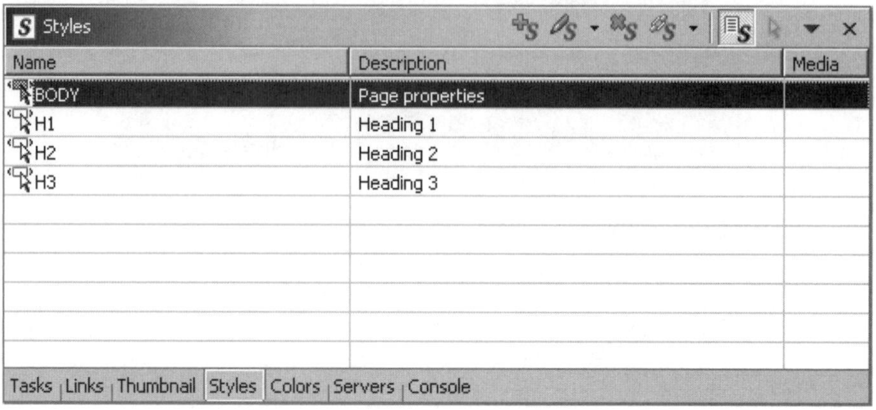

S Styles		$^{+}$S $\mathscr{O}$S ▾ $^{\times}$S $\mathscr{O}$S ▾ |▤S ▸ ▾ ×
Name	Description	Media
BODY	Page properties	
H1	Heading 1	
H2	Heading 2	
H3	Heading 3	
Tasks ｜Links ｜Thumbnail ｜Styles ｜Colors ｜Servers ｜Console		

Figure 6.19: Styles view.

Double-clicking a style will open the Style Sheet editor, where you can change the style's attributes. From the context menu of the view you can add, delete, and rename style definitions.

Colors view

The Colors view (Figure 6.20) can used to pick a color from the current color palette and apply it to an HTML element on the page.

To use a color, start by selecting the element you want to apply the color to, for example some text on the page. Pick a color from the palette and, from the Colors view menu bar, select **Text Color** → **Set as Text Color**.

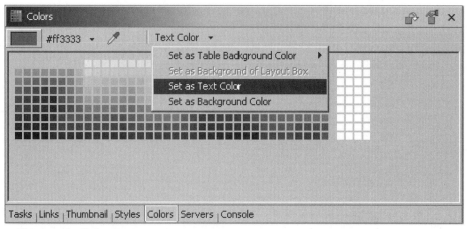

Figure 6.20: Color view.

The correct HTML tag attribute to add the selected color definition will be inserted into the page, at the correct location.

```
<FONT color="#0033ff">Business Partner Invoice Submission Service</FONT>
```

Cascading Style Sheets

Most of the time a particular Web site needs to exhibit a consistent look and feel. The size, color, and face of the fonts, the background color or bitmap, and general formatting for the elements that compose the page need to be the same. This gives the site a sense of togetherness and good organization.

Rather than coding these style parameters into every page of the site, you can define a Cascading Style Sheet (CSS) and then specify this style sheet on every page. If any thing changes on the style sheet, all pages are automatically updated.

WebSphere Studio provides a CSS Editor to manipulate style sheets and also provides a mechanism to include style sheets easily in your HTML pages. The Preview view of Page Designer correctly renders HTML pages using style sheets.

One of the options you have when creating HTML or JSP pages using Page Designer is to include a CSS. The default name for this style sheet is Master.css. In Figure 6.21, you see it opened in the CSS editor. The area below Selected Style on the lower right pane renders the style currently selected on the left-hand pane. In the figure the selected style is the one for the <H2> tag.

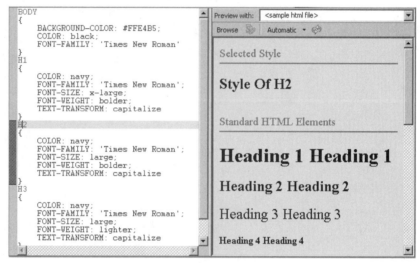

Figure 6.21: Cascading Style Sheet editor.

Including a style sheet in an HTML or JSP page is done using the <LINK> tag:

```
<LINK rel="stylesheet" href="theme/Master.css" type="text/css">
```

Of course, if you are using Page Designer, all you need to do is drag and drop the style sheet from the navigator to the page, and the <LINK> tag will be inserted automatically for you.

Exercise

In this exercise you will create the welcome page for the application that will be fully developed in the book. A complete description of the application, and how it works, is presented in its own chapter. For now all you need to know is that the welcome page, called index.html, is a static page that provides links into other parts of the application. It will be the first page shown to users when they visit the Web site.

As part of this exercise you will create the page in a static Web project. Later you will move the page to the Web project where the rest of the application resides.

1. Start WebSphere Studio Application Developer using the Chapter 6 workspace, **C:\WSCG\Workspaces\Startup\Chapter-6**.

2. Open the Web Perspective:

    a. Select **Window → Open Perspective → Other → Web**.

3. Create a new Web project called **Partners**.

    a. From the J2EE Navigator view's context menu, select **New → Project**.

    b. Select **Web → Web Project**.

    c. On the New Project wizard (Figure 6.22), click **Next**.

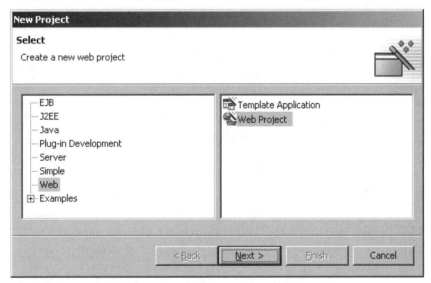

Figure 6.22: Creating a new Web project.

d. On the next page (Figure 6.23), enter **Partners** for the project's name and select the **Static Web Project** radio button; also ensure that the **Create a default CSS file** box is checked. Click **Next**.

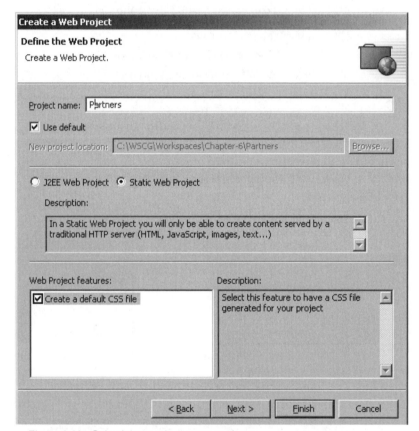

Figure 6.23: Selecting a project name and type.

e. In the next page of this dialog (Figure 6.24), you can change the document root of the Web project. The default document root is the name of the project. Change the document root to (lowercase) **partners** and click **Finish**.

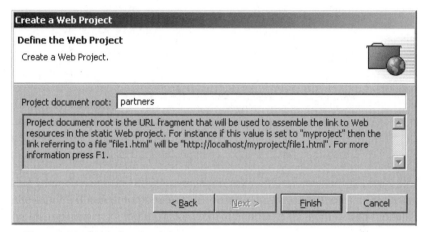

Figure 6.24: Changing the document root.

4. Verify that the project was created and that the directory structure shown in Figure 6.25 has been created. Notice that the CSS file has been created for you.

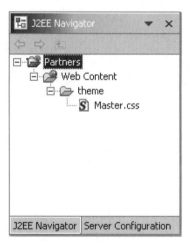

Figure 6.25: J2EE Navigator after project creation.

5. Import the banner from the file system.

   a. Select the **Web Content** folder in the navigator.

   b. From its context menu, select **Import**.

   c. Select **File System**. Click **Next**.

    d. On the Import File System dialog (Figure 6.26), click the **Browse** button next to the Directory field and navigate to **C:\WSCG\Source\Chapter-6**.

    e. Check the **images** folder checkbox. Click **Finish**.

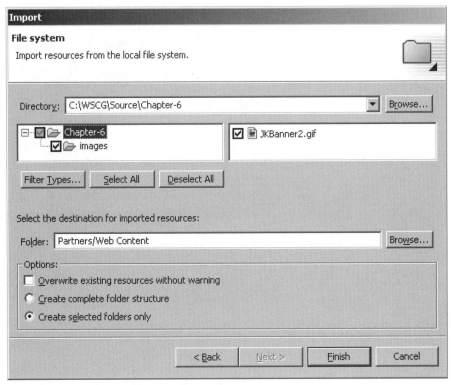

Figure 6.26: Importing banner image.

You should now have a folder named images under Web Content. In the images folder should be one file, named JKBanner2.gif.

Note: An alternative method to import the folder would be to open a Windows Explorer window, navigate to the same images folder, and drag and drop it on to the Web Content folder in WebSphere Studio.

---

6. Create a new HTML page named index.html.
   a. Select the **Web Content** folder. From its context menu select **New → HTML/XHTML File**.
   b. In the New HTML/XHTML File wizard (Figure 6.27), the folder /Partners/Web Content should be already filled in. Enter **index.html** for the File Name. Click **Next**.

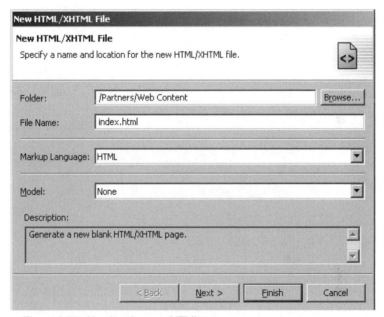

Figure 6.27: Naming the new HTML page.

   c. On the next page of the wizard (Figure 6.28), you are given a choice to change some of the generation parameters for the page before it gets created. Leave all the defaults untouched. Notice that the file Master.css will be included in the new page. Click **Finish**.

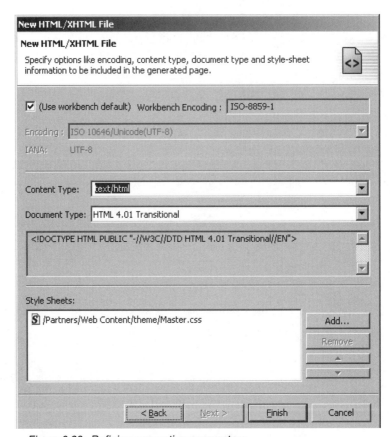

Figure 6.28: Refining generation parameters.

7. The page is created, and Page Designer opens in its Design view. Some default text has been added to the page. Select it and delete it (Figure 6.29).

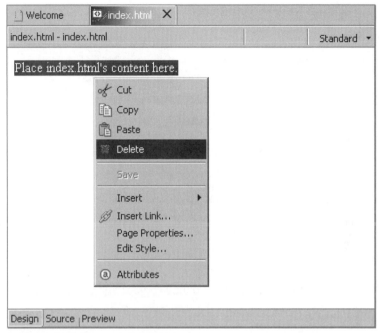

Figure 6.29: Removing default text.

8. Switch to the Source view and take a quick look at the generated code. Return to the Design view when satisfied that the generated document looks good.

Note: Several META tags have been inserted by Page Designer. These indicate what the generating program is and other data used by Page Designer itself. You can control the amount of information inserted as META tags by selecting **Windows → Preferences → Web and XML Files → HTML Files** and unchecking the appropriate check boxes.

---

9. From the navigator, select the **images** folder, and from the bottom right pane select the Thumbnail view. You should see the banner. Drag and drop the banner on top of the page.

10. Next insert a heading on the page.

   a. Select **Format → Paragraph → Heading1**. This will insert a blank paragraph with the H1 style.

   b. Enter the text **Business Partner Invoice Submission Service** above in the paragraph.

   c. Click outside the delineating box to make it disappear.

    d. Switch to the Source view and see the code that was inserted. Switch back to the Design view.

11. Insert a two-column, four-row table below the heading.

    a. Select **Table → Table** from the main menu, or click the Insert Table toolbar icon.

    b. On the dialog that opens, select **4** rows and **2** columns. Click **OK**.

    c. You should now see an empty table on the page.

    d. Switch to the Source view and see the code that was inserted. Switch back to the Design view.

12. The table will hold a list of links to the functions available on the application and a short explanation of what each function does.

    a. Click the first cell to select it.

    b. Select **Insert → Link** from the main menu or click the Insert Link toolbar icon.

    c. On the Insert Link dialog (Figure 6.30), enter **/jsp/login.jsp** for the URL.

    d. Enter **Login** for the Link text.

    e. Click **OK**.

    f. Switch to the Source view and see the code that was inserted. Switch back to the Design view.

Figure 6.30: Defining a link.

Note: If the JSP file you wanted to link to is already available on the workspace, you could have clicked **Browse** and picked it from a list. This would save you typing and would reduce the chances for error.

---

13. Select the table cell to the right of the link and enter **Login is required to access the system.** Again, switch to the source and see what was added to the code. Switch back.

14. In similar fashion, enter the links listed in Table 6.2 to complete the table:

Table 6.2

Link (Left Cell)	URL	Explanation (Right Cell)
Register	/jsp/register.jsp	New users need to register before they can login and use the system.
Invoice	/jsp/createInvoice.jsp	Submit an invoice to the system.
Add PO	/jsp/createPO.jsp	Add a purchase order. Administrators only.

15. Center the table on the page.
    a. Click the frame of the table to select it, or from the Outline view click **TABLE**.
    b. From the Attributes view select the **Table** tab. From the Alignment drop-down list, select **Center**.

16. Add a row above the first row for table headings. Make the headings **Options** and **Explanation**.
    a. Place the cursor on the first row of the table.
    b. From the main menu select **Table → Add Row → Add Above**.
    c. Enter the **Options** and **Explanation** headings into the table.
    d. Select both headings by dragging the mouse pointer.
    e. On the Cell tab of the Table Attributes view, click **Header**. Notice the change in emphasis of the heading text.
    f. Look at the generated code and come back to the Design view.

17. Next you will change the style sheet and see how the page changes accordingly. In the bottom right-hand pane click the **Styles** tab. Expand **theme/Master.css**. Notice the styles that have been predefined.

18. Double-click **H1** to open the CSS editor with the Heading1 tag selected in the Set Style Properties dialog (Figure 6.31). Make some changes, select a different font, change the size, color, and so forth. Click **Apply** to see the changes in the editor. When satisfied with the changes, click **OK** to accept them.

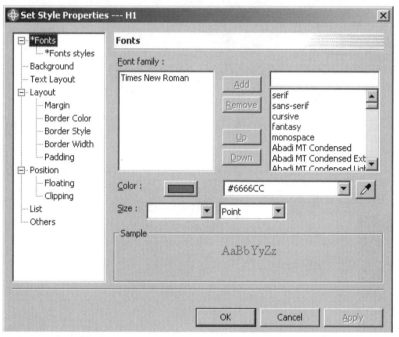

Figure 6.31: Set Styles dialog.

19. If you want to keep these changes and apply them to the pages that include the CSS. you need to save the file by pressing **Ctrl+S**.

20. Feel free to make other changes to the style sheet, such as by changing the background color of the page.

21. You may also try to add other styles for elements that have not yet been defined, such as the TH tag for table headings.

22. Finally, once more, look at the generated code; you should be able to understand all of it. Switch to the Preview view to see what the page will look like in Internet Explorer. It should look like Figure 6.32.

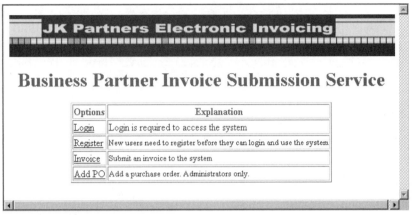

Figure 6.32: Final version of page.

Test yourself

Key terms

HTML (HyperText Markup Language)

HTTP (HyperText Transfer Protocol)

HTTPS

SSL (Secure Sockets Layer)

URL (Uniform Resource Locator)

servlet

CSS (Cascading Style Sheets)

Page Designer

HTTP response

JSP (JavaServer Pages)

Web server

DTD (Document Type Definition)

JavaScript

Web perspective

Review questions

1. Explain the request/response mechanism of HTTP.

2. What is a URL? Give an example of a URL and name its five distinct parts.

3. What are the contents of the request header?

4. What are the contents of the HTTP response?

5. Explain the flow of request/response using the HTTP GET method.

6. How is the HTML document returned to the client?

7. What tools can be used to design and develop HTML pages?

8. How can you add JavaScript or JSP code snippets to your HTML document?

9. What view can I use to modify properties of a table?

10. How can you view the Cascading Style Sheets (CSS) available?

Introduction to servlets

Chapter topics

- ❖ *Servlet lifecyle*
- ❖ *The Web Project wizard*
- ❖ *The New Servlet wizard*
- ❖ *Testing the servlet lifecycle*
- ❖ *Producing an HTTP response stream*
- ❖ *J2EE application packaging and web.xml*
- ❖ *Parameterizing servlets*

Certification objectives

- ❖ *Create J2EE projects*
- ❖ *Create Web projects*
- ❖ *Create resources in appropriate J2EE locations*
- ❖ *Work with Web Application Deployment*
- ❖ *Create server instance and server configuration*
- ❖ *Run and operate server*

The cornerstone of the Java 2 Enterprise Edition (J2EE) for Web applications is the servlet API. A servlet is a server-side Java component that executes within a J2EE Web Container. The Web Container contains a Java virtual machine along with J2EE runtime services. The typical servlet is invoked through its URL in response to an HTTP request.

A specific servlet object is an instance of a Java class that implements the **javax.servlet.Servlet** interface. For the common case, the Java class will extend (either directly or indirectly) the abstract class **javax.servlet.http.HttpServlet**.

Servlet lifecycle

The Web Container is responsible for servlet lifecycle services. Servlet instances are created and initialized by the Web Container according to the following sequence:

1. The servlet is created using the default (no-argument) constructor.

2. An instance of ServletConfig is created.

3. The servlet object's init() method is called with the ServletConfig object as argument.

4. Upon successful initialization, the state of the servlet is logically marked as Available.

Failure during the initialization sequence will cause the servlet to be marked as unavailable.

In response to an incoming request, the Web Container invokes the servlet's service() method. The service() method, defined on the Servlet interface, has the following signature:

```
public void service(ServletRequest request, ServletResponse response)
throws ServletException, IOException
```

The abstract class HttpServlet implements this method. The behavior is to create two Http specific objects for the request and response parameters. It then invokes an overloaded method that is defined in HttpServlet with the following signature:

```
public void service(HttpServletRequest request, HttpServletResponse re-
sponse)throws ServletException, IOException
```

HttpServlet also defines a set of specific request handlers structured around the HTTP request method (e.g., GET, POST, PUT). The naming of the handler methods follows a very distinct pattern. The request handler for the GET method has the following signature:

```
public void doGet (HttpServletRequest request, HttpServletResponse re-
sponse) throws ServletException, IOException
```

The corresponding request handler for the POST method has the following signature:

```
public void doPost (HttpServletRequest request, HttpServletResponse re-
sponse) throws ServletException, IOException
```

The overloaded service method checks the incoming HTTP request method and dispatches the corresponding handler method. Each handler method has default behavior (implemented in the HttpServlet class) that returns an error response (405), which corresponds to "HTTP method unsupported by URL."

The Web Project wizard

Within WebSphere Studio, servlets should be created in a special type of project: a Web project. The purpose for a Web project is to manage the resources for either a static Web site or a J2EE Web module. Web projects are best manipulated within the Web perspective. You can open the Web perspective in WebSphere Studio via **Window → Open Perspective → Other → Web**. To be able to test components developed in a Web Project within WebSphere Studio, a Web project will also be associated with a J2EE Enterprise Application project (EAR project).

To create a new Web project (and subsequently a new EAR project), you will launch the Create Web Project wizard via **File → New → Web Project**. (If you are not in the Web perspective when you try to launch this wizard, you will need to go to the **Other** dialog under **File → New**.)

The Create a Web Project wizard first asks for a project name. In Figure 7.1, the name **FirstServletProject** was entered. The second portion of the first page of this wizard lets you specify whether the project is to be used to manage J2EE resources or just a static Web site. Since you are interested in building and testing servlets, you would choose the default of **J2EE Web Project**. The bottom section of the wizard page lets you add various resources to the project. These will be visited later in this certification guide.

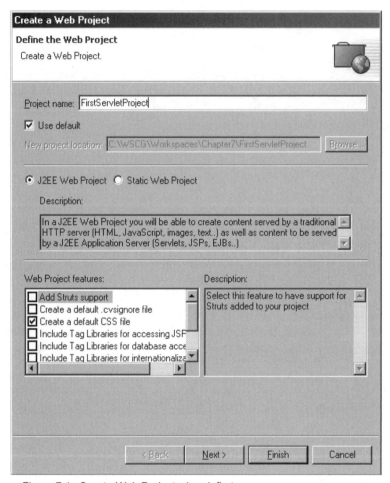

Figure 7.1: Create Web Project wizard, first page.

The second page of the Create a Web Project wizard (see Figure 7.2) lets you associate the Web project with an Enterprise Application project. If you want to create a new Enterprise Application project, select **New** and enter a project name. If you are adding the Web project to an existing Enterprise Application project, you would select **Existing** and then select the Enterprise Application project from the drop-down list.

A Web module, the J2EE resource associated with the Web project, declares a context root. A context root is a URI relative to the server. Any request to a URL that is deliv-

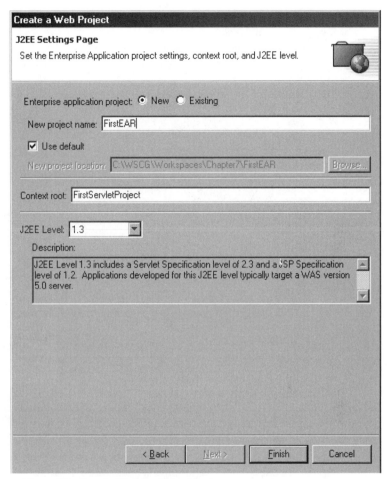

Figure 7.2: Create Web Project wIzard, second page.

ered to the server on which the Web module is deployed and is prefixed with the context root will be delivered to that particular Web module.

In Figure 7.2, the context root is *FirstServletProject*. A request to a URL such as *www.myserver.com/FirstServletProject/FirstServlet* would be delivered to this Web project, assuming it was deployed on a server addressable via *www.myserver.com*.

The final part of the wizard specifies the J2EE compliance level for resources that are part of the project. The default is J2EE 1.3.

After you have entered information within the wizard as shown on the two previous figures and the wizard completes, two new projects are added to your workspace. The resulting view within the Web perspective might look like what is displayed in Figure 7.3.

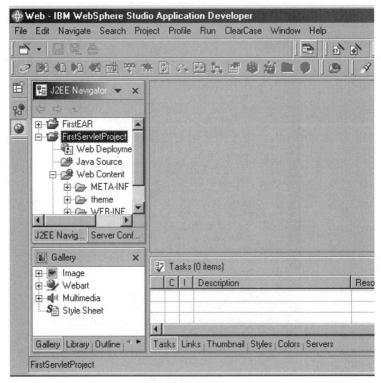

Figure 7.3: Web perspective with new Web project.

The Web project itself is configured with two top-level folders. One folder is named **Java source** and the other is named **Web Content**. Servlet and supporting Java classes will be created and managed under the Java Source folder. The Web Content folder represents the content of the Web archive (.war) file that will be deployed to a J2EE application server.

The New Servlet wizard

The easiest way to create a servlet in WebSphere Studio is via the New Servlet wizard. Once a Web project has been created, you can create a servlet. To launch the New Servlet wizard, select **File → New → Servlet**. This launches a two-screen wizard. On the first

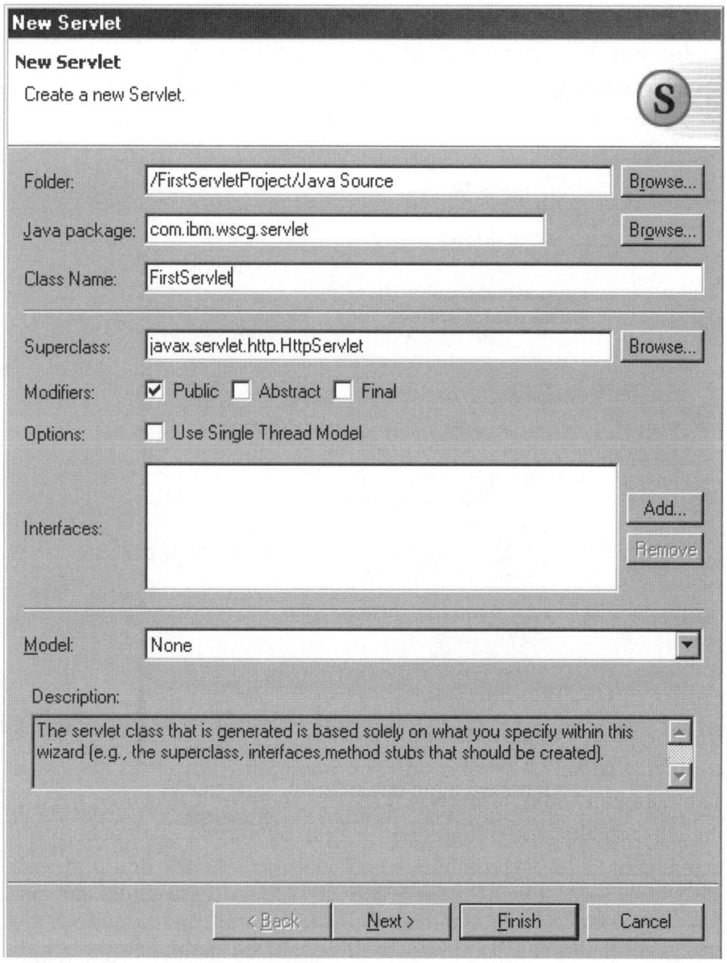

Figure 7.4: New Servlet wizard, first page.

screen (Figure 7.4), you select the fully qualified name of the servlet class to be created. The fully qualified name is specified in two parts. The first names the Java package, and the second names the servlet class.

Next, you specify the superclass, often the default HttpServlet class. There are check boxes for class modifiers (typically only **public** will be specified) and for an option to have the class implement SingleThreadModel (a bad practice). Finally, you can use the **Add** button to specify any other interfaces the class should implement. The Model specification is currently unsupported.

On the second screen (see Figure 7.5) you select which method stubs are to be generated for you. The typical choices are doGet() and doPost(). For this lifecycle exercise, we are also selecting those methods associated with the servlet lifecycle (constructor, init, and destroy).

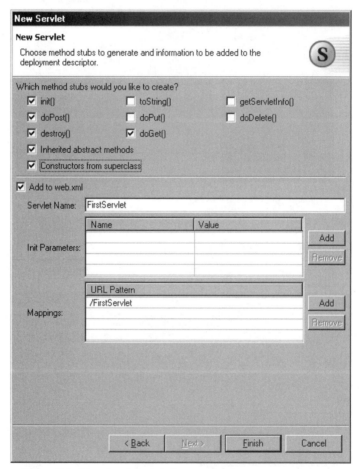

Figure 7.5: New Servlet wizard, second page.

The lower half of the second page of the wizard has to do with manipulating the Web module's deployment descriptor (the web.xml file). This is a topic for greater discussion later in this chapter. The values shown in Figure 7.5 are the defaults, which result in adding the servlet to the deployment descriptor and choosing the default URL mapping.

Exploring servlet lifecycle

One of the easiest ways to explore the servlet lifecycle is to add trace messages to a simple servlet. To examine the flow that occurs when a servlet is created, add calls to System.out.println() in both the constructor, FirstServlet(), and the init(ServletConfig) method of the servlet. To observe the call path during the service cycle, add calls to System. out.println() in the service(ServletRequest, ServletResponse), service(Http ServletRequest, HttpServletResponse), doPost(), and doGet() methods.

To override the two service methods and the init(ServletConfig) method, go to the Outline view, select the class, FirstServlet, and choose **Override Methods** from the context menu (see Figures 7.6 and 7.7.). Both service methods are implemented in the javax.servlet.http.Http Servlet class, while the init method is implemented in the javax.servlet.GenericServlet class. For all four service cycle methods that we are adding trace messages to, call System.out.println() first and then delegate to the superclass implementation; that is, call super.*methodName*().

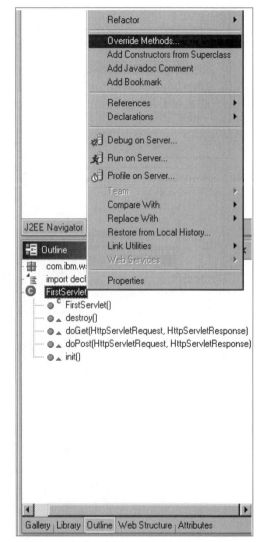

Figure 7.6: Selecting to override superclass methods.

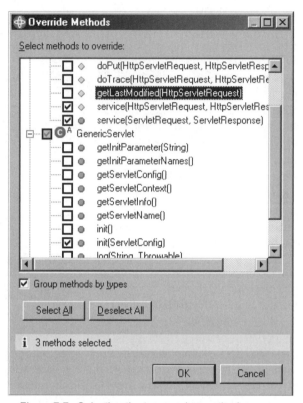

Figure 7.7: Selecting the two service methods.

For example:

```
protected void service(HttpServletRequest arg0, HttpServletResponse arg1)
        throws ServletException, IOException {
    System.out.println("FirstServlet.service_http called");
    super.service(arg0, arg1);
}
```

Finally, to trace the destruction of a servlet when it is taken out of service, also add a trace statement to the destroy() method.

Testing the servlet lifecycle

One of the most powerful tools available to J2EE developers within WebSphere Studio is the built-in WebSphere Test Environment. The various editions of WebSphere Studio ship with support for a variety of J2EE-compliant servers. The Application Developer ships with (1) WebSphere Application Server V5.0 core server, (2) WebSphere Express Server V5.0, and (3) WebSphere Application Server Advanced Single Server Edition V4.0 (AEd). It also provides support for testing on various versions of the Apache Tomcat server.

There is a separate perspective, the Server perspective, to define and configure test servers. For a module of a J2EE application, such as our FirstServletProject you can set up a new server, start the server, and run your Web application through a single context menu item: Run on Server (see Figure 7.8).

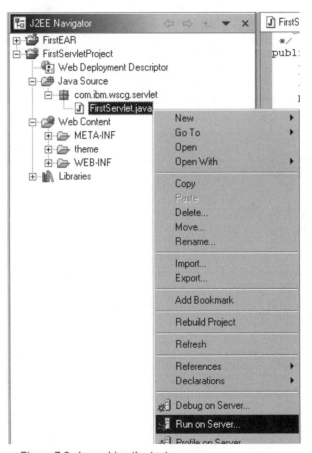

Figure 7.8: Launching the test server.

To test a servlet's response to a URL request (GET method), select the servlet and choose **Run on Server** from the context menu. If no server has been configured in the workspace, this selection will trigger a dialog allowing you to choose the type of test server to create and associate with the servlet's Enterprise Application (see Figure 7.9). In WebSphere Studio Application Developer, the default server for a J2EE 1.3 module is the WebSphere V5.0 Test Environment. This server supports the full complement of J2EE 1.3 components.

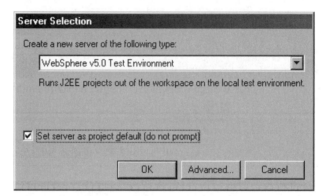

Figure 7.9: Selecting the type of server to create.

For Web applications (not for EJBs), you may consider testing on the Express Test Environment. This server supports only J2EE Web Container components. The Express Test Environment is the default server available to J2EE 1.3 Web projects in WebSphere Studio Site Developer.

A new Server project will be created, and the configuration files for a WebSphere server instance will be created within this project. In addition, the selected servlet's Web project will be associated with this newly created server instance. This association results in the servlet's Enterprise Application being installed in the server instance. In addition, future requests to Run on Server for a component of this Enterprise Application will be run on this same server.

After the server instance is created, the server will be launched (started).

Once the server has completely started, a Web browser instance will be launched, directing a request to the "test server" with the URI for the component under test. When WebSphere issues the following message to the console, the server has started:

```
WsServer      A WSVR0001I: Server server1 open for e-business
```

For **FirstServlet**, the URL issued in the browser will be *localhost:9080/FirstServletProject/FirstServlet* (see Figure 7.10). Also in Figure 7.10 you can see the server console output. Following the message that the server is open is the response to the HTTP request to the FirstServlet. The first message, *An instance of . . .*, is issued when the servlet's constructor is called. The next message is provided by the servlet engine (Web Container) itself, to indicate that a Web component is about to be initialized. Next, the trace message from the init() method is displayed.

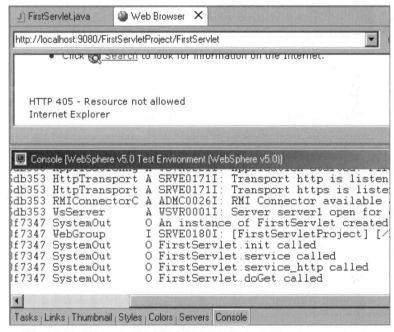

Figure 7.10: Test run showing lifecycle methods.

The next three messages are associated with the HTTP request being delivered to the now initialized servlet. First the service(ServletRequest, ServletResponse) method is called. The implementation of this method, supplied by the class javax.servlet.http.HttpServlet, creates the specialized objects that implement the HttpServletRequest and HttpServletResponse interfaces. It then calls the service(HttpServletRequest, HttpServletResponse) method. This can be seen in the second-to-last message displayed in Figure 7.10. The implementation of this overloaded service method determines the HTTP request method, in this case GET. It then calls the corresponding service handler method, doGet(), as seen by the final displayed message.

Refreshing the browser (i.e., issuing another request to the same URL, *localhost:9080/FirstServletProject/FirstServlet*) will cause the last three messages to be repeated in the console (see Figure 7.11). Thus, for each service request, the execution flow will visit each service method followed by the appropriate service handler method. The servlet is constructed and initialized only once.

```
2df72152 SystemOut    O FirstServlet.init called
2df72152 SystemOut    O FirstServlet.service called
2df72152 SystemOut    O FirstServlet.service_http called
2df72152 SystemOut    O FirstServlet.doGet called
2df72152 SystemOut    O FirstServlet.service called
2df72152 SystemOut    O FirstServlet.service_http called
2df72152 SystemOut    O FirstServlet.doGet called
```

Figure 7.11: Server console after second HTTP request.

Producing an HTTP response stream

Now that you understand the basic lifecycle of a servlet, it is time to make the component useful. Depending on the HTTP request method, the behavior of the servlet will typically be implemented in either the doGet() or doPost() method. Within these methods, you have access to two essential objects that are passed as parameters: the request and response objects. They represent the incoming HTTP request stream and the outgoing HTTP response stream.

The full complement of Java APIs is available to the servlet writer to implement application behavior. Frequently, true application logic will be written in other reusable Java classes and accessed from the servlet code. The final outcome of the processing needs to be logic that will supply content to the HTTP response stream.

The HttpServletResponse interface defines the API to interact with the HTTP response stream. This interface defines a collection of properties corresponding to HTTP stream headers. Methods include setContentType(), setStatus(), setContentLength(), setLocale(), addCookie(), setHeader(), setDateHeader(), and setIntHeader(). One of the most important methods, getWriter(), allows access to a PrintWriter that delivers its stream to the HTTP response body.

To demonstrate the use of these methods, consider coding doGet() in the manner shown in Figure 7.12. After you save the FirstServlet.java file, the servlet will be reloaded in the WebSphere Test environment (assuming the server was running while you were editing the file). Reissue the HTTP request, either by clicking Refresh on the browser or by selecting **Run on Server** again from the context menu while selecting First Servlet from the J2EE Navigator view. The resulting response can be seen in Figure 7.13.

```
public void doGet(HttpServletRequest req, HttpServletResponse resp)
        throws ServletException, IOException {
        System.out.println("FirstServlet.doGet called");

        PrintWriter out = resp.getWriter();
        // set return status to the OK status code (200)
        resp.setStatus(HttpServletResponse.SC_OK);
        // set the ContentType header to the MIME type "text/html"
        resp.setContentType("text/html");

        // now write HTML content to the response body
        out.println("<html><head><title>First Servlet</title></head>");
        out.println("<body><h1>First Servlet Output</h1> );
    out.println( <p>Hello!</p></body></html>");
}
```

Figure 7.12: doGet method.

Figure 7.13: Output from FirstServlet.

Our first servlet does not perform any interesting operations, but it does expose the very simple interaction model. In Chapter 12 we will introduce JavaServer Pages (JSP). JSP pages will be used to display an output response (page) rather than encoding HTML as Java String literals. Until then, the servlet and supporting Java classes will be responsible for generating the response content.

J2EE application packaging and web.xml

Writing a servlet is very simple, particularly using the New Servlet wizard provided with WebSphere Studio. The deployment and the test that is triggered by Run on Server may need demystification to convince everyone of this fact. A J2EE Enterprise Application is deployed and run on a J2EE Application Server. A J2EE Enterprise Application is packaged in a special Java archive file, the enterprise archive or EAR file. The file contains the application deployment descriptor, one or more Enterprise Application modules, and any dependent library files needed by the application and not provided by the application server environment.

Recall that there are three types of J2EE modules (two of which are actually deployed to the application server):

- Web application module, packaged in a Web archive (WAR) file

- EJB module, packaged in an EJB JAR file

- Application client module, packaged in an application client JAR file

For Web applications (servlet applications), all that is required is a Web archive file. WebSphere Application server, like many J2EE application servers, support installing WAR files directly to the server. Under the hood, however, the WebSphere Application Server builds a wrapper EAR file. This wrapper archive corresponds to the Enterprise Application project within WebSphere Studio. In the example you have been working through in this chapter, the Enterprise Application project is named FirstEAR and was created as a side effect of creating the Web Project, FirstServletProject (Figure 7.2).

If you were to open the application.xml Enterprise Application deployment descriptor for FirstEAR, you would see a reference to the Web module, as shown in Figure 7.14. Note the reference to the WAR file, FirstServletProject.war. As was noted earlier, the FirstServletProject.war file is built and maintained to include all of the content in the Web Content folder of the FirstServletProject Web project.

```
<module id="WebModule_1038585709209">
        <web>
                <web-uri>FirstServletProject.war</web-uri>
                <context-root>FirstServletProject</context-root>
        </web>
</module>
```

Figure 7.14: Deployment descriptor for FirstEAR.

All WAR files contain a Web application deployment descriptor, web.xml. This file is used to describe the contents of the WAR file and provide information to the application server on how the application is to be deployed (installed). Within the WAR file, the web.xml file should be found in the WEB-INF folder. This deployment descriptor is usually built by the developer and configured by a deployer in preparation for installing the associated application onto a specific application server.

From the Web perspective and the J2EE Navigator view, there is a link to the web.xml file. You can open this file in a variety of editors. The default editor for web.xml is the

Deployment Descriptor Editor (see Figure 7.15). This is a form-based, tabbed editor for manipulating the various elements of the web.xml file.

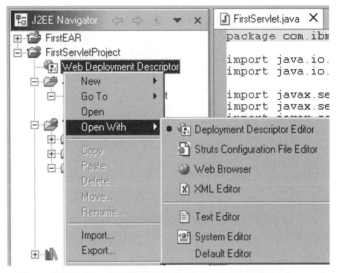

Figure 7.15: Opening the Web deployment descriptor.

The Overview tab on this editor (Figure 7.16) provides the contents organized in different sections, all available from this single page. In addition, there are tabs that provide specialized views on a subset of the contents. Finally, there is a Source tab, which allows one to view and manipulate the XML as a text file.

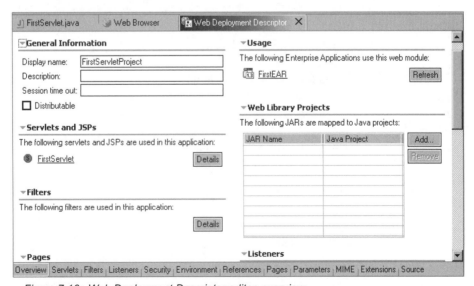

Figure 7.16: Web Deployment Descriptor editor, overview.

One of the functions of the web.xml file is to specify the Web component supplied or available in the Web application (WAR file). This is best explored from the Servlets tab (Figure 7.17). This view shows the list of Web components in the Servlets and JSPs text area. In this example there is a single Web component defined, FirstServlet. Web components can be added and removed using the appropriate buttons. Clicking the Add button causes a dialog to appear that provides a list of Java classes and JSP files from the Web project that are candidates to be added as Web components. The New button launches the New Servlet wizard. The Edit button takes you to the corresponding source file (e.g., FirstServlet.java).

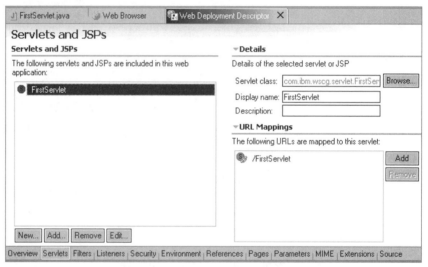

Figure 7.17: Servlets tab of the Web Deployment Descriptor editor.

Each Web component specified in the web.xml file needs to indicate the resource file that provides the component's runtime functionality. In the case of a servlet, this is the Java class file (.class). This is specified in the details section on the Servlets and JSPs page. In addition, a Web component can specify a display name and a description. These are visible to any user looking at the web.xml file (e.g. a deployer or administrator manipulating the deployment descriptor or components from an application assembly tool or application server administration console).

The last section for Web components on the Servlets and JSPs page is URL Mappings. This establishes which URLs (relative to the server and the Web application's context root) are forwarded to (that is, specify) this Web component. A Web component may have several URL mappings. What you see in Figure 7.17 for the URL mapping is the mapping that was supplied in the New Servlet wizard when the servlet was created (recall Figure 7.5). To add an additional URL mapping, click the **Add** button in the URL Mappings section. For example, in Figure 7.18 the URL mapping **/first** has been added. After this new mapping is added, you can now enter the full URL **http://localhost:9080/ FirstServletProject/first** in the browser to invoke the servlet (Figure 7.19).

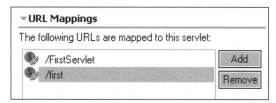

Figure 7.18: Additional URL mapping, /first.

Figure 7.19: Invoking servlet using /first URL Mapping.

Parameterizing servlets

There will be times in which a servlet will need to have one or more configuration parameters specified that can permit it to locate resources or be specialized for particular behavior on a specific application server. The Servlet API provides this behavior via initialization parameters. These parameters are set in the deployment descriptor and associated with a specific Web component.

In the Web Deployment Descriptor editor, you will set these <name, value> pairs within the initialization parameters section of the Servlets and JSPs page. Both the name and value are restricted to be java.lang.String objects. In Figure 7.20, two initialization parameters have been added, <"notify-email", help@wscg.ibm.com>, and <"version-id", "v3.1.0">.

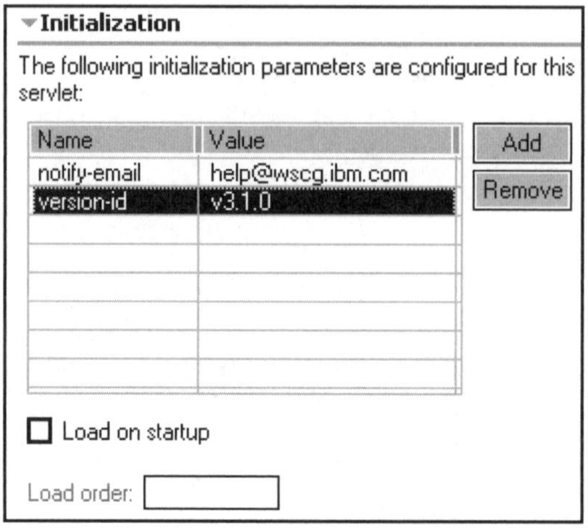

Figure 7.20: Adding initialization parameters for servlet.

The Load on startup check box enables you to specify that the servlet is loaded upon Server initialization rather than first reference. For components that are loaded on startup, you can specify their relative load order (using the Load order field) to preserve any load dependencies that may exist between the components. The resulting declaration for FirstServlet in the web.xml file can be seen by looking at the Source tab of the Web Deployment Descriptor editor.

Figures 7.21a and 7.21b show the extracted source from the web.xml file. Note that the initialization parameters are defined within the <init-param> tags. Also note that the URL mappings are defined in the <servlet-mapping> tags.

```
<servlet>
        <servlet-name>FirstServlet</servlet-name>
        <display-name>FirstServlet</display-name>
        <servlet-class>com.ibm.wscg.servlet.FirstServlet</servlet-class>
        <init-param>
                <param-name>notify-email</param-name>
                <param-value>help@wscg.ibm.com</param-value>
```

Figure 7.21a: Initialization parameters as specified in the web.xml file.

```
            </init-param>
            <init-param>
                    <param-name>version-id</param-name>
                    <param-value>v3.1.0</param-value>
            </init-param>
    </servlet>
    <servlet-mapping>
            <servlet-name>FirstServlet</servlet-name>
            <url-pattern>/FirstServlet</url-pattern>
    </servlet-mapping>
    <servlet-mapping>
            <servlet-name>FirstServlet</servlet-name>
            <url-pattern>/first</url-pattern>
    </servlet-mapping>
```

Figure 7.21b: Initialization parameters as specified in the web.xml file.

So the question should be asked, "How can the servlet access the initialization parameters?" The initialization parameters are made available to the servlet via the ServletConfig object. This object is provided as a parameter to the init() lifecycle method. It is also available in any instance method of a servlet via a call to getServletConfig().

Consider updating the init method of FirstServlet with the code listed in Figure 7.22. Two methods are used here to access the initialization parameters: getInitParameterNames() and getInitParameter(). This code saves the initialization parameters in a java.util.Properties object called properties. This step is not strictly necessary, because the doGet() method can also access the initialization parameters; however, typically, all processing on the initialization parameters will be done within the scope of the init method.

```
private static Properties properties = new Properties();
public void init(ServletConfig config) throws ServletException {
        super.init(config);
        System.out.println("FirstServlet.init called");
        Enumeration names = config.getInitParameterNames();
        while (names.hasMoreElements()) {
                String name = (String)names.nextElement();
                String value = config.getInitParameter(name);
                properties.put(name, value);
    }
}
```

Figure 7.22: Code to access initialization parameters within a servlet.

To display the parameters, add the code snippet listed in Figure 7.23 to the doGet method in place of printing "Hello!" Executing the updated servlet produces the result shown in Figure 7.24.

```
out.println("<body><h1>First Servlet Output</h1><p>");
Enumeration names = properties.keys();
while (names.hasMoreElements()) {
        String name = (String)names.nextElement();
        out.print("init-param name=" + name);
        out.println(", value=" + properties.getProperty(name) + "<br>");
}
out.println("</p></body></html>");
```

Figure 7.23: Code to display initialization parameters.

Figure 7.24: Servlet output displaying initialization parameters.

To wrap up, we will take a quick survey of the other tabs on the Web Deployment Descriptor editor. None of these topics will be covered within this book but you may come across them in your Web application development activities. The Filters and Listeners tabs allow the specification of servlet filters and lifecycle listeners, respectively. These are objects that are part of the Servlet 2.3 specification. The Security tab allows one to specify J2EE security roles and security constraints required by the Web components. These are mapped to real security credentials at deployment time. The Environment tab provides the ability to add additional environment variables available to all components in the Web application. Similarly, the Parameters tab allows entry of ServletContext parameters; again, these are available to all components in the Web application as <name, value> pairs. The References tab supports two concepts: references (indirect names for resources) and JSP tag libraries. The Pages tab defines the set of welcome pages (files to search for when the incoming URL refers to a directory rather than a resource). It also allows the specification of error page(s) for the application (resources that will be sent to the browser when either an HTTP error status or Java exception occurs). This tab also supports setting up the page to be used for login if the application is involved in form-based authentication. The MIME tab alters the MIME mappings for the built-in HTTP server of WebSphere Application Server.

Review

In this chapter you were introduced to servlets, a basic J2EE component type. The basic wizards and editors available in WebSphere studio to create, configure, and test servlets were covered. A running example, FirstServlet, was used to demonstrate the concepts of the servlet lifecycle as well as working with servlets in WebSphere Studio.

Exercise

The running example in this chapter substitutes for a separate exercise. It is recommended that you start with an empty, clean workspace and follow along the actions described throughout the chapter. The only step that is not fully elaborated on in the chapter text is the complete code written to test the lifecycle at the end of section "Exploring Servlet Lifecycle." This code is expanded for completeness as Figures 7.25a and 7.25b.

```
public FirstServlet() {
        super();
        System.out.println("An instance of FirstServlet created");
}

public void destroy() {
        super.destroy();
        System.out.println("FirstServlet.destroy called");
}

public void doGet(HttpServletRequest req, HttpServletResponse resp)
        throws ServletException, IOException {
        System.out.println("FirstServlet.doGet called");
        super.doGet(req, resp);
}

public void doPost(HttpServletRequest req, HttpServletResponse resp)
        throws ServletException, IOException {
        System.out.println("FirstServlet.doPost called");
        super.doPost(req, resp);
}

protected void service(HttpServletRequest arg0, HttpServletResponse arg1)
        throws ServletException, IOException {
        System.out.println("FirstServlet.service_http called");
        super.service(arg0, arg1);
}
```

Figure 7.25a: Servlet lifecycle test code.

```
public void service(ServletRequest arg0, ServletResponse arg1)
        throws ServletException, IOException {
        System.out.println("FirstServlet.service called");
        super.service(arg0, arg1);
}

public void init(ServletConfig config) throws ServletException {
        super.init(config);
        System.out.println("FirstServlet.init called");
}
```

Figure 7.25: Servlet lifecycle test code.

Test yourself

Key terms

servlet

Web Archive (WAR) file

Application Deployment Descriptor

J2EE

WebSphere Application Server

Enterprise Archive (EAR) file

EJB (Enterprise JavaBean)

lifecycle

Review questions

1. When is a servlet object created?

2. What is the sequence for initialization of a servlet?

3. What is the role of the methods doGet() and doPost() defined in javax.servlet.http.HttpServlet?

4. Where will you find the web.xml file within a .war file?

5. What does a URL mapping for a servlet accomplish?

6. Where are initialization parameters for servlets defined?

7. In what method does a servlet typically read and process initialization parameters?

8. What does the getWriter() method on the javax.servlet.http.HttpServlet do?

9. What is the default behavior of doGet() for a servlet?

10. What is the easiest way to test a servlet within WebSphere Studio?

Handling HTTP requests

Chapter topics

- ❖ *Introduction to the HTTP request*
- ❖ *The HttpServletRequest interface*
- ❖ *Reading the HTTP input stream*
- ❖ *Architecture of request processing*
- ❖ *Using JavaScript to perform form validation*

Certification objectives

- ❖ *Create resources in appropriate J2EE locations*
- ❖ *Create server instance and server configuration*
- ❖ *Run and operate server*

The typical user interaction with a Web application comprises many requests. These requests are delivered via the HTTP or HTTPS protocols. A great deal of information is delivered to the application server in this request. Most of this information is not application specific but is supplied by the browser in carrying out the HTTP contract. Web components need to be able to access all relevant information supplied as part of the HTTP request stream. This chapter discusses the features by which a servlet can retrieve all of the information sent from the browser.

Introduction to the HTTP request

The information contained in an HTTP request, whether specifically entered by the user or supplied automatically by the browser, is delivered to a servlet as an object that implements the javax.servlet.http.HttpServletRequest interface. As an introduction to this object and the data it encapsulates, we will consider a simple HTML page with a registration form (Figure 8.1) and consider the HTTP stream sent from the browser to the server when the form is submitted.

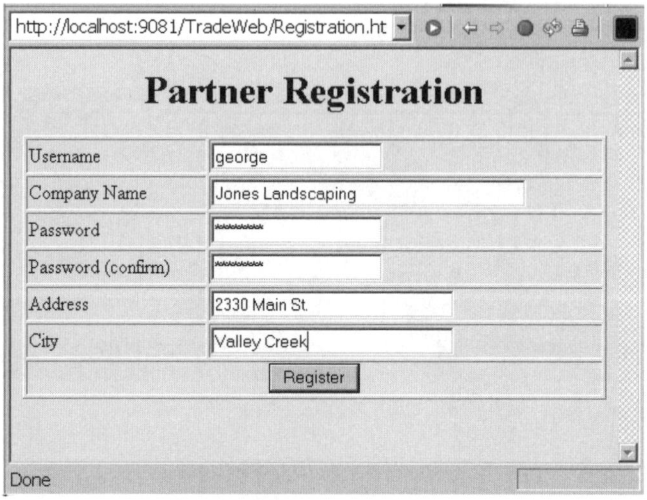

Figure 8.1: Registration Form.

```
The <FORM> tag for this page is
<form method="post" action="/TradeWeb/Register">
```

If the user enters the data shown in Figure 8.1 and presses the **Register** button, an HTTP message stream will be delivered to the server. Figure 8.2 shows the resulting message stream as captured from the TCP/IP Monitoring Server provided with WebSphere Studio. In this message stream, the first line indicates the HTTP method, POST, and the target URL, /TradeWeb/Register. The next ten lines are additional HTTP header information. Each header property is structured as a <name, value> pair. For example, the HTTP header Referer has the value *http://localhost:9081/TradeWeb/Registration.html*.

```
Request: localhost:9081
Size: 654 bytes
POST /TradeWeb/Register HTTP/1.1
Accept: image/gif, image/x-xbitmap, image/jpeg, image/pjpeg, application/vnd.ms
Referer: http://localhost:9081/TradeWeb/Registration.html
Accept-Language: en-us
Content-Type: application/x-www-form-urlencoded
Accept-Encoding: gzip, deflate
User-Agent: Mozilla/4.0 (compatible; MSIE 6.0; Windows NT 5.0; .NET CLR 1.0.370
Host: localhost:9080
Content-Length: 136
Connection: Keep-Alive
Cache-Control: no-cache

username=george&vendor=Jones+Landscaping&password1=password&password2=password&
```

Figure 8.2: HTTP message stream for registration.

Following the HTTP header is the body of the message. Since the HTTP method is POST, the form parameters are encoded and passed in the body. The parameters are also supplied as <name, value> pairs. Here the syntax is name=value with the "&" character used as a separator.

Suppose the action URI, "/TradeWeb/Register", maps to a servlet called RegistrationServlet. The following section describes the interface that RegistrationServlet uses to recover the information in this request.

The HttpServletRequest Interface

Within a servlet, the HTTP input stream is encapsulated within an object that implements the javax.servlet.http.HttpServletRequest interface, which in turn extends the javax.servlet.ServletRequest interface. As we have seen, the signatures for service(), doPost() and doGet() each have two parameters. The first of these parameters is the request object. A servlet needs to be able to access the incoming HTTP stream. The request object provides a large number of *getters* to access each element of the HTTP stream. A nearly exhaustive list of these getters in found in Table 8.1 on the following page.

Table 8.1: Getters for HttpServletRequest.

Request Method	Data accessed
getContextPath()	The portion of the URI that indicates the context of the request
getCookies()	Array of HTTP cookies sent with request
getMethod()	GET, POST, or PUT
getPathInfo()	Extra path information associated with the URL the client sent
getPathTranslated()	Extra path information after the servlet name but before the query string
getQueryString()	The query string contained in the request URL after the path. (from '?' on)
getRemoteUser()	Login of the user making the request, if authenticated, or null, if not authenticated
getRequestedSessionId()	The session id provided by the client request
getRequestURI()	The part of the request's URL from the protocol name up to the query string
getRequestURL	Reconstructed URL sent by the client
getServletPath()	The part of the request's URL that calls the servlet
getUserPrincipal()	The java.security.Principal object for the current authenticated user
getCharacterEncoding()	The character encoding for the body of the request
getContentLength()	Length in bytes of the request body
getContentType()	MIME type of the request body
getLocale()	Preferred Locale based on the Accept-Language header
getLocales()	Enumeration of Locales in decreasing order based on Accept-Language header
getProtocol()	The name and version of protocol in form *protocol/majorVersion.minorVersion*, e.g., HTTP/1.1
getRemoteAddr()	IP address of client
getRemoteHost()	Fully qualified hostname of client
getScheme()	http, https, ftp, ...
getServerName()	Hostname of server that received the request
getServerPort()	Port number on which the request was received
getHeader()	Gets a Header by name
getHeaderNames()	Enumeration of all Header names
getHeaders()	Enumeration of a particular Header values
getIntHeader()	Header value as integer
getParameter()	String value of named request parameter
getParameterNames()	Enumeration of all available request parameters
getParameterValues()	Enumeration of values of named request parameter
getParameterMap()	Map of parameters of this request

The most heavily utilized set of getters are the last four entries in Table 8.1. These methods are used to extract request parameters (usually supplied from HTML forms) from the incoming stream. There are four different methods to accommodate different programming styles. The most basic form, getParameter(), has a single argument of type java.lang.String. This argument represents the parameter name. The return value, also of type java.lang.String, will be the corresponding parameter value. This method assumes that the parameter is *single valued*. If no such named parameter exists, the value *null* is returned.

For example, given the HTTP request stream shown in Figure 8.2, execution of the following code would set variable *name* to the String, "george".

```
String name = request.getParameter("username");
```

If the parameter is multivalued, such as a choice group, you can use the method getParameterValues() to return an array of the String values. Each element of the array is a different value for the same parameter name. The method getParameterNames() returns the complete collection of parameter names supplied in the request stream. The code in Figure 8.3 uses this collection to retrieve the individual parameter values by name.

```
Enumeration paramEnum = request.getParameterNames();
while (paramEnum.hasMoreElements()) {
    String paramName = (String)paramEnum.nextElement();
    String paramValue = request.getParameter(paramName);
    // do something with <name, value>
}
```

Figure 8.3: Code for retrieving the parameters.

One final method exists for processing request parameters. getParameterMap() retrieves the complete complement of parameters as a Map. Directly or indirectly, input parameters should be processed by the servlet (or Controller layer). The business logic of your Web application should not be aware of the input channel. The business logic (Model) is interested only in a set of objects used to direct its processing. If request parameter processing, including data conversion and validation, is at all involved, this task should be encapsulated in one or more helper objects utilized by the servlet for this purpose.

Note: Input validation is typically performed at a number of different levels within a Web application. Simple validation should be performed in the browser via JavaScript. Business rule-based validation should be performed in the Model. Any other validation should be performed in the Controller layer within the request-parameter-processing helper objects.

Reading the HTTP input stream

Sometimes the HTTP request stream needs to be processed as a binary or character stream, rather than a preparsed set of properties. Examples include requests that upload files and Java client-to-servlet interactions. The request stream associated with file upload typically uses a multipart MIME encoding. The HttpServletRequest interface provides support for reading the request as a Stream. Two specific methods provide this support: getInputStream() and getReader(). The first opens a ServletInputStream on the request, and the second method opens up a BufferedReader.

For the more common case, how does this dual mode of interacting with the request stream affect the J2EE developer working within WebSphere Studio? The most notable impact is interpreting the Variables view from the debugger. To support this dual mode, implementations of the HttpServletRequest interface perform a trick known as lazy instantiation. None of the properties of the HttpServletRequest object is populated (i.e., the stream is not parsed) until the first runtime request is made for some distinct property. At that time, the request stream is parsed and all the properties are populated. The implementation class can safely do this because the Servlet API Specification explicitly stipulates that for a particular request a servlet may interact with the request stream only in one of the two modes. This is illustrated by the following two code snippets and the corresponding comments. If an attempt is made to access a request object in a "second mode," the implementation throws an IllegalStateException indicating the improper access attempt.

```
String username = request.getParameter("username");
    //The following will generate an Exception
ServletInputStream in = request.getInputStream();
```

```
BufferedReader reader = request.getReader();
username = request.getParameter("username"); //will generate an Exception
```

To inspect the contents of the request stream when debugging a servlet, you will want to look at the _proxiedRequest field of the request object. But remember that prior to execution of any method that accesses a request property, nothing will be available to inspect. To demonstrate this consider the following lines from a doPost() method.

```
String username = request.getParameter("username"); // one
if (username != null ) {                             // two
```

Figure 8.4 shows the variables view prior to executing the line labeled "one." Note that the field *parameters* is null. This is the object that provides the request parameters to the application.

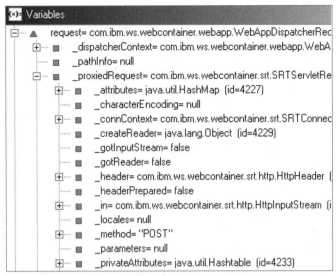

Figure 8.4: _proxiedRequest prior to execution of line one.

Contrast this to what is visible after a single Step Over operation in the debugger (i.e., line "one" has been executed). The status after this operation is shown in Figure 8.5. The figure shows that there is a Hashtable that holds seven parameters.

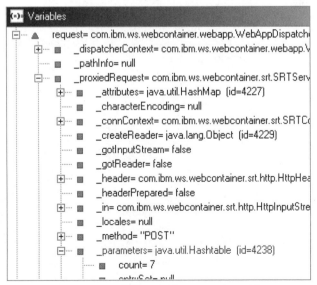

Figure 8.5: _proxiedRequest after execution of line one.

Architecture of request processing

So what is the best way to handle input request parameter processing within your Web application? As was indicated earlier, the parameters should be quickly encapsulated within one or more distinct Objects. The characteristics of these objects depend on the application architecture. Frequently, the encapsulating JavaBean will be what is known as a *value bean*. "Value bean" is the term used in J2EE literature to describe an object whose purpose is to communicate data between application layers. Value beans often are JavaBeans that just expose a set of Properties. A special type of value bean, one that transmits form parameter data, is often called a form bean.

For example, consider building a form bean to encapsulate the data supplied in our registration form. Start by creating a Java class (specifically, a JavaBean) that implements java.io.Serializable. Consider building a class com.ibm.wscg.formbeans.Registration-FormBean (Figure 8.6).

Figure 8.6: Creating a JavaBean to encapsulate HTTP form parameters.

Next, add private fields to the class to represent each form parameter. These should be primitive types. The default type for each field should be java.lang.String, as in Figure 8.7. However, make the type be appropriate to the expected data and the way the application prefers to interact with this data (e.g. boolean, int,java.lang. BigDecimal, java.util.Calendar).

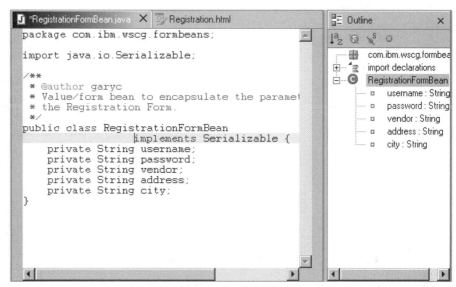

Figure 8.7: Adding private fields to the Form bean for each form parameter.

To be most useful, the fields of this JavaBean should be exposed as read/write Properties. This means there will be a public getter and setter for each field. Within WebSphere Studio, this is easily accomplished from the Outline view. From the Outline view, select any field and choose the context menu item **Generate Getters and Setters** (see Figure 8,8). Then on the resulting dialog, click the **Select All** button and click **OK** (see Figure 8.9).

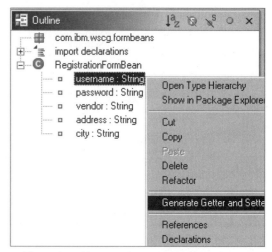

Figure 8.8: Menu option to generate getters and setters.

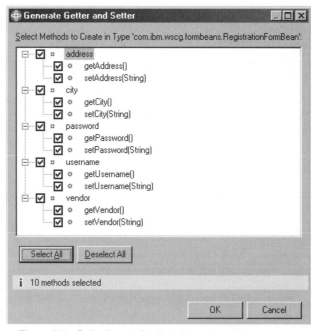

Figure 8.9: Selecting methods to be generated.

The last step is to decide where to place the logic to actually create and populate this JavaBean from the request parameters. The logical options include

- Directly in the servlet (either inline or refactored into a stand-alone method)

- By providing a populate/create method on the form bean class itself

- By creating a Factory method on a form bean Factory object.

Each of these options is very plausible, and in the end the same code needs to be written in each one. Let's briefly consider these options and why you would choose to prefer one over another. There are two related issues to be considered:

1. Form parameter names may change and are under the control of the Web page designer. Try and lock down these names at design time and have them be consistent across your enterprise. If change does occur, consider what elements of your application will be affected. This issue encourages encapsulating the populate code within the form bean itself by isolating this information in a single object whose role is directly associated with the HTML form.

2. What application-layer-specific information flows across application layer boundaries? This issue discourages providing a public populate() method on the form bean if it is passed on to other application layers.

The most involved and most flexible solution is to create a Factory class whose role is to encapsulate the form parameter names to form bean mappings. It can even externalize this mapping to either a Java properties file or an XML file. Thus, changes to form parameter names do not require code modification.

Fortunately, with good refactoring tools, one isn't locked into the design up front. One incremental approach, working with a tool such as WebSphere Studio, is to start by creating the form bean within the servlet processing method (doGet() or doPost()). Then follow this with the code to populate the bean from the request parameters. This way you can easily test this code, setting a breakpoint within the servlet and stepping through the form-bean-populating code. You can then inspect the contents of the resulting form bean.

Next, you can refactor this code into a separate utility method within the servlet. The Extract Method refactoring tool is great for this task. This is started by selecting a block of code that you wish turn into a method. The context menu selection **Refactor → Extract Method** (Figure 8.10) then does the rest.

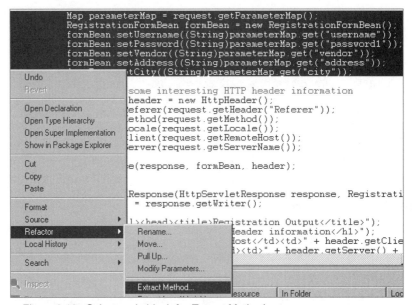

Figure 8.10: Select code block for Extract Method.

The refactoring option launches the Extract Method wizard, where you supply a method name (Figure 8.11). You are then given the option to review the changes that will be made as a result of the refactoring. Once you accept the changes, the new method will be created, and the code block will be replaced with a call to the newly created method.

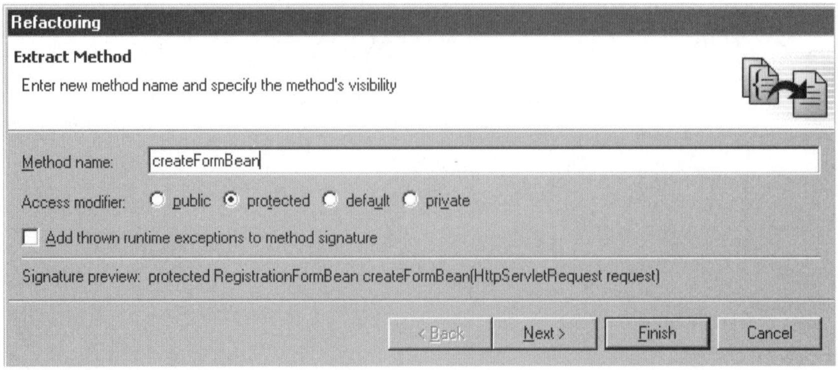

Figure 8.11: Extract Method dialog.

After adding some error-handling code to the method and further testing, you may decide that you would like to move the method to the RegistrationFormBean class. The options are either to move the method as it is and turn it into a public static factory method, or to extract the "populate" portion of the method first and move it as an instance method of the RegistrationFormBean class (Figure 8.12). If it is first turned into a public static method on the RegistrationServlet class, you can use the **Refactor → Move** tool to complete the refactoring.

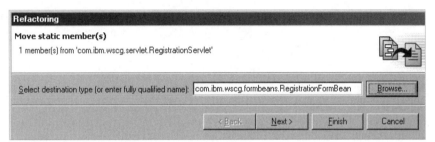

Figure 8.12: Moving a static member.

Using JavaScript to perform form validation

Before completing the topic of handling HTTP requests, let's return to the topic of input validation. Simple validation that required fields have been provided is best handled in the browser with JavaScript. WebSphere Studio has good support for writing JavaScript. The basic model for form validation is to create a JavaScript function to be invoked onSubmit. This function will return true if the validation succeeds and false if it fails. In addition, you will usually provide a pop-up alert with information about what validation rule failed.

Note: The use of JavaScript, which runs on the browser, brings up issues of testing compatibility between different clients. In most cases, using the elements included in the ECMAScript standard and requiring more recent browsers will minimize browser compatibility issues.

To enter this function, open up the HTML or JSP page (e.g., Registration.html) that contains the form that you want to validate. In the Page Designer editor, switch to the source view. Place the cursor right before the </HEAD> end tag and select **Insert → Script**. This will add the <SCRIPT> tag, within which you can write your JavaScript function.

Figure 8.13 lists a simple function definition used to validate that (1) all fields contain data and (2) both password fields contain the same data. The function, validateForm, takes a single argument that is the form object that is being validated. The text entered in a field is accessed through the method call theForm.*input_name*.value. The first condition checks to see whether any input value corresponds to the empty String, " ". This would imply that no data was entered. The call to window.alert generates a modal dialog containing the parameter text and an OK button.

```
function validateForm(theForm) {
    if ( (theForm.username.value == "") || (theForm.vendor.value == "")
||
        (theForm.password1.value == "") ||
        (theForm.password2.value == "") || (theForm.address.value == "")
        || (theForm.city.value == "") ) {

        window.alert("All fields require a value!")
        return false
    }
    if ( (theForm.password1.value != "") && (theForm.password2.value != "")
        && (theForm.password1.value == theForm.password2.value) ) {
        return true
    }
    else {
        window.alert("The two passwords supplied do not match!")
        return false
    }
}
```

Figure 8.13: Simple validation function in JavaScript.

To have the validateForm function called upon trying to submit the FORM requires adding an Event to the FORM tag. The following represents the updated FORM tag for the Registration form.

```
<form method="post" action="/TradeWeb/Register" name="RegForm"
    onsubmit="validateForm(document.RegForm)">
```

The onsubmit event is triggered when the form's Submit button is pressed. It is bound to the event handler validateForm. The parameter, document.RegForm, identifies the named form. Prior to issuing the HTTP request, the event handler is called. If the event handler returns true, the HTTP request is made. Otherwise, no request is sent.

Review

A client interaction with a Web application starts from a browser. The communication transport protocol is HTTP. The HTTP request stream is composed of a header and a body. A servlet needs easy access to the content of the input request stream. This content is delivered to the servlet via an object that implements the HttpServ-letRequest interface. This object permits two different, but exclusive, modes for reading the stream. Under most circumstances, a servlet will access the request data via the large set of Properties (getters) of the HttpServletRequest object. This includes access to preferred Locale, user Principal, miscellaneous headers, cookies, and parameters.

Processing form data starts with potential validation in the browser via JavaScript. Within the servlet, it is best to populate a form bean immediately so as to encapsulate the incoming form parameters and to make them available to the application model.

Exercise

This exercise will have you create a registration Web page. You will create the RegistrationServlet to process the incoming registration data. You will then create a Java-Bean to capture the form data. The Registration servlet will then return a response stream that echoes back some of the request stream properties. On this pass, you will not be adding any data to a database but will be testing your code by use of the debugger.

1. Start WebSphere Studio Application Developer using the Chapter 8 workspace, **C:\WSCG\Workspaces\Startup\Chapter-8**.

Creating the registration Web page

1. Open the Web perspective. In the **TradeWeb** project, select the Web Content folder and create a new HTML file named Registration.html.
   a. Launch the New HTML/XHTML File wizard via **File → New → HTML/ XHTML File**.
   b. Set the File Name to **Registration.html** and the Markup Language to **HTML**.
   c. Click **Finish**.

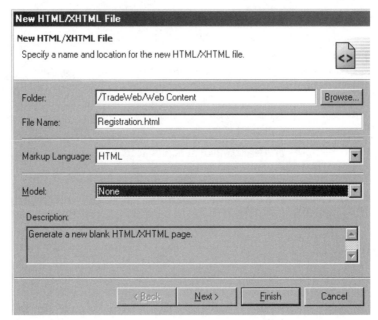

Figure 8.14: New HTML/XHTML File Wizard.

2. Switch to the Design view of PageDesigner if you are not already there. Delete the existing text.

3. Insert a Heading 1 paragraph with the text "Partner Registration."
   a. Select **Insert → Paragraph → Heading 1**.
   b. Type **Partner Registration**.

4. Ensure that the cursor is at the end of the line "Partner Registration" and insert a Form.
   a. Select **Insert → Form and Input Fields → Form**.

5. Insert a 7 row, 2 column table within the form.
   a. Select **Insert → Table**
   b. Specify **7**-rows and **2**-columns.

6. Add input field names in the first column and Text Fields in the second column. To insert a Text Field, use **Insert → Form and Input Fields → Text Field** and set the values shown in Table 8.2. The Input type, Names, Columns, and Maximum length are entered on the Attributes view, shown in Figure 8.15). Also add a Submit button with text **Register** to the seventh row, joining the two columns in that row.

Table 8.2: Input data for Registration Form.

Label (Column 1)	Input type	Names	Columns	Maximum length
Username	text	username	20	16
Company Name	text	vendor	40	40
Password	password	password1	20	16
Password (confirm)	password	password2	20	16
Address	text	address	30	30
City	text	city	30	30

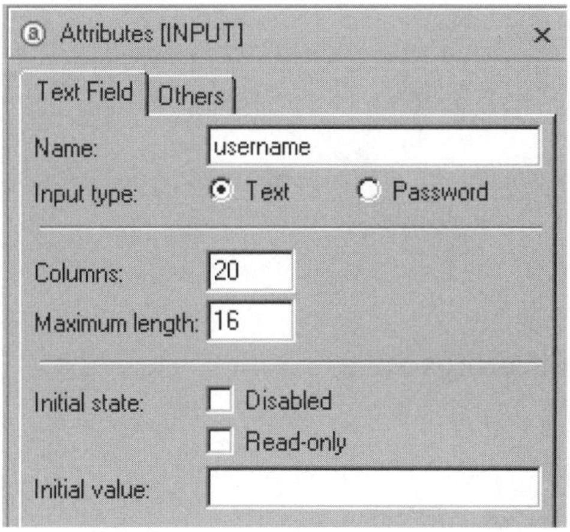

Figure 8.15: Text field attributes.

Figure 8.16 shows the resulting table as seen in the Design view.

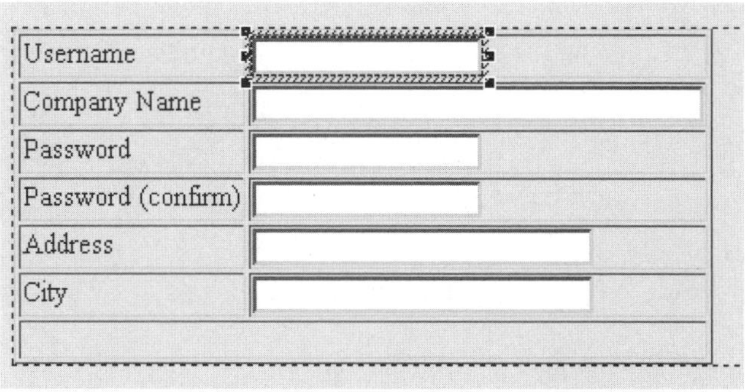

Figure 8.16: Design view of registration input fields.

7. To validate the settings fully, you can look at the Source view. It should look the same as that shown in Figure 8.17.

```
<TR>
    <TD>Username</TD>
    <TD><INPUT type="text" name="username" size="20" maxlength="16"></TD>
</TR>
<TR>
    <TD>Company Name</TD>
    <TD><INPUT type="text" name="vendor" size="40" maxlength="40"></TD>
</TR>
<TR>
    <TD>Password</TD>
    <TD><INPUT type="password" name="password1" size="20" maxlength="16"></TD
</TR>
<TR>
    <TD>Password (confirm)</TD>
    <TD><INPUT type="password" name="password2" size="20" maxlength="16"></TD
</TR>
<TR>
    <TD>Address</TD>
    <TD><INPUT type="text" name="address" size="30" maxlength="30"></TD>
</TR>
<TR>
    <TD>City</TD>
    <TD><INPUT type="text" name="city" size="30" maxlength="30"></TD>
</TR>
<TR>
    <TD colspan="2" align="center">
    <INPUT type="submit" name="register" value="Register"></TD></TR>
```

Figure 8.17: Table contents.

Creating the registration servlet

1. Create the RegistrationServlet.
   a. Select **File → New → Servlet**.
   b. Browse for the Java package **com.ibm.wscg.servlet**.
   c. Set the class name to **RegistrationServlet**.
   d. Click **Next**.

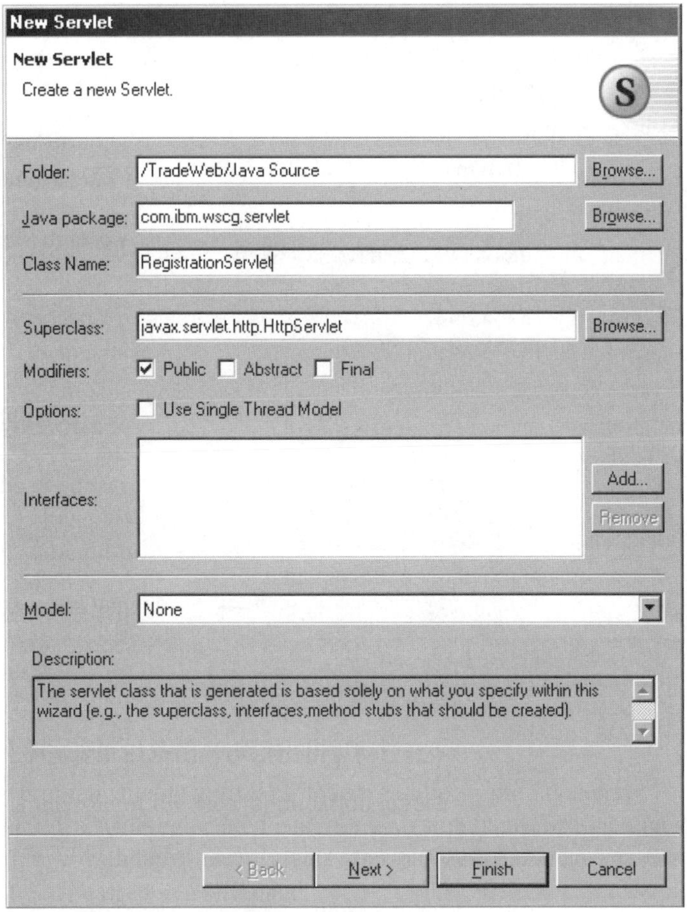

Figure 8.18: New Servlet wizard.

2. Set the URL mappng to /Register and elect not to create doGet().

   a. On the second page of the New Servlet wizard (Figure 8.19), uncheck **doGet()**.

   b. In Mappings, add a new URL Pattern for **/Register** and remove the one **/RegistrationServlet**. Click **Finish**.

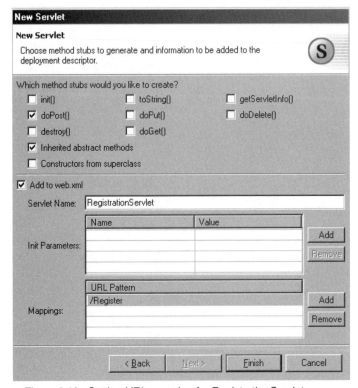

Figure 8.19: Setting URL mapping for RegistrationServlet.

3. Add two lines of code to the **doPost()**:

```
String username = req.getParameter("username");
if (username != null) {}
```

4. Save the file.

5. Return to Registration.html. Locate the Form tag from the Outline view (Figure 8.20).

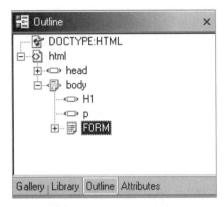

Figure 8.20: Outline view of HTML page.

6. Switch to the Attribute view (Figure 8.21) and choose **Servlet. . .** from the drop-down menu.

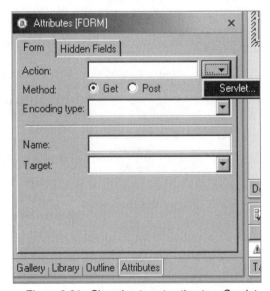

Figure 8.21: Choosing to set action to a Servlet.

7. Select **RegistrationServlet** from the list on the Select Servlet dialog Z (Figure 8.22).

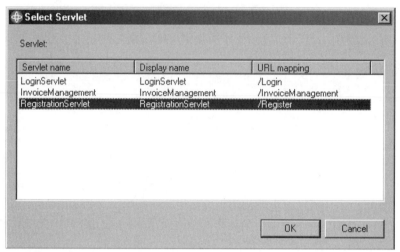

Figure 8.22: Selecting RegistrationServlet.

8. In the Attributes view for the form (Figure 8.23), select **Post** for the Method.

Figure 8.23: Choosing Post for the method.

9. Save Registration.html.

Setting up the TCP/IP monitoring server

1. Set up a new TCP/IP monitoring server named Snoop.

   a. Switch to the Server perspective.

   b. In the Server Configuration View, select **Servers**,

   c. Choose **New → Server and Server Configuration** from context menu.

   d. In the Create a New Server and Server Configuration wizard (Figure 8.24), select **TCP/IP Monitoring Server** from the list as Server type.

   e. Enter **Snoop** as the Server name.

2. Click **Finish**.

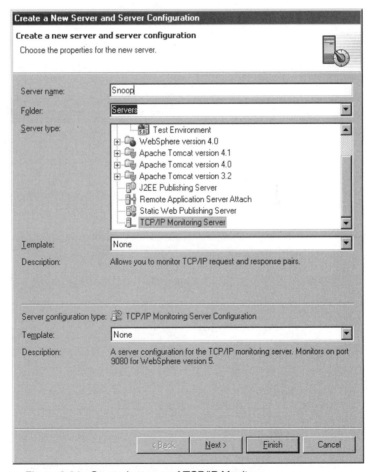

Figure 8.24: Create Instance of TCP/IP Monitor.

Inspecting the HTTP Request

1. From Navigator view, select Registration.html. Click on **Debug on Server** from the context menu.

2. In the Select a Server Client dialog (Figure 8.25), choose **Web browser (via TCP/IP monitor)**.

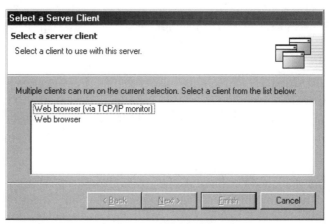

Figure 8.25: Selecting to run via the TCP/IP monitor.

3. Click **Finish.**

4. After the server starts, enter data into the registration form as shown in Figure 8.26.

Figure 8.26: Entering registration data.

5. When the Step-by-Step Debug dialog (Figure 8.27) pops up, click **OK**.

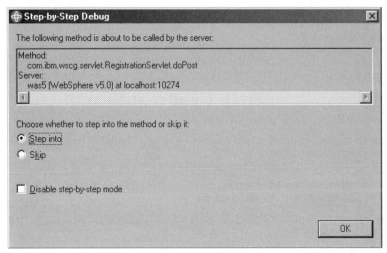

Figure 8.27: Stepping into a Web component.

6. From the Variables view, look at the various data values. In particular, expand **req**, then expand **_proxiedRequst**. Note that _method is set to "POST" and _requestURI is set to "/TradeWeb/Register".

7. Then step over the first statement.

8. Expand _proxiedRequest again and look at the incoming parameter values (_parameters).

9. Click **Resume** to let the request complete.

10. Back on the Server perspective, double-click on the title bar for the TCP/IP Monitor view. Under localhost:9081, select **/TradeWeb/Register**. Look at the request stream.

Adding output parameter processing and output rendering

1. Switch back to the Web perspective and RegistrationServlet.java. Update the contents of the servlet to match that found in the file **C:\WSCG\source\ RegistrationServlet-v1.0.java**.

2. Resubmit the form. Using the debugger, step through the code and inspect the local variables that get populated. Then look at the servlet output in the browser (see Figure 8.28).

Figure 8.28: Servlet response.

3. Create a form bean.
   a. Create a class **com.ibm.wscg.formbeans.RegistrationFormBean**.
   b. The RegistrationFormBean class should declare five private fields, each of type java.lang.String, with names **username**, **password**, **vendor**, **address**, and **city**.
   c. Use the **Generate Getters and Setters** menu item to generate the accessor methods.
   d. Check your class against the one provided in C:\WSCG\source\RegistrationFromBean.java.

4. Create an application exception class.
   a. Create a class **MissingParameterException**.
   b. The MissingParameterException class should extend java.lang.Exception and should implement the superclass constructors.
   c. Check your class against the one provided in C:\WSCG\source\MissingParameterException.java.

5. Next, add the code listed in Figure 8.29 to the doPost() method of the servlet, just before the call to sendresp().

```
Map parameterMap = req.getParameterMap();
RegistrationFormBean formBean = new RegistrationFormBean();
formBean.setUsername((String) parameterMap.get("username"));
formBean.setPassword((String) parameterMap.get("password1"));
formBean.setVendor((String) parameterMap.get("vendor"));
formBean.setAddress((String) parameterMap.get("address"));
formBean.setCity((String) parameterMap.get("city"));
```

Figure 8.29: Code to add to doPost() method.

6. Add an argument of type **RegistrationFormBean** to the sendresp() method to be able to pass formBean.

7. Also update sendresp() to display the submitted vendor name.

8. Save **RegistrationServlet** and resubmit your data. You should see something like the display shown in Figure 8.30. Compare you code to that found in C:\WSCG\source\RegistrationServlet-v1.1.java.

Figure 8.30: Servlet output showing form parameter.

9. Use the Extract Method refactoring tool to move the form bean creation code to a **static** method named **createFormBean()**.

10. Add error handling to the method and test.

11. Finally, move the createFormBean() method to your RegistrationFormBean class and test one final time.

Test yourself

Key terms

HTTP headers
form bean
value bean
JavaScript

Review questions

1. Under what circumstances will a servlet receive an IllegalStateException when accessing a method of the HttpServletRequest interface?

2. What method should you use to retrieve HTTP cookies delivered by the browser?

3. JavaScript should be used to apply business rules to input values. True or false?

4. The TCP/IP monitor server can be used to observe both the HTTP request stream and the response stream. True or false?

5. A form bean is used to encapsulate an HTML form layout. True or false?

6. Explain what the Extract Method refactoring tool accomplishes.

7. Why do you want to create a JavaBean that encapsulates request parameter values?

8. Under what circumstances would you want or need to access the request stream as either a ServletInputStream or a BufferedReader?

9. Why do some values of the HttpServletRequest object not show up immediately in the Variables view of the debugger?

10. List what the getParameterValues() method returns.

9

Case study

Chapter topics

❖ *Case study data model*
❖ *Application use cases*

Certification objectives

❖ *This chapter does not address any specific certification objectives*

Before continuing to cover J2EE Web application development using WebSphere Studio, we are going to introduce a very simple case study that will be used for the remainder of the certification guide. This Web-enabled application permits vendors (business partners) to submit invoices for services provided.

The application supports new vendors to register on the system. Once registered, a vendor representative can log into the partner site and submit invoices against existing purchase orders (POs). Administration personnel can also create new purchase orders on the system.

Case study data model

The back end for the application is composed of a database with three primary tables. The database is implemented using the Java-based Cloudscape database. The Cloudscape runtime ships with WebSphere Test Environment (WebSphere Studio). Cloudscape uses the local filesystem as the data repository. A fully compliant JDBC 2.0 driver for Cloudscape also ships with the WebSphere Test Environment.

The partially populated database can be found in the WSCG\Database directory. You can connect to this database from the DB Servers view in the Data perspective (Figure 9.1).

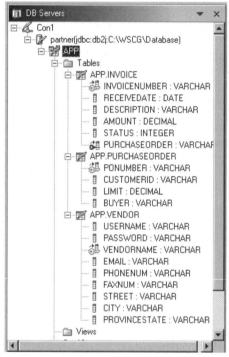

Figure 9.1: Case Study database.

The *vendor* table contains records for each partner who can access the Web application. The columns include a username and password to authenticate access to the application; *vendorname*, the primary key, the vendor ID; and then a number of columns that provide contact information including, email, phone, fax, and address.

The *purchaseorder* table contains records for each purchase order. The columns include *ponumber*, the primary key; *customerid*, corresponding to a vendorname found in the vendor table; *limit*, the total value of the PO; and *buyer*, identifying the representative that created the PO.

The *invoice* table contains records for each submitted invoice. The columns include *invoicenumber*, part of the compound primary key; the *purchaseorder* number, the other part of the primary key; the *receivedate*, indicating when the invoice was submitted; the *description*, identifying what products or services are being paid for; *amount*, the total price to be paid; and *status*, indicating the workflow status of the invoice.

Chapter 15 will concentrate on JDBC, the technology used to access the persistent store. Within the case study, value beans are created to represent the persistent data as Java objects. Mapper classes are used to encapsulate the database access routines used to map between the Java objects and the database records. The value beans can be found in the Java package com.ibm.studiocertguide.model. Figure 9.2 shows this package and the three value beans: Invoice.java, Partner.java, and PurchaseOrder.java. The mappers are located in the com.ibm.studiocertguide.mapping package.

Figure 9.2: Java Source organization for Case Study.

Other necessary packages are

■ com.ibm.studiocertguide.servlet, which contains the application's servlets

■ com.ibm.studiocertguide.formbeans, which encapsulates data received via HTML forms

■ com.ibm.studiocertguide.view, which represents dynamic data supplied on application Web pages

Figure 9.3 shows the class diagrams for the model (value beans) objects.

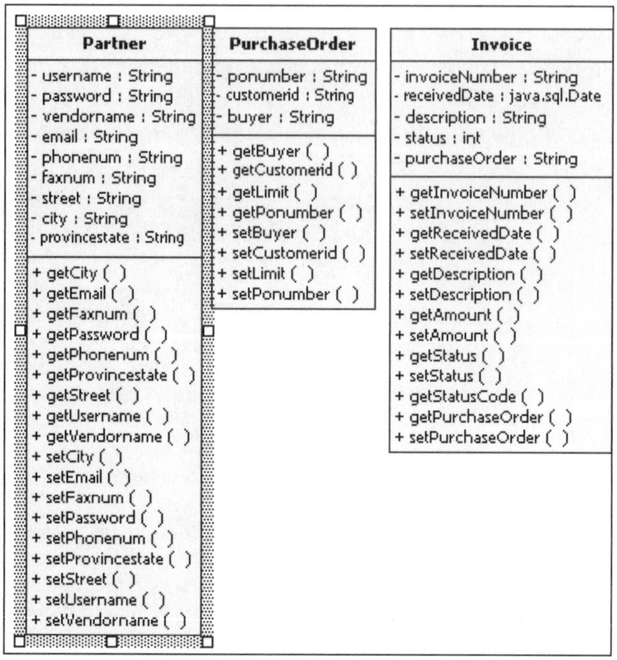

Figure 9.3: Class diagrams for value beans.

Application use cases

Having outlined the code organization and the back-end datastore, we will now look at each of the use cases highlighted in this certification guide:

- Vendor registration

- Vendor login

- Vendor review and submission of invoice

- Vendor submission of invoice

- Administration creation of purchase orders

- Vendor update of account profile

The basic structure is to have a dedicated servlet to process each use case.

Use case: vendor registration

Description

A vendor navigates to the registration page and is presented with a registration form (Figure 9.4). When the vendor enters data into the HTML form and clicks the Create Vendor button, a new entry is added to the vendor table. The complete registration form is validated within the browser. Other error conditions include a nonunique combination of vendorname and username.

The processing servlet is RegistrationServlet.

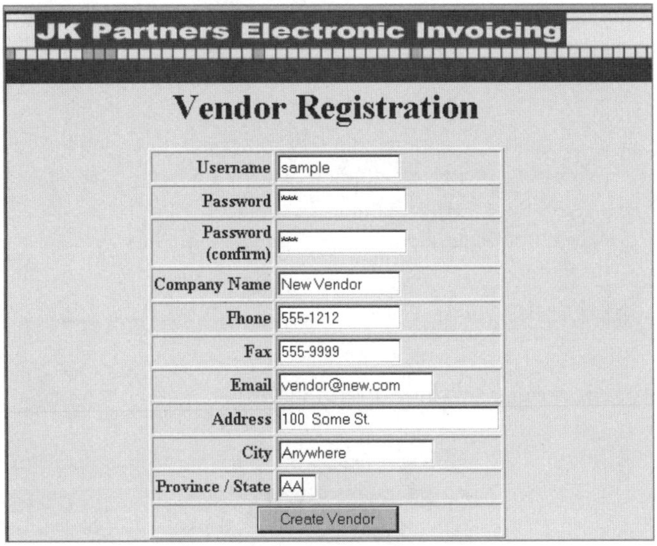

Figure 9.4: New vendor registration.

The response is a simple acknowledgment of successful update of the persistent store (Figure 9.5).

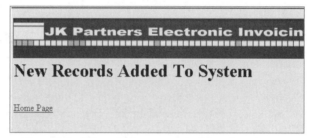

Figure 9.5: Acknowledgment to vendor registration.

Use case: vendor login

Description
A vendor navigates to the login screen and enters username and password created during registration (Figure 9.6). Upon clicking the Login button, the vendor is authenticated via matching username and password stored in the vendor table. Upon successful login, a list of available services is displayed (Figure 9.7).

The processing servlet is LoginServlet.

Figure 9.6: Partners login screen.

Figure 9.7: List of services available to vendor.

Use case: vendor review and submission of invoice

Description

Vendor, after logging in, is taken to the available services page. From there Vendor can select to Review and Submit Invoices. Clicking this option displays the status of the vendor's previously submitted invoices. There is also a form on which a Vendor can enter a new invoice by selecting an existing purchase order number from a drop-down list (see Figure 9.8), filling out the additional information fields, and clicking the Submit Invoice button.

The processing servlet is DisplayUpdateProfileServlet.

Select Purchase Order	Invoice #	Invoice Amount	Description		
5000765139 ▼		$			
	Submit Invoice				
			Invoice History		
Invoice #	PO #	Date	Description	Amount	Status
IBM03001	5000765139	2002-12-23	20 bags of mulch	75	ACCEPTE

Figure 9.8: Review and Submit Invoices page.

Use case: vendor submission of invoice

> ## Description
>
> A vendor, after logging in, selecting Review and Submit Invoices, selecting a purchase order number, and completing the additional information needed to submit an invoice (Figure 9.9), clicks the Submit Invoice button. New invoice is added to the persistent store, and an updated Review and Submit Invoices page is displayed (Figure 9.10).

The processing servlet is InvoiceManagement.

Select Purchase Order	Invoice #	Invoice Amount	Description
5000765139 ▾	IBM03077	$ 275.00	Monthly maintenance
	Submit Invoice		

Invoice History

Invoice #	PO #	Date	Description	Amount	Status
IBM03001	5000765139	2002-12-23	20 bags of mulch	75	ACCEPTE

Figure 9.9: Submitting a new invoice.

Select Purchase Order	Invoice #	Invoice Amount	Description
5000765139 ▾		$	
	Submit Invoice		

Invoice History

Invoice #	PO #	Date	Description	Amount	Status
IBM03001	5000765139	2002-12-23	20 bags of mulch	75	ACCEPTE
IBM03077	5000765139	2003-01-05	Monthly maintenance	275	ACCEPTE

Figure 9.10: Response to adding a new invoice.

Use case: Administration creation of purchase order

Description

A company representative selects the option to add a PO. This displays the Create New Purchase Order page. After the vendor enters data for a new purchase order (Figure 9.11) and clicks the Create PO button, a new purchase order is added to the persistent store. A New Record Added to System response page is returned to acknowledge the new PO.

The processing servlet is CreatePOServlet.

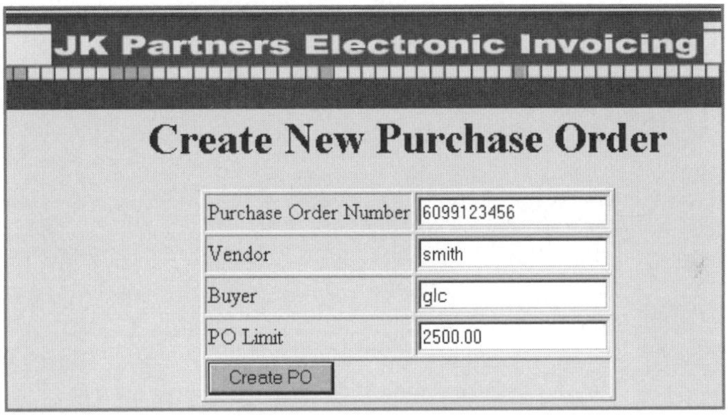

Figure 9.11: Create a new purchase order.

With this introduction to the case study, we will proceed with covering the rest of the technology needed to build J2EE Web applications in WebSphere Studio. In so doing, many of the pieces of the case study will be developed, providing a hands-on example for you, the developer.

Application state with servlets

Chapter topics

- ❖ *Application state*
- ❖ *Session lifetime*
- ❖ *Session scaling*

Certification objectives

- ❖ *Understand session managers*
- ❖ *Create resources in appropriate J2EE locations*
- ❖ *Run and operate server*

Having looked at the specification for the case study, you can now start to implement it and use it as a vehicle for exploring more advanced servlet concepts. To start, you will create a servlet that will authenticate the client (i.e., a LoginServlet). Like the RegistrationServlet built in Chapter 8, the LoginServlet will be called from an HTML form. For the form tag

```
<FORM action="/TradeWeb/LoginServlet" method="post">
```

the logic of the LoginServlet will be initially placed in the doPost() method. Consider the design for the LoginServlet. The logical steps are the following:

1. Extract the username and password parameters from the HttpServletRequest object.

2. Call logic that will look up the record in the database whose username matches that submitted on the login form. Retrieve this record as a Java object (Partner).

3. If no matching partner record is found, login fails.

4. If the submitted password does not match the password retrieved in the database, login fails.

5. If login is successful, display a page showing the available services that the partner can perform through the Web application.

A couple of points should be noted about this design. First, on login failure, consider redisplaying the Login.html page. A more robust design would add a message to the page indicating that login failed. Second, it is very likely that downstream services need to know which partner is making the request. That information is application state.

Application state

Typically, when you want to manage state in Java classes, you create instance variables. For example, you could consider having the LoginServlet have an instance variable, *vendor*, that keeps track of the currently logged-in vendor.

What is wrong with this approach? How many vendors can be concurrently logged into the application? How many instances of the LoginServlet are involved in servicing each of these individual vendors? The number of concurrently logged-in vendors can be quite large; consider 20 for the current discussion. By default, the Web container will instantiate exactly one instance of the LoginServlet. Thus, there is a conflict. At any given point in time the value of the instance variable vendor, in the servlet, will be bound to the Vendor who most recently logged in. This is not the behavior you are looking for.

Servlets are multi-threaded. As such, servlets need to be written in a *thread-safe* manner. The most basic approach to enforce thread safety is to make servlets *stateless*. In other words, servlets should not have any instance variables. More accurately, any servlet class fields (instance or class) should be read-only.

Note: The servlet specification does permit servlet writers to relinquish their responsibility to ensure that a servlet is thread-safe. A servlet class can specify that it implements the javax.servlet.SingleThreadModel interface. In that case, it is the Web Container's responsibility to ensure that only one thread is active within a servlet instance at any given time. Use of this feature is generally considered to be a *worst practice*. Making servlets stateless is, by contrast, a fundamental *best practice!*

So the question remains, "How do you manage application state in Web applications?" The state is associated with a client. Thus, one approach is to manage the application state in the browser. A couple of options exist for browser-based state management: HTTP cookies and hidden form fields. Depending on the nature and encoding of your application state, either of these options may be considered. Among the downsides of these options are the additional (HTTP) data traffic, the visibility of application state values (at least to packet sniffers), and the challenge with storing data other than Strings.

An alternative approach is to store the application state on the server and use a single HTTP cookie to store a key (id), such that the application state can be retrieved using this key. Such an approach is provided via the HttpSession API. The javax.servlet.http.HttpSession interface provides a mechanism to store and track arbitrary application state (session data). The HttpSession interface defines the following methods to manipulate individual state:

- Object getAttribute(String)

- Enumeration getAttributesNames()

- void setAttribute(Sting, Object)

- void removeAttribute(String)

The HttpSession object ("session" for short) manages a collection of <name, value> pairs, where values can be any Java object and the names are restricted to Java Strings. State is stored and retrieved by name (key).

The creation and management of session objects is provided by the Web Container. A servlet *binds* to the appropriate session object via a factory method provided by the HttpServletRequest interface. These factory methods are

- HttpSession getSession()

- HttpSession getSession(boolean)

The first of the two overloaded methods is equivalent to calling the second version with an argument of *true*. Therefore, the full semantics of the factory method can be discussed by covering the details of the second version. The purpose of the getSession method is to retrieve the HttpSession object that holds the application state for the client represented by the current HttpServletRequest. If the incoming request is associated with an existing HttpSession object, a <name, ID> pair will be supplied with the request, in the form of either an HTTP cookie or a query string parameter. The name portion is fixed for a given Web Container. For the WebSphere Web Container, the session ID is identified by the cookie or parameter name of JSESSIONID. If no session ID is provided along with the HTTP request and the servlet requests a session via the getSession() method, a new session object (assigned a unique ID) will be created and returned to the servlet.

For only one case does the getSession() method behave differently if a *false* argument is passed. For this usage, should no matching session exist, instead of creating a new session the method returns *null*.

Let's consider the use of HttpSession in the context of a couple of servlets. The first of these will be our LoginServlet. Consider the code snippet in Figure 10.1:

```
public void doPost(HttpServletRequest req, HttpServletResponse resp)
                        throws ServletException, IOException {
    LoginFormBean formBean = new LoginFormBean();
    Partner partnerLoginInfo = formBean.getLoginInfo(req);

    PartnerModelHelper model = new PartnerModelHelper();
    Partner partner = model.login(partnerLoginInfo);

    if (partner == null) {
        // handle failed Login
        resp.sendRedirect("/TradeWeb/Login.html");
    } else {
        // save partner in session and forward to Management servlet
        HttpSession session = req.getSession();
        session.setAttribute("partner", partner);
        displayPage(resp, session, partner);
    }
}
```

Figure 10.1: Use of HttpSession in login servlet.

The first two lines use a FormBean to retrieve the username and password from the Login form and return this as a partially populated object of type Partner. The next pair of lines creates an object that will perform the authentication task, returning the fully populated Partner object if login is successful and *null* otherwise.

Next is the servlet's error handling. If login failed, the servlet sends a redirect request back to the browser with the URL pointing to the login page.

If login is successful, a session is retrieved (more than likely this will be a new session), and the Partner object is stored into this session under the key "partner". Next, a method that generate the response page, displayPage(), is called. This displayPage() method will use the Partner object to personalize the response page. Within this servlet we are not utilizing any data stored in the session. Instead, this servlet is providing the foundation where other elements of the application (other servlets) have access to the effective Partner object. Although the session is not used to retrieve application state, the (newly) assigned session ID is displayed so that session creation can be tracked. The displayPage() method is shown in Figure 10.2. Logging in with username=smith and pwd=password results in the response shown in Figure 10.3.

```
private void displayPage(HttpServletResponse resp, HttpSession session,
                         Partner partner) throws IOException {
    PrintWriter out = resp.getWriter();

    out.println("<HTML><HEAD><TITLE>Login.jsp</TITLE></HEAD><BODY>");
    out.println("<TABLE border=\"0\" width=\"100%\"><TBODY><TR>");
    out.println("<TD bgcolor=\"#155927\" align=\"center\"" +
            "valign=\"bottom\"><IMG border=\"0\"" +
            "src=\"/TradeWeb/images/JKBanner2.gif\" width=\"640\"" +
            "height=\"68\"></TD>");
    out.println("</TR><TR><TD><H1 align=\"center\">Welcome " +
            "<font color=\"red\">");
    out.println(partner.getVendorname());
    out.println("</font>, to <BR>Partner Services</H1></TD></TR>");
    out.println("<TR><TD><A href=\"/TradeWeb/InvoiceManagement\">" +
            "Review and Submit Invoices</A>");
    out.println("<A href=\"/TradeWeb/DisplayProfile\"><BR>" +
            "Update partner profile</A></TD></TR>");
    out.println("</tbody></table>The session id=" + session.getId() +
            "</body></html>");
}
```

Figure 10.2: displayPage() method, displaying session ID.

Figure 10.3: Result of logging in as user=smith.

Consider the downstream access to the application state via a second servlet that displays the vendor profile. For this task it is not necessary to include the full functionality of displaying the complete profile, nor is it necessary to provide the logic to update the profile. Those tasks can follow later, when more productive tools for display page development have been considered.

The string "Update partner profile" has an associated hypertext link to the URI /TradeWeb/ DisplayProfile. This will be a Web path bound to this display vendor profile servlet. Consider the doGet() method listed in Figure 10.4 for this second servlet:

```
public void doGet(HttpServletRequest req, HttpServletResponse resp)
            throws ServletException, IOException {

    Partner partner = (Partner)req.getSession().getAttribute("partner");

    if (partner == null) {
            // handle missing application state
            resp.sendRedirect("/TradeWeb/Login.html");
    } else {
            displayPage(req, resp, partner);
    }
}
```

Figure 10.4: doGet() method for vendor profile servlet.

The critical piece of this code is the first line, which retrieves the Partner object from the HttpSession. The code first retrieves the session from the request object and then requests the application state object stored under the key "partner". Note that the returned object must be cast to the type Partner, because the return type for getAttribute() is java.lang.Object.

The conscientious programmer will check to see that the expected application state has been found by testing to see whether the variable *partner* has been bound to *null*. When might this value be *null*? What happens if a user bookmarks the URI "/TradeWeb/ DisplayProfile" and then goes directly to that link without logging in first? In such a case, the call to getSession() in this method will have the side-effect of creating a new *empty* HttpSession object. Thus, this check for application state *precondition* is necessary to ensure reliable application behavior.

To simplify the example, we will just use the sendRedirect() method of the HttpServletResponse interface to redirect to the Login page. No message indicating why this redirect occurred will be displayed. Selecting the "Update partner profile" link (see Figure 10.3) invokes the code shown in Figures 10.5a and 10.5b, causing the page shown in Figure 10.6 to be displayed. As you can see, the vendor email is clearly returned from the Vendor object stored in the session with id=UZVDWK4BJMEQQIOZZSJ1RPI.

```
private void displayPage(HttpServletRequest req, HttpServletResponse resp,
            Partner partner) throws IOException {
    PrintWriter out = resp.getWriter();
```

Figure 10.5a: displayPage() method for vendor profile update.

```
out.println("<html><head><title>Vendor Update Profile</title></head>");

out.println("<body><TABLE border=\"0\" width=\"100%\"><TBODY><TR>" +

       "<TD bgcolor=\"#155927\" align=\"center\" valign=\"bottom\">");

out.println("<IMG border=\"0\" src=\"/TradeWeb/images/JKBanner2.gif\"+

       "width=\"640\" height=\"68\"></TD></TR><TR><TD align=\"center\">");

out.println("<h1>Vendor Profile Update</h1>");
out.println("<table border=\"1\"><tbody>");
out.println("<tr><th align=\"right\">Username</th>");

out.println("<td><input type=\"text\" name=\"username\" size=\"15\"" +

       "maxlength=\"15\" value=\"");
out.println(partner.getUsername());
out.println("\"/></td></tr>");
out.println("<tr><th align=\"right\">Email</th>");
out.println("<td><input type=\"text\" name=\"email\" size=\"30\"" +

       "maxlength=\"30\" value=\"");
out.println(partner.getEmail() + "/></td></tr>");

out.println("</tbody></table></TD></TR></TBODY></TABLE>session id=" +

       req.getSession().getId() + "</body></html>");
}
```

Figure 10.5b: displayPage() method for vendor profile update.

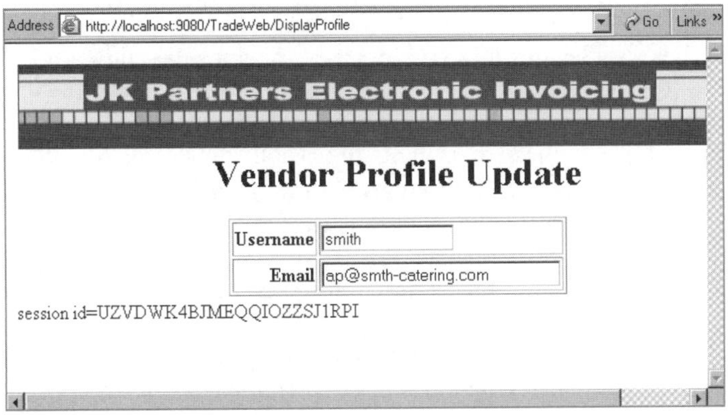

Figure 10.6: Display partial vendor profile.

Session lifetime

One of the issues associated with the use of HttpSessions within your J2EE applications, is the lifetime of application state managed by this object. The intent is to support a client visiting the application in a single browser session. This is supported by default by storing the session id in an HTTP cookie on the browser with expiration set to −1. This expiration directs the browser to keep the cookie around only as long as the browser is open. Thus, if a user were to close her browser and then revisit the site from a different browser session, the previous session ID (cookie) would no longer be available and the Web Container would respond by creating a new session.

What happens to the old session? Since the object is stored within the application server (not the browser), how is this abandoned session detected by the server? How does the server clean up the memory resources associated with this now *orphaned* session? When a session is created on the server, this object is associated with a maximum inactive interval. This interval can be explicitly set via the method setMaxInactiveInterval() on the session object itself. The behavior of the inactive interval is to have the server force the invalidation (removal) of the session if no client request associated with the session occurs within the interval. A typical default inactive interval might be 30 minutes. This allows the server to limit the otherwise-ever growing number of HttpSession objects.

An application can programmatically invalidate a session whenever the client indicates completion of a session, such as by logging off. The invalidate() method on the session object accomplishes this task.

Even with the invalidation framework, an application needs to manage session data wisely. For a long-running interaction (session), the application may place many objects onto the session. These objects (application state) are not available for garbage collection while "stored" on the session, even if the application is done with them. If some application state is applicable only for a certain *phase* of the application, then the application can explicitly remove the object(s) from the session when it is no longer needed, using the removeAttribute() method.

There is a small set of best-practice rules for dealing with HttpSessions within your applications:

1. Keep the size of the HttpSession controlled. A general rule of thumb is to keep it to less than 4 kilobytes. At first glance that appears to be very generous, and in some ways that is true. However, note that the size includes all storage "reachable" from objects directly stored on the session. So avoid storing complex objects on the session unless you can be sure of their reach.

2. If the realized application state is larger than can be efficiently managed directly in memory on the session, then the bulk of the application state should be stored

in some persistent store, such as a database. Then only the keys needed to retrieve the application state from the database need to be stored on the session.

3. Be sure that all objects stored on the session are Serializable. This is required by nearly all mechanisms that support session scalability or fail-over.

4. When working with sessions, be aware that the expected session may have been invalidated by the expiration of the inactive interval, and program accordingly.

Session scaling

When deploying an application that is using HttpSession objects, there are a handful of configuration settings that can be specified for how sessions will be handled for an application by the session manager. In WebSphere Application Server these configuration settings include: enabling or disabling the use of cookies to handle session ids, enabling or disabling URL rewriting to handle session ids, specifying the mechanism to be used to support session sharing within a clustered server environment.

When an application is being run on multiple servers to provide higher throughput and/or failover support, a mechanism must be provided to support accessing session objects from somewhere other than the JVM's object heap. WebSphere Application Server can be configured to support **session persistence**, storing active sessions in a relational database accessible by all servers in the cluster. An alternative session scaling architecture supported by WebSphere uses the messaging infrastructure with active servers directly sharing session data. Note, these session scaling options are not available in the WebSphere Express offering provided on the CD that is included with this book.

Review

Building Web applications requires management of application state. One of the tools provided by J2EE to manage application state is the HttpSession interface.

Exercise

This exercise will have you create two separate servlets: LoginServlet and DisplayUpdateProfileServlet.

1. Begin by starting WebSphere Studio, pointing to the Chapter 10 startup workspace, **c:\wscg\workspaces\Chapter-10-startup**.

2. Create class com.ibm.wscg.servlet.LoginServlet using the New Servlet wizard (**File → New → Other → Web → Servlet**), filling in the information shown in Figure 10.7.

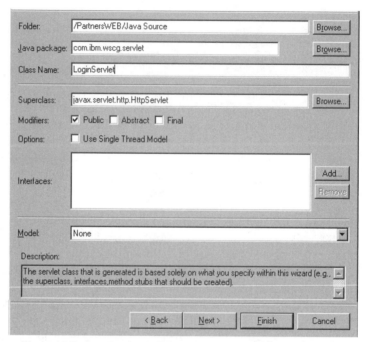

Figure 10.7: Creating LoginServlet using the New Servlet wizard, first page.

3. On the second page of the wizard (Figure 10.8), set the check boxes to create a stub only for the doPost() method.

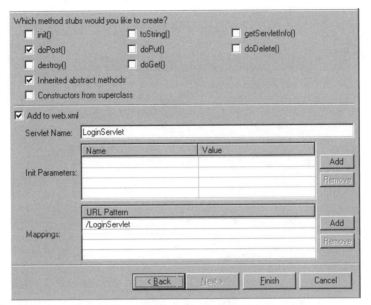

Figure 10.8: New LoginServlet wizard, second page.

4. Refer to the code earlier in this chapter to implement the doPost() and displayPage() methods for LoginServlet. This code will make use of a couple of classes that are provided for you in the startup workspace. You should be able to code as provided in the chapter text.

5. Create a WebSphere Express Test Environment Server to test the LoginServlet. Note that you could choose to create a WebSphere Version 5 Test Environment, but for this exercise we will take you through the process for the Express Test Environment.

   a. Start by launching the Create a New Server and Server Configuration wizard, **File → New → Other → Server → Server and Server Configuration**.

b. Enter a name for the test environment server to be configured. In
Figure 10.9, we use **WSCG Test Environment**.

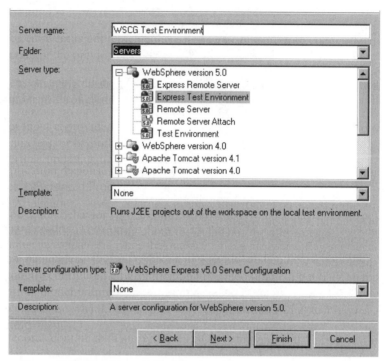

Figure 10.9: Create a new Test Server wizard.

c. Select the server type as **WebSphere version 5.0** → **Express Test
Environment**. Click **Finish**.

6. Open a Server perspective, **Window** → **Open Perspective** → **Other** → **Server**.
In the Server Configuration view, notice the new server. Add PartnerEAR application to the server configuration.

a. Right-click on **WSCG Test Environment**. From the context menu, select **Add**
→ **PartnerEAR** (see Figure 10.10).

Figure 10.10: Adding a project to the test environment.

7. Next, you will edit the server configuration itself.

   a. Double-click on **WSCG Test Environment**. The server configuration editor will open (Figure 10.11).

Figure 10.11: Server configuration editor.

8. The only configuration change you need to perform is to add a Data source so that the application can talk with the Cloudscape database that contains the Partner database tables.

   a. Click on the **Data source** tab.

b. Under the Server Settings, select the **Cloudscape** entry in the JDBC provider list. In the next section ("Data source defined in the JDBC provider selected above"), click the **Add** button (Figure 10.12).

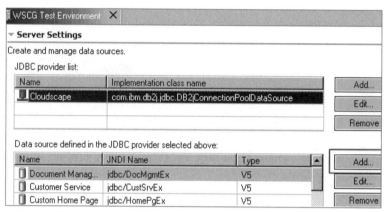

Figure 10.12: Adding a data source.

c. On the first page of the resulting Create a Data Source wizard, click **Next** to accept the default JDBC provider (Cloudscape JDBC Provider 5.0) and Version 5.0 data source.

d. On the second page of the wizard, enter **InvoiceDS** as the Name and **jdbc/partnerds** as the JNDI name for the named field, as shown in Figure 10.13.

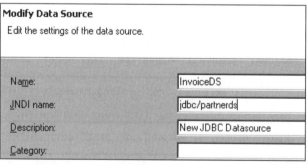

Figure 10.13: Data Source data.

e. On the last page of the wizard, select databaseName. For the value enter: **c:/wscg/database** (see Figure 10.14).

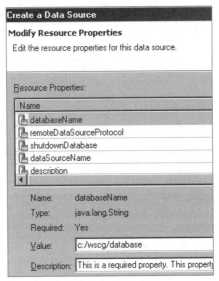

Figure 10.14: Set file path for Cloudscape database.

    f. Click **Finish**. Save the server configuration.

9. Publish and start the test environment you just created.

    a. Locate **Login.html** in either a Navigator or J2EE Navigator view. Right-click and select **Run on Server**.

    b. A Web browser comes up, displaying the Login screen (Figure 10.15). Once this appears, enter **smith** and **password** for the username and password, respectively.

Figure 10.15: Login screen.

c. Click **Login**. If all goes well, you should see the response page as shown in Figure 10.16.

Figure 10.16: Login response.

d. Note the creation of the Session and the displayed session ID.

10. Create the DisplayUpdateProfileServlet servlet class.

a. Launch the New Servlet wizard, **File → New → Other → Web → Servlet**.

b. Choose the Folder to be **/PartnersWEB/Java Source**, the package to be **com.ibm.wscg.servlet**, and Class Name to be **DisplayUpdateProfileServlet** (see Figure 10.17). Click **Next**.

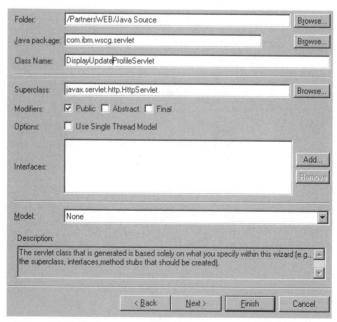

Figure 10.17: Creating the DisplayUpdateProfileServlet.

c. On the subsequent page of the New Servlet wizard (Figure 10.18), check **doGet().** Also click on the **Add** button next to the Mappings section and create a mapping for **/DisplayProfile**. You can then optionally remove the mapping to **/DisplayUpdateProfileServlet**.

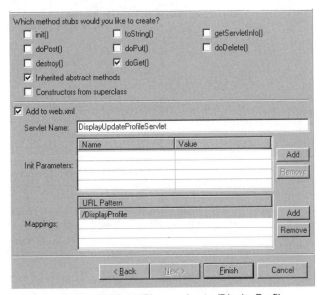

Figure 10.18: Setting URL mapping to /DisplayProfile.

d. Add the logic for both **doGet()** and **displayPage()** from earlier in the chapter. Save the servlet (make corrections to the code and repeat as needed until it validates with no errors).

11. Restart the test server to pick up the modified web.xml file (new servlet). Again, login with **smith/password**. Note the session ID; it will be different from the last time, because the server restarted.

12. Click on the link to **Update partner profile**. You should now see the Partner profile displayed, with the email field loaded from the database with the value ap@smith-catering.com. Also note the same session ID being displayed.

13. Go in and explore the session object, by setting a breakpoint in the doGet() method and restart the server in debug mode. Use the Variables view of the Debug perspective to look at the HttpSession object (see Figure 10.19).

14. Next, close all of your browser instances. This will remove the session ID cookie from the browser. Restart the browser and enter the URL **http://localhost:9080/ TradeWeb/DisplayProfile**. Note that this is an attempt to go directly to the Update Profile page. This will fail and should redirect you to the login screen.

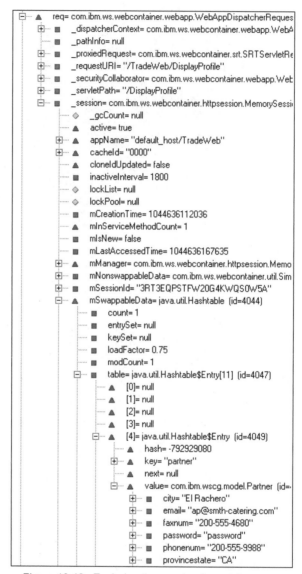

Figure 10.19: Exploring the session from debugger.

Test yourself

Key terms

HttpSession
HTTP cookie
application state
thread-safe

Review questions

1. When using HttpSessions, where is the application state (session) stored? On the browser or in the Application Server?

2. Why can't application state be stored directly within the servlets themselves?

3. The HttpSession object manages a collection of _____ pairs.

4. For the WebSphere Web Container, the session ID is identified by the cookie or parameter name of _____.

5. When working with HttpSessions, be sure that all objects on the session are _____.

6. Which of the following is (are) true regarding servlets?
   a. They are multi-threaded.
   b. They are stateless.
   c. They are stateful.
   d. They are read-write.

7. What are the different ways to maintain state in a Web application?
   a. Cookies
   b. Hidden from fields
   c. Http Sessions
   d. Application Server Console

8. Which of the following HttpSession methods do *not* manipulate individual state?
   a. Object getAttribute(String)
   b. Enumeration getAttributesNames()
   c. HttpSession getSession()
   d. Void setAttribute(String)

9. The creation and management of session objects is provided by the
   a. WebSphere Studio
   b. servlet
   c. Web Container
   d. JSP

10. Which of the following methods can be used to invalidate sessions?
    a. Invalidate()
    b. cleanSession()
    c. setMaxInactiveInterval()
    d. cleanup()

Model-View-Controller basics

Chapter topics

- ❖ *The servlet as a controller*
- ❖ *Refactoring view logic from controller servlets*
- ❖ *Passing object references between servlets*

Certification objectives

- ❖ *Use refactoring features*
- ❖ *Create resources in appropriate J2EE locations*
- ❖ *Run and operate server*

At this point we have taken a good survey of servlet basics. Next, we need to consider effective application design, with the goal of building robust and maintainable Web applications. A basic best practice for software design involves the establishment of distinct application layers, each of which is single purposed for the type of service it provides. Each layer also provides a limited interface with which other layers interact.

A very coarse layering of Web applications distributes the application components into one of three layers: model, view, and controller.

The *view* (or *presentation*) *layer* consists of components that accept user input and present application output. In a J2EE, thin-client-based application, the typical components will consist of HTML pages, JavaServer Pages (JSP) pages, and dedicated presentation servlets.

The *model layer* consists of components that encapsulate the business logic of the application. It is frequently implemented via a number of distinct sublayers. What is important when designing model-layer components is to ensure that they are independent of the input-output channel. The model should not need to change in order to support another client model (e.g., thick client or J2EE application client). Practically, this means that such controller-specific objects as HttpSession and HttpServletRequest should not be passed along to the model layer.

The *controller layer* consists of components that interpret an incoming request, extract any input parameters from the request, and select (and delegate to) the appropriate model components to carry out the operation. The controller acts as traffic cop. When the operation is complete (model layer), the controller packages up any result data and forwards it to the appropriate view component to deliver the application response.

The controller also frequently updates *application state* variables so that, on subsequent requests, the controller is easily aware of the application state. Consider a commerce type application and a request to check out. This operation has a precondition that there be a nonempty shopping cart available to the application as well as potentially other related objects (e.g., shipping and billing addresses). The controller needs to assess quickly whether the inbound *checkout* request for a user is viable (i.e., that the precondition is met). Only then would the controller forward the request to the appropriate business logic (model layer). If it is found that the precondition is not met, then the controller would forward to an appropriate view component to reestablish state consistency between the client (browser) and the application.

The servlet as a controller

Servlets are the J2EE component that is dispatched to respond to an incoming HTTP request. As such, if we are to place servlets into one and only one application layer, servlets must act as controllers. The servlet has access to the following:

- Input parameters, supplied in the HttpServletRequest object

- Application state, generally stored directly or indirectly via the HttpSession object

Thus the servlet has the ability to extract input parameters and perform validation on those parameters. It is a best practice to factor the input parameter (form) management task to a dedicated object. These so-called *form bean* objects encapsulate the knowledge of the input format and generally create one or more *domain* objects that represent this data. The domain object(s) are input neutral and are appropriate to be passed along to the model layer for processing. The form beans are also considered to be part of the controller layer. The RegistrationFormBean class that was developed in Chapter 8 is an example of this practice.

Once the input parameters have been processed and validated (if appropriate), the current application state is interrogated. This involves retrieving data from the HttpSession. This data item might be as simple as a *state marker.* A state marker is an object that represents a logical application state. This state may be encoded in different forms but is typically marked by a simple Integer or String. With the combination of input data and application state, the servlet should be able to determine (1) whether the operation's precondition has been met and service can continue and (2) what specific operation is to be performed.

Next, the controller accesses the model layer, either directly (perhaps instantiating a model-processing object) or indirectly via an Adapter. In the latter case, an adapter object can encapsulate knowledge on how to communicate with the model layer. This is often the case when the model is implemented via Enterprise JavaBeans (EJBs).

The controller passes data along to the model layer in the form of parameters, which include domain objects returned from the form bean(s) and objects retrieved from the session. Again, it is important that the model not be aware of any controller-specific objects.

The net effect of the completion of processing by the Model is the generation of some result. The result may simply be status (e.g., "operation completed successfully" or "operation failed"). Often the result will be more involved (e.g., data retrieved from back-end persistent store).

Any result data needs to be packaged in a form that is convenient for the view layer to consume and display. The object(s) that provide the raw display data are typically called *value beans.* Often the data consists of part or all of the state of business objects. However, business objects may be transactional and provide many services beyond their data values. The view layer does not need to access business services; thus, the result data is "repackaged" as one or more value beans.

With the processing result status and any associated value beans, the controller is ready to select the appropriate object in the view layer to use to generate the presentation for the current user request. This view selection is typically a binary decision. If the operation succeeded, dispatch the view object to display the corresponding presentation of the result data. Otherwise, choose the view object that will display the notification of operation failure.

In addition to choosing the view object, the controller may also update the application state by adding or removing objects from the session as well as by updating the state marker stored in the session.

Refactoring view logic from controller servlets

Up until this point we have demonstrated isolating the presentation generation logic into private methods on the servlet. For example, consider the displayPage() method in each of the two servlet classes written as part of Chapter 10. But what if we want to separate the controller and view into at least two different objects? How can that be accomplished?

The Servlet API provides an interface for calling out to other services from within a servlet. The RequestDispatcher interface represents a mechanism to involve the Web Container in delegating part of the servlet's processing to another resource. These resources are typically other servlets (Web components) that are part of the Web application. The resources can also be static Web resources (e.g., HTML pages).

The RequestDispatcher interface defines two methods, include() and forward(). These two methods differ in how the associated resource interacts with the HTTP response stream. If a resource is asked to include(), that resource will add its contribution to the current HTTP response stream. This way a servlet could compose its output response by including a set of static resources (Web pages). If on the other hand, a resource is asked to forward(), the current (calling) servlet abandons any right to supply content to the HTTP response stream and instead fully delegates that responsibility to that resource.

It is the forward() method that is most typically called from a controller servlet. This will be invoked on a RequestDispatcher associated with a dedicated presentation Web component (servlet or JSP page).

A RequestDispatcher is obtained from the ServletContext object. The ServletContext is the interface between the servlet and the Web Container. It is via the ServletContext that container services are accessed. The typical Java snippet used by a controller servlet to forward to a presentation servlet looks like the following:

```
RequestDispatcher dispatch = getServletContext().
            getRequestDispatcher("MyPresentationServlet");
dispatch.forward(request, response);
```

By providing the presentation servlet with the current request and response object, the calling servlet can enable the other resource to take over the completion of processing for the current HTTP request.

What service method should be implemented when coding a view-layer servlet? Since it is the controller layer's responsibility to interpret the incoming request semantics fully, a view-layer servlet need not concern itself with issues such as whether the incoming request was a GET or a POST. Thus, the typical approach for these servlets is to override the base service() method.

Passing object references between servlets

One of the challenges when refactoring logic into multiple Web components is passing object references from the calling servlet to the receiving servlet. In previous chapters, when we considered linkage of application logic between subsequent HTTP requests, this issue has been managed by storing object references on the HttpSession. This same technique can easily be used to communicate object references between multiple Web components operating on a single HTTP request.

The disadvantage of using the HttpSession as a scope object for managing shared object references is the default lifetime of the corresponding reference. Even if data is needed only to complete the current HTTP request, any object reference to that data, if stored on the HttpSession, will remain available until that reference is explicitly removed from the session or the session is invalidated.

A better scope to be used for sharing object references is the HttpServletRequest object itself. Recall that just like the HttpSession object, the HttpServletRequest has methods getAttribute() and setAttribute(). These can be used just as in the session interface to store an object reference by name to be picked up "downstream" in the processing. The advantage of using the request scope is that the request object is destroyed explicitly by the Web Container when control returns to it from the servlet that was originally dispatched to handle the HTTP request. Thus, if the shared object is "temporary" and needed only to present the resulting view, the object(s) will be immediately available for garbage collection upon the completion of the HTTP request.

In general, both the HttpSession and the HttpServletRequest objects are used to share object references between the controller servlet and the view servlet. If the shared object is needed by both the view servlet and downstream servlets, the HttpSession is the most appropriate scope. In all other circumstances the request scope should be used.

In the exercise to follow, you will refactor the LoginServlet from Chapter 10's exercise. This will show the ability to have one servlet delegate to a different servlet during the service of a single HTTP request. Chapters that follow will examine a special form of Web component, the JSP page, for use as the dedicated technology for creating these view-layer servlets.

Review

Success in building robust and maintainable applications is the effective use of application layers. The very basic Model-View-Controller pattern is a common decomposition of Web applications into three basic and complementary layers. In this pattern, the servlet plays the role of controller by managing the processing flow for an incoming request. Several additional specialized roles were also discussed to facilitate the implementation of MVC layering. The first of these, FormBean, encapsulates processing incoming form parameters. Application state and input parameters are usually packaged up as a set of Domain objects that are consumed by the model layer and are free from any controller-specific artifacts. Finally, ViewBean objects are used to transmit application results to the view layer.

Exercise

1. Start WebSphere Studio Application Developer using the Chapter 11 startup workspace, **C:\WSCG\Workspaces\Startup\Chapter-11** (or your own version of the completed Chapter-10 workspace).

Creating the view servlet

2. Open the Web perspective and select the PartnersWEB project. Launch the New Servlet wizard and create a Servlet class, com.ibm.wscg.servlet.DisplayUser OptionsServlet.

   a. Select **File → New → Servlet**.

   b. In the New Servlet wizard, browse and select the **com.ibm.wscg.servlet** package as the Java package.

   c. Enter **DisplayUserOptionsServlet** for the Class Name.

   d. Click **Next**.

   e. On the second page of the New Servlet wizard, uncheck all method stub selections.

   f. Check the **Add to web.xml** check box and set the Servlet Name to **DisplayUserOptions**.

   g. In Mappings, add the corresponding URL pattern **/DisplayUserOptions**, and then delete the default Mapping (/DisplayUserOptionsServlet).

   h. Click **Finish**.

3. From the Outline view, select the **DisplayUserOptionsServlet** class and choose **Override Methods** from the context menu as shown in Figure 11.1.

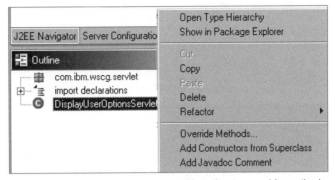

Figure 11.1: Class context menu with option to override methods.

4. In the Override Methods dialog, select **service(HttpServletRequest, HttpServletResponse)** from the list, as shown in Figure 11.2, and click **OK.**

Figure 11.2: Selection to override the service() methods.

5. Change the names of the generated arguments for this service() method to be **req** and **resp**, respectively, and also on the call to **super.service().**

6. Next, open **LoginServlet.java**. Copy the contents of the displayPage() method to the body of DisplayUserOptionsServlet's service() method.

7. After organizing imports, save **DisplayUserOptionsServlet**. Note that there are two errors in the Task view. The two variables *session* and *partner* are unknown. Of course, partner refers to the Partner object placed on the HttpSession by the LoginServlet. Add the following lines of code to the beginning of the new service() method:

```
HttpSession session = req.getSession();
Partner partner = (Partner)session.getAttribute("partner");
```

8. Organize Imports, one more time.

9. Save DisplayUserOptionsServlet.

10. Back in the Login servlet, remove the method displayPage().

11. In the doPost() method, replace the call to displayPage() with the following lines of code:

```
getServletContext().getRequestDispatcher("DisplayUserOptions").
                    forward(req, resp);
```

This call will delegate processing to the DisplayUserOptions servlet. This will have the same runtime effect as calling the private method displayPage(). The advantage is that this service (view layer) can be independently managed as a distinct Web component.

12. Save LoginServlet and test.

13. You should see the same results upon logging in as when you tested the project from Chapter 10.

14. Set a breakpoint in the service() method of the DisplayUserOptions Servlet to see the delegation via the RequestDispatcher. To do this step you'll have to stop the server and start it in Debug mode.

Test yourself

Key terms

Model-View-Controller

application layers

Domain object

form bean

value bean

state marker

Review questions

1. What is the difference between using the HttpServletRequest object as a scope for sharing object references between two servlets and using the HttpSession object for the same purpose?

2. The RequestDispatcher interface supports what two mechanisms for delegation to other Web resources?

3. What is the role of the controller application layer?

4. What is the role of the model application layer?

5. What is the role of the view application layer?

6. The _____ layer encapsulates your business logic components.

7. The _____ acts as a traffic cop.

8. The state of an application can be interrogated by retrieving data from _____.

9. The objects that provide the raw display data are called _____.

10. A RequestDispatcher is obtained from a _____ object.

Introduction to JavaServer Pages

Chapter topics

- ❖ *JSP document structure*
- ❖ *Runtime model and page compilation*
- ❖ *Overview of JSP document structure*
- ❖ *Building JSP pages with WebSphere Studio*
- ❖ *Testing and debugging JSP pages in WebSphere Studio*

Certification objectives

- ❖ *Create J2EE projects*
- ❖ *Use the content assist function*
- ❖ *Create a Web project*
- ❖ *Create resources in appropriate J2EE locations*
- ❖ *Use Page Designer to add and modify HTML and JSP content, including the use of JavaScript*
- ❖ *Use content assist*
- ❖ *Use Web Page wizards*
- ❖ *Run/operate server*
- ❖ *Perform JSP debugging*

By this time you are probably fed up with creating HTML content as Java String literals inside servlets. Certainly the RequestDispatcher interface explored in Chapter 11 could be used to include a partial or complete HTML document into the servlet response stream. However, there is a better alternative for developing and delivering Web pages that contain both static and dynamic content.

JavaServer Pages (JSP) is a server-side scripting technology designed to provide the ease of development of Web pages (using Web page design tools) along with the flexibility and expressiveness of servlets.

Overview of JSP document structure

A JSP source file (JSP page) is a standard markup file (e.g., HTML or XML) with the addition of specific JSP tags. This additional JSP syntax serves the purpose of supplying dynamic content to the rendered presentation. For the most part, JSP "tags" correspond to directly executable Java code. Figure 12.1 shows the Source view of a very simple JSP page. The JSP tag <%= new java.util.Date() %> causes the current (at the server) date and time to appear on the displayed page, as shown in Figure 12.2.

```
<!DOCTYPE HTML PUBLIC "-//W3C//DTD HTML 4.01 Transitional//EN">
<HTML>
<HEAD>
<META http-equiv="Content-Type"
      content="text/html; charset=ISO-8859-1">
<META name="GENERATOR" content="IBM WebSphere Studio">
<META http-equiv="Content-Style-Type" content="text/css">
<LINK href="/TradeWeb/theme/Master.css"
                    rel="stylesheet" type="text/css">
<TITLE>Simple JSP</TITLE>
</HEAD>
<BODY>
<H1>The current time on the Server is:<BR>
<%=new java.util.Date()%><BR>Thank you for visiting!
</H1>
</BODY>
</HTML>
```

Figure 12.1: A simple JSP page, source view.

The Current Time On The Server Is:
Thu Apr 03 10:26:10 EST 2003
Thank You For Visiting!

Figure 12.2: Browser display of the simple JSP page listed in Figure 11.1.

If you were to view the HTML source in the Web browser, you would just see the text displayed in Figure 12.2. In other words, no reference to java.util.Date() appears on the client browser.

Runtime model and page compilation

JSP is really just an alternative source model for building servlets. The runtime manifestation of a JSP is a servlet. This servlet is generated by a process known as *page compilation*. Page compilation reads and parses the JSP source file. This source file is composed of a collection of static markup (HTML) tags with interspersed JSP tags. The parser collects each section of static markup as a String. Thus, all of the static markup for a JSP file can be represented as an array of Strings.

For example, consider the JSP source shown in Figure 12.1. The non-JSP content is represented by two Strings. The first String includes the markup up to and including the first <BR> tag. The second String includes the markup starting with the second <BR> tag through to the end of the file. In WebSphere Application Server's implementation of JSP page compilation, each unique "static" String results in a write to the response output stream with that static content (just as you might do in a manually coded servlet). These writes occur within the JSP implementation class described below.

The page compiler then creates a class that implements the interface. This interface, defines a _jspService() method, which is called by the Web Container to provide the runtime service. The body of the _jspService() method is a series of calls that write to the HTTP response stream via an instance of javax.servlet.jsp.JspWriter (those same statements described in the previous paragraph). These calls are interspersed with Java code generated to correspond with the JSP tag(s) that appeared in the original JSP source file.

The resulting runtime behavior is for the servlet to emit the static (HTML) content composed with the dynamic content in the appropriate sequence.

JSP Syntax overview

JSP specification provides a very rich API. However, in practice, JSP "programming" is very simple. The JSP specification defines a set of "tags" that are grouped into three categories:

- Directives

- Scripting elements

- Actions

Directives

The JSP 1.2 specification defines three JSP directives: *include, taglib*, and *page*. The original syntax for specifying a directive is

```
<%@ directive_name attributes %>
```

(An alternative, XML-document-style syntax is <jsp:directive.*directive_name attributes* />.) Directives provide a way to affect the generation of the Java runtime class.

The *include* directive is used to include a file "in place" statically at translation time. The full syntax is

```
<%@ include file="relativeURLspec" %>
```

For example:

```
<%@ include file="header.html" %>
```

This include is done at translation time, not at runtime. So, if the resource that you are including changes, and those changes need to be picked up by those JSP that includes them, then you want to use the runtime include *action*, not this include directive. If, on the other hand, the resource does not change, then the include directive should be used, because there is no runtime impact.

The second directive is the *taglib* directive, which is talked about in detail in Chapter 14. This directive is used to supply information about a tag library that is to be used by the translator during page compilation.

The third directive is the *page* directive. This directive has a large number of attributes that provide direction to the translator about various characteristics to be associated with the generated class. These attributes are shown in Table 12.1.

Table 12.1: Attributes for JSP page directive.

Attribute name	Attribute value range	Description
language	Compliant JSP scripting language	Default value is "java".
extends	A Java class that implements HttpJspPage interface	This should not be used without consideration, because it prevents the JSP Container from providing specialized superclasses that provide enhanced quality of service.
import	A comma separated list of fully qualified Java package or type names	The default import list is java.lang.*, javax.servlet.*, javax.servlet.jsp.*, and javax.servlet.http.*. This is the only attribute that may appear in more than on page directive within the page. Multiple import attributes are interpreted as the set union of all listed types and packages.
session	"true"	"false"	Indicates whether the JSP is session aware or not. The default value is "true".

Table 12.1: Attributes for JSP page directive. (Continued)

Attribute name	Attribute value range	Description
buffer	"none" | *size*; size is something like "12kb"	Specifies the buffering model for the JspWriter opened to handle content output form the page. A specific buffer size guarantees that the output is buffered with a buffer size not less than that specified.
autoFlush	"true" | "false"	Default is "true". If false, and the stream is buffered, an exception is thrown when the buffer overflows. If true, the stream is flushed.
isThreadSafe	"true" | "false"	Default is true. If "false", the typical implication is that the generated class implements SingleThreadModel.
info	Arbitrary String	This can be retrieved using the Servlet.getServletInfo() method.
isErrorPage	"true" | "false"	Indicates whether the page is used to handle errors. If "true", the implicit script variable *exception* is defined and bound to the offending Throwable from the source JSP page in error.
errorPage	A URL	The JSP will catch all exceptions and forward processing to the names target resource.
contentType	"Type" | "Type; charset=CHARSET"	The default value for type is "text/html"; the default value for the character encoding is ISO-8859-1.

Scripting elements

There are three distinct flavors of scripting elements in JSP:

- Declarations

- Scriptlets

- Expressions

Declarations

Declarations are used to define class-level members (e.g., fields and methods). They are most frequently used to permit the implementation of the jspInit() and jspDestroy() methods. The syntax is

```
<%!
  public void jspInit() {
    // do some initialization operation.
  }
%>
```

The XML-compliant version of the declaration tag is

```
<jsp:declaration></jsp:declaration>
```

Implicit and explicit objects

Both scriptlets and expressions are used to add Java code to the body of the _jspService() method. Within the body of this method there will be both *implicit* and *explicit* scripting objects (variables). Implicit scripting objects, listed in Table 12.2, are variables that are already bound by the tool-generated code.

Table 12.2: JSP implicit objects.

Implicit Object (local variable name)	Java type	Object represented by reference
request	javax.servlet.http.HttpServletRequest	The request associated with this invocation.
response	javax.servlet.http.HttpServletResponse	The current response object.
out	javax.servlet.jsp.JspWriter	A writer connected to the output stream
session	javax.servlet.http.HttpSession	The current session object for the requesting client.
pageContext	javax.servlet.jsp.PageContext	The pageContext (a utility object) for this JSP.
application	javax.servlet.ServletContext	The servlet context for this JSP.
config	javax.servlet.ServletConfig	The ServletConfig for this JSP Servlet.
page	java.lang.Object	Usually corresponds to the object "this".
exception	java.lang.Throwable	The Throwable that resulted in the error page being invoked.

Implicit objects can only be used. Explicit objects correspond to scripting variables and can be defined and assigned within scriptlets and expressions.

Scriptlets

The scriptlet is the most versatile element of JSP. It permits the insertion of Java code fragments into the JSP source. An example of the syntax for the scriptlet is shown in Figure 12.3.

```
<%
  Invoice invoice = (Invoice)request.getAttribute("invoice");
  out.println(invoice.getDescription());
%>
```

Figure 12.3: Scriptlet.

With the need to intermix HTML and scripting elements seamlessly on the page, scriptlets often do not completely specify full Java statements. Consider the code block in Figure 12.4 and the corresponding scriptlets. Note that the first and last scriptlets combine to specify the start and end of the while loop. This mixed-mode "code" takes some time to get used to, both reading and writing. (Of course, one of our goals is to minimize or eliminate scriptlet code from our JSP, in part so as to improve the readability and maintainability of the code.)

```
<%
  while (iter.hasNext()) {
    PurchaseOrder po = (PurchaseOrder)iter.next();
%>
  <tr>
    <td><%out.print(po.getCustomerid());%> </td>
      <td><%out.print(po.getLimit()); %> </td>
  </tr>
<% } %>
```

Figure 12.4: Mixed HTML and scriptlet code.

The XML form of the scriptlet tag is

```
<jsp:scriptlet></jsp:scriptlet>
```

Expressions

JSP expressions are a shortcut for displaying content to the output stream. Notice that in both of the scriptlet examples, Figure 12.3 and 12.4, there are several instances of code that performed an out.print (or out.println). The JSP expression allows specifying the Java expression that is to be displayed. For example, the scriptlet <% out.print(po.getCustomerid()); %> from the table cells in Figure 12.4 could be written as the expression <%= po.getCustomerid() %>. Note that the implied out.print(...) wrapper is left off, as well as the semicolon that terminates the Java statement. Also note the "=" added to the tag delimiter, which distinguishes the expression from the scriptlet. JSP expressions are very useful and generally easy to read. The XML form of the expression tag is

```
<jsp:expression></jsp:expression>
```

Actions

The final group of JSP tags comprises the actions. There are two broad types of actions: those that are predefined in the JSP specification (so-called standard actions) and custom actions, specified via tag libraries. We will look at custom actions in Chapter 14. The standard actions are listed in Table 12.3.

Table 12.3: JSP standard actions.

Action Tag	Description
<jsp:include page="*urlSpec*" />	Provides for the runtime inclusion of a resource available in the same Web component into the current response stream.
<jsp:forward page="*urlSpec*" />	Forwards all the runtime dispatch of the current request to a resource available in the same Web component.
<jsp:useBean""id=scope="" *typeSpec* ></jsp:useBean>	Associates an instance of a Java object defined within a given scope and available with a given ID, with a declared scripting variable (whose name is the same as the ID value).
<jsp:setProperty>	Allows for the initialization of a bean's property from either request parameters or runtime expressions. Typically used within the body of the jsp:useBean tag.
<jsp:getProperty>	Places the value of a bean instance property, converted to a String, into the implicit out object for display.
<jsp:plugin>	Used to generate the appropriate client browser constructs (OBJECT or EMBED) that will result in download of the Java Plugin (if required) and the subsequent execution of the applet or JavaBean component.

Table 12.3: JSP standard actions. (Continued)

Action Tag	Description
<jsp:param>	Used in conjunction with the <jsp:plugin> action. Used to specify applet parameters (name, value pairs).
<jsp:params>	Used in conjunction with the <jsp:plugin> action. Block that encloses the <jsp:param> tags.
<jsp:fallback>	Used in conjunction with the <jsp:plugin> action. Provides text to display whether applet can load.

A couple of these standard actions need to be covered in more detail. The most important of these is the <jsp:useBean> tag. This is used as a convenient way of populating an explicit scripting variable with an Object from one of the four storage scopes: *page, request, session,* or *application*. The default scope is *page*. The page scope is created per JSP page per execution. It is an important scope for communication of objects between a JSP page and custom tags (refer to Chapter 14). The request scope refers to attributes of the HttpServletRequest object. The session scope refers to attributes of the HttpSession object. Finally, application scope refers to attributes of the SessionContext object.

The typeSpec attribute set includes the following configurations:

- type="Java type"

- class="Java class type"

- type="Java type" class="Java class type"

- type="Java type" beanName="serialized bean filename"

This attribute set determines whether and how to instantiate the Java object if it is not located in the specified scope. The first variant indicates that no object should be created if one is not found in the specified scope. Both the second and third variants create a new object using the default (no-argument) constructor of the Java class specified in the *class* attribute. The final variant will instantiate an object from a serialized bean (.ser) file. If an object is instantiated, it will then be stored in the specified store scope, and if there is a body to the jsp:useBean tag, that body will be executed. It is within the jsp:useBean tag body that you might commonly use the jsp:setProperty tag. This tag will be used to initialize the properties of the newly instantiated bean.

Consider the following code snippet:

```
<jsp:useBean id="invoice" class="com.ibm.wscg.model.Invoice" scope="request">

<jsp:setProperty param="description" property="description" />
// . . .
</jsp:useBean>
```

Here the generated code will locate an instance of the Invoice class via the equivalent of request.getAttribute("invoice"). If the call to getAttribute() returns null, then a new Invoice object will be created and stored (setAttribute()) on the request object, and setters will be called on the new object corresponding to the specification in the jsp:setProperty tag(s) found in the body of the <jsp:useBean>.

Building JSP pages with WebSphere Studio

WebSphere Studio provides a wizard for creating new JSP pages. Once a JSP page is created, you can use the Design and Source views of WebSphere Studio Page Designer to add and modify its content.

Creating a new JSP page

The quickest way to create a JSP source file in WebSphere Studio is to use the New JSP File wizard. This can be launched by selecting **File → New → Other → Web → JSP file**.

The first screen of the wizard, shown in Figure 12.5, asks for the JSP filename and folder. The markup language can also be chosen. Here the basic choice is between HTML and XHTML. If you are using HTML frames, you can also choose HTML Frameset or XHTML Frameset.

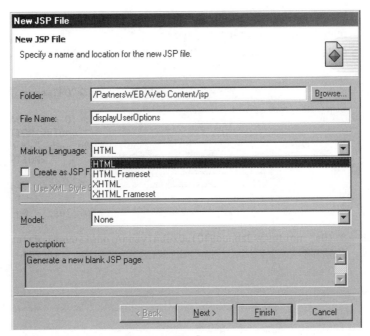

Figure 12.5: New JSP File wizard, first page.

The Create as JSP Fragment check box, partially hidden in Figure 12.5 by the Markup Language drop-down list, specifies whether the JSP file is to be complete (that is, include page-level tags, e.g., <HTML>, <HEAD>, <BODY>) or is to be "included" within some other file that provides these page-level tags. Checking the box specifies the latter case. (Note that, when building JSPs for portlets, one would always select to create a JSP fragment.)

If the selected markup is XHTML, the Use XML Style Syntax check box will be enabled, giving you the option to have the XML-style tag syntax used. If you are generating XHTML, you should use the XML-style tag syntax so that the resulting source file can be manipulated as a well-formed XML document.

The second page of the New JSP File wizard, shown in Figure 12.6, lets you choose to include tag libraries on the page (see Chapter 14). The result of adding a tag library will be to generate a taglib directive in the generated JSP file.

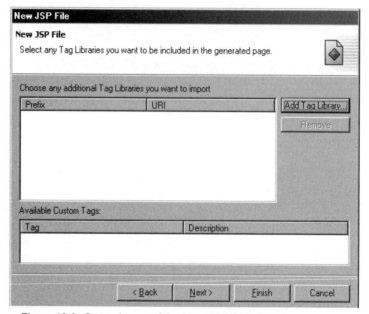

Figure 12.6: Second page of the New JSP File wizard.

The third page of the New JSP File wizard, shown in Figure 12.7, allows you to specify a page directive for the JSP file. You will certainly want to do this if you want to override any defaults (for example, setting the page *not* to be session aware) or you want to specify a Java package or type imports.

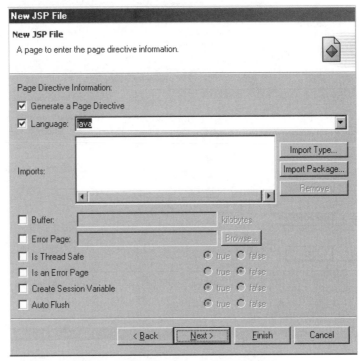

Figure 12.7: Third page of the New JSP File wizard.

The fourth page of the New JSP File wizard (Figure 12.8) let you configure the content type and encoding information. It also permits the specification of external cascading style sheets to be associated with the JSP page.

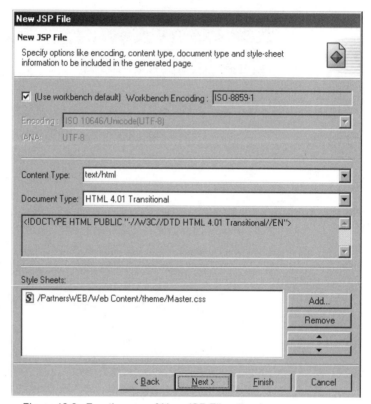

Figure 12.8: Fourth page of New JSP File wizard.

The fifth and final page of the New JSP File wizard (Figure 12.9) enables you to stub out either init() or destroy() methods as JSP declarations. You can also add the JSP page, explicitly, as a Web component to the Web module's deployment descriptor (web.xml).

Which method stubs would you like to create?
☐ init()   ☐ destroy()

☐ Add to web.xml

Servlet Name: displayUserOptions.jsp

Name	Value

Init Parameters: Add   Remove

URL Pattern
/displayUserOptions.jsp

Mappings: Add   Remove

< Back   Next >   Finish   Cancel

Figure 12.9: Final page of the New JSP File wizard.

Adding content in Design view

Depending on your preferences, you can build a JSP page using the Design or Source view of Page Designer (see Chapter 6). After completion of the New JSP File wizard, the file will be opened within the Page Designer in Design view (Figure 12.10).

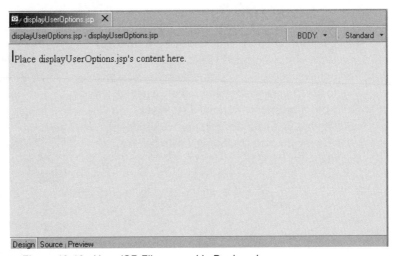

displayUserOptions.jsp ✕

displayUserOptions.jsp - displayUserOptions.jsp   BODY ▾   Standard ▾

Place displayUserOptions.jsp's content here.

Design | Source | Preview

Figure 12.10: New JSP File opened in Design view.

In Design view, static content can easily be added via extensive sets of menus and toolbar buttons. For instance, the banner graphic, paragraphs, and links can easily be added, resulting in the page shown in Figure 12.11. In general, much of a JSP page will be standard HTML markup and will be built by an organization's Page Designer role. For this content, the design mode of WebSphere Page Designer is probably the most productive.

Figure 12.11: JSP page populated with static HTML content.

The JSP menu can be used to enter individual JSP tags directly in either Design or Source view (see Figure 12.12). Consider adding a scriptlet to access an object supplied in the HttpSession. Place the cursor at a position where you would like to insert the scriptlet and select **Insert Scriptlet** menu item from the **JSP** menu. The corresponding Attributes view provides an entry area to type the corresponding Java code fragment (Figure 12.13).

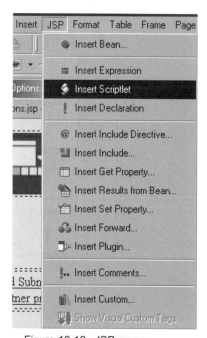

Figure 12.12: JSP menu.

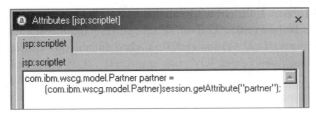

Figure 12.13: Scriptlet entry.

The scriptlet will show up as a visual element in the Design view, as seen in Figure 12.14.

In a similar way, adding a JSP expression will permit typing the Java expression within the attribute view (Figure 12.15). In Figure 12.16 you can see that the Design view visual element representing the JSP expression has an "=" sign.

In general, however, when entering scriptlets and expressions, you will be well advised to work in the Source view.

Figure 12.14: Scriptlet visual representation.

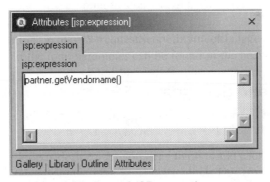

Figure 12.15: Entry of JSP expression.

Figure 12.16: Visual representation of JSP expression.

Editing in Source view

The WYSIWYG Design view is great for entering basic HTML elements and simple JSP tags. However, the power of content assist is available only from the Source view (Figure 12.17). Content assist is available for HTML, JavaScript, and JSP scripting. It makes building pages very efficient.

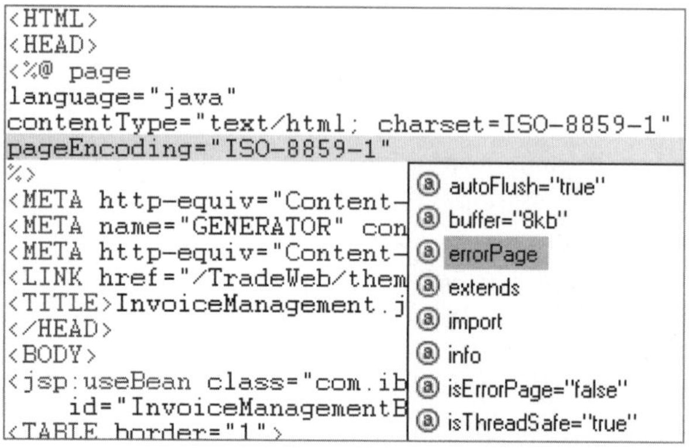

Figure 12.17: Content assist for a JSP tag.

Three other valuable views available when you are editing JSP pages are the Outline, Properties, and Library views. The Outline view shows the structure of the document as a tree. It can be used to navigate around the JSP page, whether in Design or Source mode. The Properties view shows all available attributes for the currently selected tag. The Library view provides easy access to insert JSP tags while providing a rich set of JavaScript functions.

Testing and debugging JSP pages in WebSphere Studio

One of the true productivity aids in building JSP pages in WebSphere Studio is the validator. When a JSP page is saved, then the JSP Compilation validator is automatically started (although the validator can be turned off for a project and then run manually under developer control). The validator will run page compilation and Java compilation on the generated page. Thus, it detects both JSP syntax errors and Java compilation errors and reports them in WebSphere Studio's Task view (Figure 12.18).

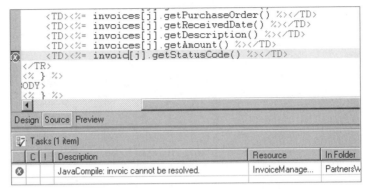

Figure 12.18: Syntax error detected by JSP Compilation Validator.

Once your JSP page has been built and validated to be free of syntax errors, you will be ready to test and debug your JSP page. Like any other Web resource, a JSP page can be invoked via a URL. Selecting the JSP file in either the J2EE Navigator or Navigator view and then selecting either Run on Server or Debug on Server will publish the enclosing Web project to its associated test server, start the server if necessary in the corresponding mode (debug or not), and finally issue the URL to a Web browser. It may be that the JSP page that you are testing needs to have one or more objects available within some storage scope in order to operate correctly. Under such circumstances you would choose to launch a URL and run through associated application logic to invoke your JSP page in the proper context.

JSP pages can easily be debugged. You can set breakpoints from the source view of Page Designer (Figure 12.19). You can set a breakpoint only on a line in which a JSP tag is present (that is, you can't set a breakpoint on a line with only HTML or XML tags).

```
    </TR>
    <% for (int j=0; j<invoices.length; j++) { %>
    <TR>
        <TD><%= invoices[j].getInvoiceNumber() %></TD>
        <TD><%= invoices[j].getPurchaseOrder() %></TD>
        <TD><%= invoices[j].getReceivedDate() %></TD>
        <TD><%= invoices[j].getDescription() %></TD>
        <TD><%= invoices[j].getAmount() %></TD>
        <TD><%= invoices[j].getStatusCode() %></TD>
    </TR>
    <% } %>
/TBODY>
```

Figure 12.19: Setting a breakpoint in a JSP page.

When suspended at a breakpoint within a JSP file, the debugger will show the JSP source file with the current "approximate" line of code highlighted. Of course, the code actually executing and being debugged is the generated servlet. Thus, inspection of the variables will reflect the state of the runtime element of the JSP page (Figure 12.20).

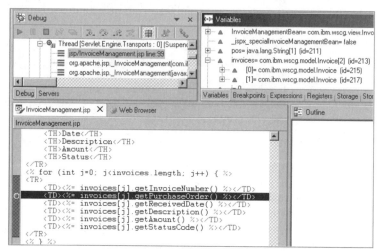

Figure 12.20: Suspended at a breakpoint in JSP.

During debugging, should you find an error and make a change to a JSP page, all that you need to do to check that the update has fixed the problem is to (1) let the current suspended thread continue to the point where the HTTP response is sent back to the Web browser; (2) save the JSP; and (3) click the **Refresh** button on the browser to reissue the last HTTP request. The JSP page will be compiled on the fly, and your breakpoint(s) will once again be active.

Note that JSP pages, like servlets, are Web components. By default the WebSphere Test Environment (server), when run in debug mode, will be launched in the step-by-step debug configuration. This automatically provides a breakpoint at the entry point of each Web component. Upon entry to a new Web component, you will be prompted to single-step into the component or to skip over it (not stop except at internal, explicit break-points). You are also given the option to disable the step-by-step debug mode.

There are some challenges with handling runtime errors that occur during the execution of a JSP page. This is one of the topics of Chapter 13, along with building more robust Web applications.

Review

JavaServer Pages is a powerful scripting technology best suited for developing a Web application's view layer. The source code is basically an extension of HTML, while the runtime artifact is a servlet. Thus JSP pages, like servlets, execute within the Web Container. The typical application flow will have an HTTP request being initially handled by a servlet (controller). This controller servlet will then forward to the appropriate JSP page (view layer) after invoking the model layer.

Exercise

This exercise will build the InvoiceManagement.jsp file. This is called from the Invoice-Management servlet and provides a FORM to submit an invoice against a choice of purchase orders. The page will also display the invoice submission history for the customer. The dynamic data can all be found in an instance of InvoiceManagementBean stored in the request scope under the ID "InvoiceManagementBean" by the InvoiceManagement servlet.

1. Start WebSphere Studio with workspace **c:\WSCG\Workspaces\Startup\ Chapter-12**.

2. From the Web perspective, launch the New JSP file wizard, **File → New → JSP File**. Enter **InvoiceManagement.jsp** for the filename and **/PartnersWEB/ Web Content/jsp** for the folder. Have the Markup Language be **HTML**. Don't include any tag libraries at this time (see Chapter 14 for details on tag libraries). Click **Finish** (taking the defaults on the remaining pages of the wizard).

3. Add a <jsp:usebean> tag by dragging the **com.ibm.wscg.view.Invoice ManagementBean** file onto the page, near the top, in Design mode. In the Attributes view (Figure 12.21), set the ID to be **InvoiceManagementBean** and the scope to be **Request**.

Figure 12.21: Attributes view for <jsp:useBean> tag.

4. Replace the text on the JSP page with a 1-column, 2-row table. Then drag the JKBanner2.gif image (from the partnersWEB/WebContent/images folder) into the first row (Figure 12.22).

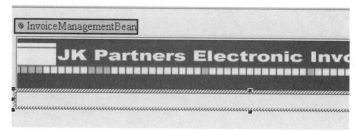

Figure 12.22: Banner added to table.

5. In the second row put an additional table. This table should have 2 rows and 1 column. (We will have a couple more nested tables before finishing up.) On the Attributes view, on the Table tab, set the Table width to be **100%**.

6. In the first row of this new table add a table with 3 rows and 4 columns. Set this table's width to be **100%**. In the second row, add a table with 4 rows and 6 columns. Also set this table width to be **100%**. The result should look like Figure 12.23.

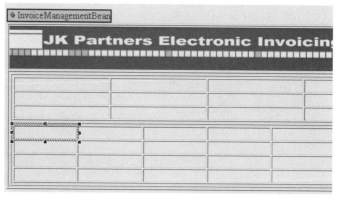

Figure 12.23: Nested tables.

7. Switch to Source view. Use the Outline view to navigate around the document. Locate the first <TD> tag within the first nested table (the contents of this <TD> tag is the table with 3 rows of 4 columns). Insert a <FORM> tag. Move the closing </FORM> tag right after the subsequent </TABLE> tag. Use content assist to set

the attributes for the FORM tag (method **"POST"** and action **"/TradeWeb/ InvoiceManagement"**). You could use the Attributes view to set these values also.

8. On the enclosed table, set the bgcolor attribute to **"#40c23d"**. In this table's first row, set the row bgcolor attribute to **"#ffff40"**. In each of the four columns, add table headers with the text **Select Purchase Order**, **Invoice #**, **Invoice Amount**, and **Description**, respectively, as shown in Figure 12.24.

Figure 12.24: First set of table headers.

9. On the next row, set the bgcolor attribute to **"#cccccc"**.

10. In the first cell we want to place a drop-down menu that is populated from the array of purchase orders available from the InvoiceManagementBean. Note that the getPOs() method on this JavaBean returns an array of Strings, each of which is a PO ID. Figure 12.25 lists a series of scriptlets and JSP expressions to accomplish the task.

```
<TD><%
        String[] pos = InvoiceManagementBean.getPOs();
        if (pos != null) {%>
            <SELECT name="PO">
            <% for (int i=0; i<pos.length; i++) {%>
                <OPTION value="<%= pos[i] %>">
                    <%= pos[i] %>
                </OPTION>
            <% } /* end for loop */
        } %>
        </SELECT>
</TD>
```

Figure 12.25: JSP code to populate the array of purchase orders.

Note the various Java code fragments within each scriptlet. This pattern is common with conditional and loop structures. Also note the use of the scripting variable InvoiceManagementBean, which was introduced by the jsp:useBean tag.

11. In each of the three other cells on this row, you will provide HTML Text Fields to allow the input of an invoice id, invoice amount, and description respectively. For the first of these, use the **Insert → Form and Input Fields → Text Field** menu to bring up the Insert Text Field dialog. Fill it in with the data shown in Figure 12.26.

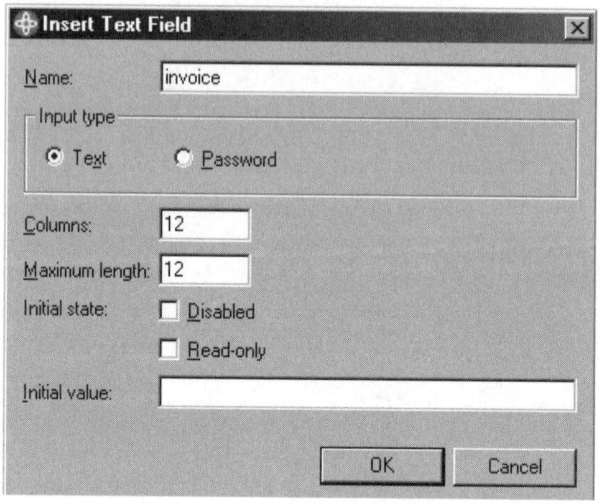

Figure 12.26: Insert Text Field dialog.

12. If you set the Name, Columns, and Maximum length values to be **amount, 10, 10** and **description, 40, 80** respectively for the last two columns, you should have the following code:

```
<TD><INPUT size="12" type="text" maxlength="12" name="invoice"></TD>
<TD>$<INPUT size="10" type="text" maxlength="10" name="amount"></TD>
<TD><INPUT size="40" type="text" maxlength="80" name="description"></TD>
```

13. In the second column of the third row insert a Submit Button (**Insert → Form and Input Fields → Submit Button**). Set the name to be **Submit** and the label to be **Submit Invoice**.

14. Just before the next <TABLE> tag add the following scriptlet to display the table *only* if there are any "past" invoices (InvoiceManagementBean.getInvoices() != null). Also create a local script variable, **invoices**, to hold the array of Invoice objects.

```
<TD><%
  com.ibm.wscg.model.Invoice[] invoices =
InvoiceManagementBean.getInvoices();
  if (invoices != null) { %>
    <TABLE border="1" width="100%">
```

15. In the second row, fourth column of the subsequent table, enter an <H2> paragraph with text value **Invoice History**.

16. Change all of the third-row cells to table headers (<TH>). Enter the following header texts: **Invoice #**, **PO #**, **Date**, **Description**, **Amount**, and **Status**.

17. Just before the fourth table row tag, add a scriptlet to loop (repeat the fourth row) based on the number of Invoice objects in the invoices array.

```
</TR>
<% for (int j=0; j<invoices.length; j++) { %>
<TR>
```

18. In the fourth row place the following JSP expressions to display properties of the "current" Invoice object:

```
<%= invoices[j].getInvoiceNumber() %>
<%= invoices[j].getPurchaseOrder() %>
<%= invoices[j].getReceivedDate() %>
<%= invoices[j].getDescription() %>
<%= invoices[j].getAmount() %>
<%= invoices[j].getStatusCode() %>
```

19. Add a scriptlet to close the for loop immediately after the </TR> tag for the fourth row.

20. Add a scriplet to close if statment immediately, after the end table tag </TABLE>.

21. Save your file and verify that there are no tasks in the task view. If you switch to the Design view, your display should look something like Figure 12.27.

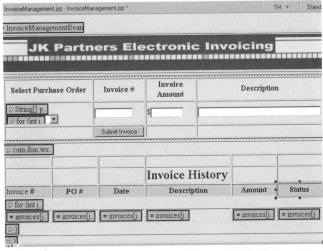

Figure 12.27: Final Design view of the InvoiceManagement.jsp file.

22. Before testing the JSP page, let's take a brief moment to understand the application flow that will result in this JSP page being invoked. After logging in to the application, the user is presented with a list of available services. One of these is to Review or Submit Invoice. This link invokes the InvoiceManagement servlet. Open up com.ibm.wscg.servlet.InvoiceManagement.java. Take a look at the handleRequest method. This method calls methods that retrieve all Purchase Orders for the current customer as well as all Invoices previously submitted by that same customer. This information is used to populate the instance of the InvoiceManagementBean that you manipulated within the JSP page. Then, just as in our servlet-calling-servlet example from Chapter 11, the servlet adds the InvoiceManagementBean to the request scope (setAttribute()) and then gets a RequestDispatcher for the resource/jsp/InvoiceManagement.jsp and forwards to our JSP page. This, of course, is the typical interaction between the controller servlet and the view JSP.

23. Test the JSP page. For this we will set a breakpoint in the JSP page and debug the application. This way you can practice orienting yourself with the task of debugging JSP pages.

24. Back in the Source view, locate the <jsp:useBean> tag. Set a breakpoint on that line of code (Figure 12.28).

```
</HEAD>
<BODY>
<jsp:useBean class="com.ibm.wscg.view.InvoiceManagementBean"
    id="InvoiceManagementBean" scope="request"></jsp:useBean>
<TABLE border="1">
    <TBODY>
        <TR>
```

Figure 12.28: Breakpoint set on useBean action.

25. Next, select index.html in the Navigator (or J2EE Navigator) view and select context menu item **Debug on Server**.

26. From the browser, click on the **Login** button.

27. On the login page, enter the userid of **smith** and a password of **password**. On the resulting dialog, asking about step-by-step debug, disable Step-by-step and Skip.

28. Next, click on the **Review and Submit Invoices** link.

29. Once the debugger is up, step over one time. Then look at the Variables view (Figure 12.29). Expand **InvoiceManagementBean**.

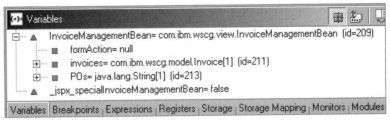

Figure 12.29: New script variable after execution of useBean action.

30. In this sample run, Smiths Catering has one active PO and one invoice in the invoice history.

31. Continue to step through the JSP page, exploring the control flow and the scripting variables that go in and out of scope. Upon completion, click on the **Continue** button to release the thread. Then look at the resulting page returned to the browser (Figure 12.30).

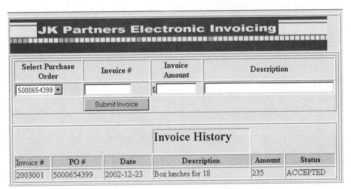

Figure 12.30: Resulting page rendered by the JSP page.

32. You can now go back and clean up the presentation by removing borders on the tables and selecting color schemes for various table cells.

Test yourself

Key terms

JavaServer Pages   *expressions*

XML   *page compilation*

scriptlets

Review questions

1. What is JavaServer Pages technology?

2. List the three categories of tags in JSP.

3. What are the three directives in the JSP 1.2 Specification? Provide an example of a JSP directive.

4. Explain the use of the page directive. List a few attributes of the page directive.

5. List three flavors of scripting elements.

6. How do you publish a JSP file in WebSphere Studio?

7. What is the syntax for using a scriptlet in a JSP file?

8. What is page compilation?

9. Which of the following scripting elements is used to define class-level members?
   a. Scriptlets
   b. Expressions
   c. Declarations
   d. Actions

10. Which of the following does the <jsp:useBean> action tag allow?
   a. Runtime inclusion of a resource available in the same Web component into the current response stream
   b. Association of an instance of a Java object defined within a given scope and available with a given ID, with a declared scripting variable
   c. Initialization of a bean
   d. Obtaining a value from a bean

Considerations for building robust Web applications

Chapter topics

- ❖ *Input data errors*
- ❖ *Application-level exceptions and error pages*

Certification objectives

- ❖ *Create resources in appropriate J2EE locations*
- ❖ *Work with Web Application Deployment Descriptor using web.xml editor*
- ❖ *Run/operate server*

Now that the Web Container technologies have been covered, it is important to step back and look at the big picture of application design. We have described the Model-View-Controller (MVC) design principle, which organizes application components into three distinct layers. Two of these layers, the controller and view layers, have been the focus of most of the discussion. (It should be pointed out that one aspect of model design is presented in Chapter 15.) The controller works hand in hand with the view to provide the user interface (UI) of the application to the end user. It is likely that different controller and view "pairs" might be involved in providing different UIs, such as the following:

- ■ A stand-alone GUI application front end

- ■ A thin-client Web browser front end

- ■ A thin-client wireless PDA front end

However, in each of these different front ends, the roles of the controller and view stay the same. They provide the reliable and robust user interface to the application model. In the Web browser client case, the elements we are dealing with can be briefly described as follows:

- The controller is implemented as a servlet or one or more classes delegated to by a servlet.

- Access to application state is provided by the HttpSession; by data that makes round trips through the browser, such as hidden form fields; or by both.

- User input is provided via HTML form parameters, by HTTP URL query string parameters, or by both.

- Application response is produced as a full or partial HTML page being generated via a JSP page.

- Application behavior (processing) is provided by Java classes and back-end systems that know nothing about the details of the user interface.

Within these parameters we want to take a look at how to handle exceptional issues, such as an improperly configured environment, bad or incomplete input data, inappropriate state transition, model failures or exceptions; all the while providing a reliable and user-friendly interface. So what kinds of problems can arise, and what techniques are available to handle them?

Input data errors

The first big problem area we have covered to some degree in Chapter 8. This has to do with input data errors. These could be simple missing data or involve more complex incorrect data typing. In Chapter 8 we introduced the notion of a FormBean, an object responsible for encapsulating the input user data in a validated, correct form ready for consumption by the model. Validation can take place at a couple of different levels. The first of these involves the use of JavaScript function(s) within the browser itself that perform some simple checks on the data (completeness) before allowing the HTTP request to be issued. This practice eliminates a large set of input problems without the need to call upon server-side code.

The second of these input error-handling steps is involved in the creation and validation of the FormBean(s) itself. Here more elaborate data checks can be performed, including data type exceptions (numeric expected) and data range exceptions. But what do you do if a data validation exception occurs? Where the input is coming from an HTML form, the most common approach is to redisplay the input page, pre-populated with the data previously entered and an additional display (error) message indicating the problem and requesting the user to correct the problem and resubmit.

To accomplish this most easily, consider including a <jsp:useBean> tag on the input form page, where the type of the bean is your FormBean. Set the scope to be the HttpRequest, and, on each form entry field, supply its initial value from the corresponding bean property. Generally, each property directly associated with the form will be a String type. The FormBean should have redundant properties for those entries that the model expects to receive as some other type. In addition, if there are errors, the error text for each is captured in a FormErrors bean and placed into the request scope to be displayed by the JSP page. Let's look at each of these pieces more closely through an example from the complete casestudy workspace. The scenario consists of the InvoiceManagement servlet and the InvoiceManagement.jsp view.

For handling the easy validation, we will look at adding JavaScript to the page. The two code snippets are listed in Figures 13.1 and 13.2.

```
<SCRIPT language="JavaScript">
function validateForm(theForm) {

//      ** Make sure there are no blank fields
//  Not really checking everything
//      -- to support the other error handling example
        if((theForm.PO.value == "") ||
          (theForm.invoice.value == "")) {
          alert("All fields are required.")
          return false
        }


//      ** Form values acceptable
        return true
}
</SCRIPT>
</head>
```

Figure 13.1: JavaScript function for validating that all fields have been filled in.

```
<FORM name="submitInvoice" method="POST" action="/partner/InvoiceManagement"

    onsubmit="return validateForm(document.submitInvoice)">
    <TABLE width="100%" bgcolor="#40c23d"><TBODY>
        <TR bgcolor="#ffff40">
            <TH>Select Purchase Order</TH>
            <TH>Invoice #</TH>
            <TH>Invoice Amount</TH>
            <TH>Description</TH>
        </TR>
        <TR bgcolor="#cccccc">
                <TD bgcolor="#cccccc">
<%
try {
  java.lang.String[] _a0 = InvoiceManagementBean.getPOs();
  java.lang.String _p0 = _a0[0]; // throws an exception if empty.
  %>
                <SELECT name="PO">
<%
    for (int _i0 = 0; ; ) { %>
                    <OPTION value="<%= _p0 %>"><%= _p0 %></OPTION>
<%
    _i0++;
    try {
      _p0 = _a0[_i0];
    }
    catch (java.lang.ArrayIndexOutOfBoundsException _e0) { break; }
} %>
                </SELECT><%
}
catch (java.lang.ArrayIndexOutOfBoundsException _e0) {
} %>

        </TD>

            <TD><INPUT size="12" type="text" maxlength="12" name="invoice"

                value="<%= invoiceForm.getInvoiceNumber() %>">
            </TD>

            <TD>$<INPUT size="10" type="text" maxlength="10" name="amount"

                value="<%= invoiceForm.getAmount() %>"></TD>
            <TD><INPUT size="40" type="text" maxlength="80"

                name="description" value="<%= invoiceForm.getDescription() %>"></TD>

    </TR>
```

Figure 13.2: JSP page invoking the JavaScript validation function.

In the code in Figure 13.1 you see the JavaScript function validateForm() defined. This is then called via the onsubmit event handler in the <FORM> tag shown in Figure 13.2. When the Submit button is clicked, the JavaScript function is called. If there is an input validation error (in this case, if either the PO or invoice field is left blank), an alert is displayed and a value of false is returned to the event handler, preventing the HTTP request from taking place (Figure 13.3). On the other hand, if both fields are populated, the request will be submitted (function returning true).

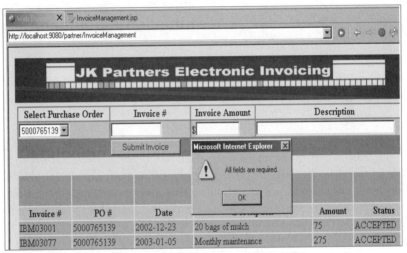

Figure 13.3: Alert being displayed upon failed validation.

The second part of the form validation involves several additional pieces. On submission, the responding servlet (InvoiceManagement) will call a method to populate a FormBean. The FormBean is com.ibm.wscg.formbeans.InvoiceForm (Figures 13.4a, 13.4.b, 13.4.c). It provides a Factory method, getForm(), that can be called from the servlet to populate the bean.

```java
package com.ibm.wscg.formbeans;

import java.io.Serializable;
import java.math.BigDecimal;
import java.util.ArrayList;

import javax.servlet.http.HttpServletRequest;

import com.ibm.wscg.model.Invoice;

/**
 * FormBean to collect Form fields from Invoice Submission form
 */
public class InvoiceForm implements Serializable {
        private String purchaseOrder;
        private String invoiceNumber = "";
        private String amount = "";
        private String description = "";
        private BigDecimal amt;

        public String getAmount() {
                return amount;
        }

        public String getDescription() {
                return description;
        }

        public String getInvoiceNumber() {
                return invoiceNumber;
        }

        public String getPurchaseOrder() {
                return purchaseOrder;
        }

        public void setAmount(String amount) {
                this.amount = amount;
        }

        public void setDescription(String description) {
                this.description = description;
        }
```

Figure 13.4a: FormBean code for the invoice form.

```
        public void setInvoiceNumber(String invoiceNumber) {
            this.invoiceNumber = invoiceNumber;
        }

        public void setPurchaseOrder(String purchaseOrder) {
            this.purchaseOrder = purchaseOrder;
        }

        public BigDecimal getAmt() {
            return amt;
        }

        public void setAmt(BigDecimal amount) {
            this.amt = amount;
        }

        public String[] validate() {
            int errorCnt = 0;
            ArrayList errorMsgs = new ArrayList();

            /* valid PO generated from drop down list
            if (getPurchaseOrder() == null) {
                errorCnt++;
                errorMsgs.add("Select a valid PO number");
            }
            */
```

```
        if (getInvoiceNumber() == null || getInvoiceNumber().equals("")) {
```

```
                errorCnt++;
                errorMsgs.add("Invoice number cannot be empty");
            }
```

```
        if (getDescription() == null || getDescription().equals("")) {
```

```
                errorCnt++;
                errorMsgs.add("Description cannot be empty");
            }
            if (getAmount() == null) {
                errorCnt++;
                errorMsgs.add("Invoice amount must not be empty");
            } else {
                try {
                    setAmt(new BigDecimal(getAmount()));
                } catch (NumberFormatException nfe) {
                    errorCnt++;
```

Figure 13.4b: FormBean code for the invoice form.

```
                        errorMsgs.add("Invoice amount must be numeric");

                }
        }

        if (errorCnt == 0)
                return null;

        // else build array of Strings for error message
        String[] errors = new String[errorCnt];
        for (int i = 0; i < errorCnt; i++) {
                errors[i] = (String) errorMsgs.get(i);
        }
        return errors;

}

public static InvoiceForm getForm(HttpServletRequest request) {
        InvoiceForm form = new InvoiceForm();
        form.setPurchaseOrder(request.getParameter("PO"));
        form.setInvoiceNumber(request.getParameter("invoice"));
        form.setAmount(request.getParameter("amount"));
        form.setDescription(request.getParameter("description"));
        return form;
}

public Invoice getInvoice() {
        Invoice invoice =
                new Invoice(
                getInvoiceNumber(),
                getPurchaseOrder(),
                getAmt(),
                getDescription());
        invoice.setStatus(0);

        invoice.setReceivedDate(new java.sql.Date(System.currentTimeMillis()));

        return invoice;
}
}
```

Figure 13.4c: FormBean code for the invoice form.

The code snippet from the servlet is shown in Figure 13.5. Here you can see the call to create the InvoiceForm bean (getForm()). Next, the servlet code calls the validate() method on the InvoiceForm object. This code verifies that all of the fields are non-empty and, further, that a valid BigDecimal (amount) property is successfully generated. If any of these checks fail, a String error response is collected and added to an array of Strings returned by the validate() method. Back in the servlet code, if there are any error Strings, then both the current FormBean and a newly created FormErrors bean are added to the request (to be displayed on the response page).

```
protected void doPost(HttpServletRequest request, HttpServletResponse response)

    throws ServletException, IOException {
    // Post is used to submit new invoice

    // retrieve the input form
    InvoiceForm invoiceForm = InvoiceForm.getForm(request);
    String[] errors = invoiceForm.validate();
    if (errors != null) {
        request.setAttribute("invoiceForm", invoiceForm);
        request.setAttribute("errors", new FormErrors(errors));
        handleRequest(request, response);
    }

    // else perform update
    Invoice invoice = invoiceForm.getInvoice();
    InvoiceFactory factory = new InvoiceFactory();
    factory.insertInvoice(invoice);

    // Now go and do display work
    handleRequest(request, response);
}
```

Figure 13.5: Servlet method to populate the form bean.

If there are no errors, then the FormBean again supplies a method to create our model object, Invoice. This invoice is then added to the database using the InvoiceFactory object (Chapter 15 discusses the database and JDBC side of Web application development in detail). Finally, the handleRequest method is called, which generates the InvoiceMangement bean to be displayed in response to the request.

The code in the InvoiceManagement.jsp page associated with this processing is shown in Figure 13.6 and 13.7, In the first figure you can see the two additional jsp:useBean tags used to define the explicit objects invoiceForm and errors, respectively. This figure also shows the conditional HTML being generated to display the error Strings if any form validation failed. The code in Figure 13.7 shows initializing the values of the form fields from invoiceForm. (Note that, when no errors have occurred, a new "empty" invoiceForm object will be created as a result of execution of the jsp:useBean tag.) If invalid data is entered, you will receive a response similar to what is shown in Figure 13.8.

```
<jsp:useBean id="invoiceForm" class="com.ibm.wscg.formbeans.InvoiceForm"
        scope="request" />
<jsp:useBean id="errors" class="com.ibm.wscg.formbeans.FormErrors"
        scope="request" />
<jsp:useBean id="InvoiceManagementBean"
        class="com.ibm.wscg.view.InvoiceManagementBean" scope="request" />
<TABLE border="0" width="100%">
        <TBODY>
        <TR>
```

```
<TD bgcolor="#155927" align="center" valign="bottom"><IMG border="0"
```

```
        src="/partner/images/JKBanner2.gif" width="640" height="68">
</TD>  </TR>
<TR>
<TD>
<TABLE width="100%">
        <TBODY>
        <TR>
            <TD><% String[] msgs = errors.getErrors();
            if (msgs != null) {
                int cnt = msgs.length;
            %> <font color="red">
```

```
            <h2 align="center">Errors in Invoice Submission!</h2>
```

```
                <ul>
                <% for (int i=0; i<cnt; i++) { %>
                <li><%= msgs[i] %> <% } %>
                </ul>
            </font> <% } %>

    <FORM name="submitInvoice" method="POST"
            action="/partner/InvoiceManagement"
```

```
        onsubmit="return validateForm(document.submitInvoice)">
```

Figure 13.6: JSP code to create invoice form bean and report invoice errors.

```
<TD><INPUT size="12" type="text" maxlength="12" name="invoice"
    value="<%= invoiceForm.getInvoiceNumber() %>"></TD>
<TD>$<INPUT size="10" type="text" maxlength="10" name="amount"
    value="<%= invoiceForm.getAmount() %>"></TD>
<TD><INPUT size="40" type="text" maxlength="80"
name="description" value="<%= invoiceForm.getDescription() %>"></TD>
```

Figure 13.7:   Populating form fields from form bean.

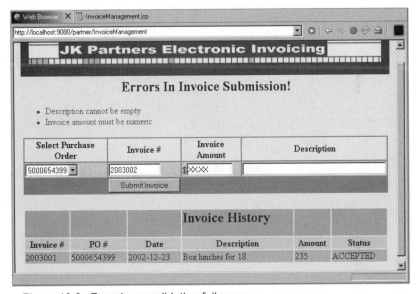

Figure 13.8:   Form bean validation failure.

This use of a FormBean with validation is a very common approach to this problem. In fact it has been formalized as one of the key features of the Apache Struts framework (an open framework for building Web applications, available from *jakarta.apache.org/struts* and used by IT shops worldwide, which provides a generic controller and strong support for development of the view layer using JSP pages). In Struts, form beans extend the class ActionForm, while equivalent to our FormErrors are the ActionError and ActionErrors classes.

Before we leave the topic of input validation, it is important to note that some input range checking can be characterized only as enforcing *business rules*. Such business rules validation should be performed only in the model layer. Moving this checking to the controller greatly impairs maintenance, particularly when multiple client front-end technologies are used with the same model. Also, as business rules change, developers should go only to the model to define these changes.

Application-level exceptions and error pages

Handling and controlling data input errors is a significant step forward in building more robust Web applications. But what happens when something else goes wrong? The answer to that question involves a quick aside to talk about exceptions, both in Java software development in general and in the servlet infrastructure specifically. The Java Exception mechanism provides the most robust way to handle both expected and unexpected errors within your applications. In any Java application development project, application-specific Exception classes are defined to encapsulate known exceptional conditions. Within an organization or even within a project, each application-level Exception extends some base class to make it easier to handle the "catch-all exceptions that we have control over" situation.

The servlet API does exactly that: provide the capability to use application-specific Exceptions. There is a base class, ServletException, which is a checked Exception. In addition, the service() method in GenericServlet catches all uncaught Exceptions that pass through and throws a ServletException on to higher layers in the Web Container. This Exception object generally wraps the so called "root cause" Exception as a Throwable. One can interrogate the ServletException via the method getRootCause() to retrieve the wrapped Exception.

Most typically, your application's model layer will generate many different application-specific exceptions. How can your controller respond? In general, your controller(s) will need to catch these exceptions and route the response to an appropriate view that corresponds to the desired application response for that particular error condition.

In the situation where the application response is identical for a given Exception irrespective of the application state and specific request, coding for this response can be eliminated and instead handled by a J2EE Error page mechanism. For example, consider the login or authentication activity that occurs within our case study. For this and other error handling, we might create a couple of classes, com.ibm.wscg.exception.PartnersException (which extends javax.servlet.ServletException) and com.ibm.wscg.exception.InvalidPartnerException (which extends our PartnersException).

If this were the case, we would change the signature of the login() method on PartnerModelHelper to declare that it throws an InvalidPartnerException. The client code (Figure 13.9) would no longer check for the returned null.

```
public class PartnerModelHelper implements Serializable {

public Partner login(Partner loginInfo) throws InvalidPartnerException {
        String username = loginInfo.getUsername();
        if (username == null)
                return null;
        PartnerFactory factory = new PartnerFactory();
        Partner partner = factory.findPartnerByName(username);
        if (partner != null) {
                // check for match of password
                String validPass = partner.getPassword();
                String enteredPass = loginInfo.getPassword();
                if (validPass != null && validPass.equals(enteredPass))
                        return partner;
                else

                        throw new InvalidPartnerException("Invalid Password");

        }
        throw new InvalidPartnerException("Partner Not Found");
}
}
```

Figure 13.9: Servlet code that throws InvalidPartnerExceptions.

Suppose there is a simple forwarding servlet, mapped to the URI /InvalidLogin, that just adds a message bean to the request and forwards to the Login.jsp. In that case the client can completely ignore this error condition. Instead it can be declaratively specified in the Web deployment descriptor. In WebSphere Studio the Pages tab of the Web Deployment Descriptor editor provides the entry for setting both error code-based error pages and the Java Exception-based error pages (Figure 13.10).

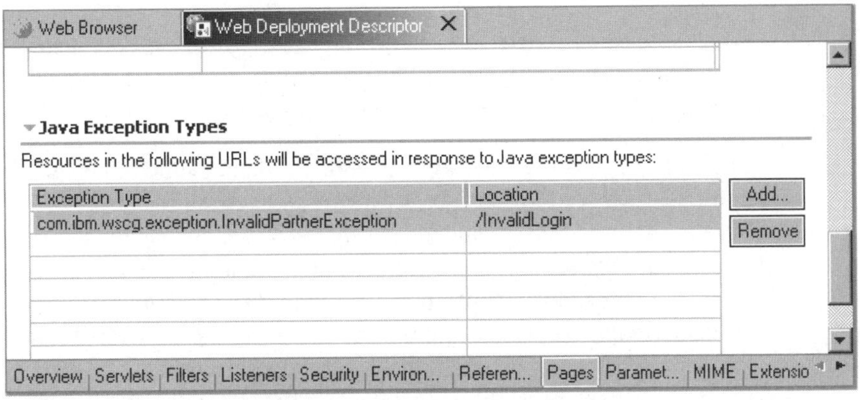

Figure 13.10: Setting declarative error page.

Now logging in with an invalid login name gets routed to our InvalidLogin servlet and then back to the Login.jsp page (Figure 13.11).

Figure 13.11: Error page results.

One final item before leaving this section deals with logging and tracing. Frequently during error handling, you would like to make a log or trace entry. The GenericServlet class provides three log() methods to allow servlets to log a String, a Throwable, or both to the server's log file. If we add a call in our error servlet, the trace shown in Figure 13.12 will appear on our console (see InvalidLogin.service() for details.)

```
[PartnersAcctPay] [/partner] [Servlet.LOG]: InvalidLogin: init
[PartnersAcctPay] [/partner] [Servlet.LOG]: InvalidLogin: Invalid login: gary/johns
[PartnersAcctPay] [/partner] [Servlet.LOG]: /jsp/Login.jsp: init
```

Figure 13.12: Writing to the servlet log.

For a more extensive tracing and logging framework, consider incorporating Apache's log4j framework (which will be integrated within J2EE 1.4). This allows one to control and filter what log and trace messages get issued to the servlet log (or dedicated trace file).

Before we leave the topic of error handling, there is one more very important error condition that we need to consider: a *precondition* check, mentioned in Chapter 11. With the stateless nature of HTTP and the ability for someone to enter any URL from a browser or network appliance, it is very possible that an incoming request may be inappropriate from an application state perspective. In all of the examples above, the model operated only on inputs supplied during that request from the browser. Most application processing will utilize a combination of current request input data and current application data. In such circumstances, the expected input data may be valid, but additional (available or unavailable) application state is invalid for the current request.

The techniques described thus far would tend to push that responsibility back onto the model layer. However, it is usually much better for the controller to take on this responsibility. A couple of design patterns can be used to encode the application state machine. One, the *state pattern,* explicitly manages an object (on the HttpSession) that represents the current application state. This object will hold references to the detailed application state and also be able to determine which incoming requests represent valid requests, given the current application state.

The alternative pattern, typically known as the *action pattern,* creates a unique controller object representing a particular incoming request. One of the responsibilities of this Action object is to validate the current application state prior to delegating application behavior on to the model layer. Again, the Struts framework organizes its controller implementation around the action design pattern.

However you choose to implement your application precondition checking, don't forget to do it.

Review

The MVC framework provides a clear path toward building and maintaining robust Web applications. This chapter has surveyed some of the more common issues surrounding building these stable applications.

Test yourself

Key terms

error page

Exceptions

Struts

log4j

Review questions

1. What are the basic elements of a Web application?

2. A controller component in a Web application is implemented using which Java technology?

3. What are the exception design issues facing developers of Web applications?

4. What are the different levels at which input validation can take place?

5. How is a data validation exception handled?

6. What is the base class in the servlet API for exception handling?

7. What are the two design patterns that facilitate precondition checking?

8. Business rules validation should only be performed in the _____ layer.

9. The _____ provides the most robust way to handle both expected and unexpected errors within your applications.

10. The application-specific errors that your application's model layer will generate will need to be handled by your _____.

14

JSP tag libraries

Chapter topics

- ❖ *Motivation for using JSP tag libraries*
- ❖ *Existing tag libraries*
- ❖ *Using custom tag libraries in WebSphere Studio*
- ❖ *Creating your own custom action tags*

Certification objectives

- ❖ *Create resources in appropriate J2EE locations*
- ❖ *Run/operate server*

In the last few chapters we went on a journey that began with understanding how servlets can be used as the gateway to Web applications. We also saw how servlets can be used to produce output directly back to the user, but we made an argument why not to do that. Afterward, we introduced JavaServer Pages (JSP) and explained why JSP pages should be used to produce dynamic output, how JSP pages consist of a mixture of HTML and Java code, and how they provide a better alternative to generating the output stream on the servlet itself.

Creating JSP pages in WebSphere Studio is a fairly simple process because the tools it provides make it easy to compose vibrant pages with dynamic content. However, the dynamic component is still coded in terms of JSP syntax, mainly as scriptlets or expressions.

In this chapter we will cover another way to produce dynamic output and extract the information contained in the JavaBeans that hold the output data to be displayed. This time, however, we will not use any scriptlets or JSP expressions. This chapter is about the magic of JSP tag libraries.

Motivation for using JSP tag libraries

The main motivation for using JSP tag libraries is to provide the Page Designer a way to include dynamic content in JSP pages without requiring knowledge of the Java programming language. Page Designers are for the most part very creative individuals who can produce excellent quality, eye-appealing Web pages. Java programmers are, on the other hand, well . . . programmers; very logical and organized people, who have mastered the Java language. However, their artistic ability usually leaves a lot to be desired. (There are, of course, exceptional individuals who can perform both roles well.)

Using the custom tags that JSP tag libraries make possible further separates the responsibilities and skills required for these two roles. The Java programmers create the libraries, and the Page Designers use the custom tags, usually with little or no concept of programming required.

In this chapter we explore how the tag libraries are presented to the Page Designer in an HTML-like way and how to use them.

The final motivation, or goal, is to have fully functional, clean-looking JSP pages that contain no scriptlets or JSP expressions—pages that look as though they were completely composed using HTML (or HTML-looking tags).

Existing tag libraries

Before we look at using custom tags, let us take a look at some of the most commonly used libraries.

There are many types of class libraries available to you. In fact, there are too many for us to include a complete reference in this book. Our advice is that, before you embark in writing your own specialized tag library, you search the Internet and see whether you can find an already existing library that will suit your needs.

WebSphere Studio makes available several JSP tag libraries. One or more of these libraries can be included in a JSP page as needed.

Jakarta tag libraries

Table 14.1 shows the libraries provided by the Jakarta Group, which are readily available. To learn more about the Jakarta tag libraries, visit *jakarta.apache.org/taglibs/*.

Table 14.1: Jakarta Group tag libraries available in WebSphere Studio.

Library function	URI
Mail	http://jakarta.apache.org/taglibs/mailer-1.1
General utilities	http://jakarta.apache.org/taglibs/utility
String manipulation	http://jakarta.apache.org/taglibs/string-1.0.1
Date and time manipulation	http://jakarta.apache.org/taglibs/datetime-1.0
Struts framework	http://jakarta.apache.org/taglibs/struts-1.0
Session object	http://jakarta.apache.org/taglibs/session-1.0
Request object	http://jakarta.apache.org/taglibs/request-1.0
Response object	http://jakarta.apache.org/taglibs/response-1.0
Page object	http://jakarta.apache.org/taglibs/page-1.0
Application object	http://jakarta.apache.org/taglibs/application-1.0

JavaServer Pages Standard Library (JSTL)

Another tag library, available with WebSphere Studio, is the JavaServer Pages Standard Tag Library (JSTL). Although called a tag library (singular), JSTL contains multiple tag libraries. Each one of the tag libraries represents a collection of actions that encapsulate functions that can be used in a JSP page.

JSTL provides functionality for most actions required by a Page Designer. According to the JSTL specifications, the four major areas covered are

- General purpose, conditional, iterator, and URL-related actions (Core)

- Internationalization (i18n) and text formatting actions

- Relational database access (SQL) actions

- XML processing actions

The URIs for each of these tag libraries are shown in Table 14.2:

Table 14.2: JSTL EL Libraries and their URIs.

Library	URI
Core	http://java.sun.com/jstl/core
Internationalization	http://java.sun.com/jstl/fmt
SQL	http://java.sun.com/jstl/sql
XML	http://java.sun.com/jstl/xml

Each of these tag libraries needs to be defined in the JSP page before its actions can be used. For example, the core tag library is defined as shown in the following JSP taglib directive:

```
<%@ taglib uri="http://java.sun.com/jstl/core" prefix="c" %>
```

Note that the URIs and prefixes differ depending on the library being used. The preceding directive defines the Core library. The prefix is used to identify the library custom action in the JSP page; it is used as part of the action name space. This way, different libraries can have actions that have the same name but are differentiated by the prefix.

There are two versions of each of the libraries in JSTL: an expression language (EL) version and a runtime (RT) version.

The EL version introduces an expression language to the library syntax, which allows you to evaluate and perform simple arithmetic and logic functions while using the library's custom actions. Object attributes can be accessed directly by name without having to enter an explicit <jsp:usebean> JSP action to make the object available to the JSP page.

```
//Assume an object of type Car is available in the request scope with id=car
```

```
//Also assume the Car class has an attribute called color
//To display the color of the car using the EL library you would use:
<c:out value = "${requestScope.car.color}"/>
```

The RT versions of the tag libraries, listed in Table 14.3, provide exactly the same custom tags as the EL versions. However, any operations on the scoped objects must be represented in the form of JSP expressions or scriptlets. The same code shown using the RT version of the library could be written as

```
...
<jsp:usebean id="car" class="com.ibm.wscg.view.Car" scope="request"/>
...
<c_rt:out value = "<%= car.getColor() %>" />
```

Table 14.3: JSTL RT libraries and their URIs.

Library	URI
Core	http://java.sun.com/jstl/core_rt
Internationalization	http://java.sun.com/jstl/fmt_rt
SQL	http://java.sun.com/jstl/sql_rt
XML	http://java.sun.com/jstl/xml_rt

To learn more about JSTL, visit *java.sun.com/products/jsp/jstl*.

Using custom tag libraries in WebSphere Studio

When using WebSphere Studio, you can select which Tag libraries are potentially available to JSP pages by using the Create a Web Project wizard, as shown in Figure 14.1.

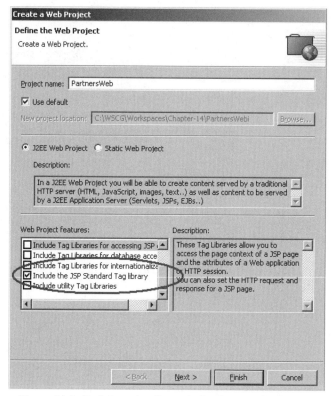

Figure 14.1: Defining a tag library in the Create a Web Project wizard.

You can also add a tag library definition to an existing Web project through the Properties view of the project, under Web properties item (Figure 14.2).

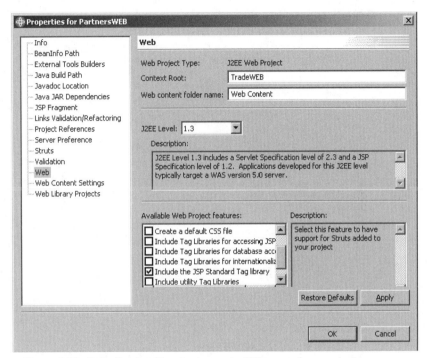

Figure 14.2: Selecting tag libraries to use in JSP pages for a project.

Either way, selecting a tag library causes several actions to happen automatically: Definitions for the tag libraries are added to the Web project deployment descriptor, web.xml (Figure 14.3), and the JAR file containing the libraries is imported into the proper place in the directory structure for the Web project.

```
Web Deployment Descriptor  ×
        <url-pattern>/DisplayProfile</url-pattern>
    </servlet-mapping>
    <welcome-file-list>
        <welcome-file>index.html</welcome-file>
        <welcome-file>index.htm</welcome-file>
        <welcome-file>index.jsp</welcome-file>
        <welcome-file>default.html</welcome-file>
        <welcome-file>default.htm</welcome-file>
        <welcome-file>default.jsp</welcome-file>
    </welcome-file-list>
    <taglib>
        <taglib-uri>http://jakarta.apache.org/taglibs/datetime-1.0</taglib-uri>
        <taglib-location>/WEB-INF/lib/taglibs-datetime.jar</taglib-location>
    </taglib>
    <taglib>
        <taglib-uri>http://jakarta.apache.org/taglibs/string-1.0.1</taglib-uri>
        <taglib-location>/WEB-INF/lib/taglibs-string.jar</taglib-location>
    </taglib>
    <taglib>
        <taglib-uri>http://jakarta.apache.org/taglibs/utility</taglib-uri>
        <taglib-location>/WEB-INF/lib/utility.jar</taglib-location>
    </taglib>
    <taglib>
        <taglib-uri>http://jakarta.apache.org/taglibs/mailer-1.1</taglib-uri>
        <taglib-location>/WEB-INF/lib/taglibs-mailer.jar</taglib-location>
    </taglib>
</web-app>
```

Overview | Servlets | Filters | Listeners | Security | Environment | References | Pages | Parameters | MIME | Extensions | Source

Figure 14.3: Tag library definition entered in web.xml deployment descriptor.

Note that the <taglib> element in the deployment descriptor defines the unique URI for the tag library. It also defines where the JAR file containing the classes that implement the library are located. According to the JSP specification, these files must be located under the WEB-INF directory; because they are JAR files, they are in the lib folder under WEB-INF (Figure 14.4).

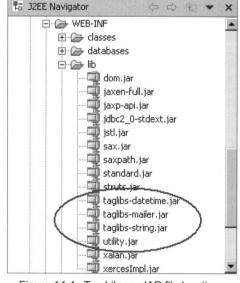

Figure 14.4: Tag Library JAR file location.

Once the desired tag libraries have been defined, they will be available when you create a new JSP file. The New JSP File wizard, on its second page (Figure 14.5), lets you select from the libraries defined for the Web project. In the figure you see the page of the wizard where you select the prefix. This prefix is used in combination with the action tag to qualify the action fully. Only tag libraries that were chosen when the Web project was created are available for selection when creating a JSP page. The custom tags available for the selected library are displayed in the Available Custom Tags list box.

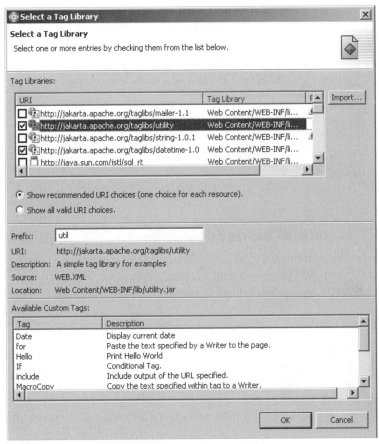

Figure 14.5: Selecting a tag library for use in JSP.

Once the wizard completes creating the new JSP page, the proper taglib page directives will be automatically inserted in the JSP. Notice that the prefix selected for each of the libraries is also part of the taglib page directive. In the example shown in Figure 14.6, the prefixes are *util* and *dt*.

```
UsingTL.jsp

<!DOCTYPE HTML PUBLIC "-//W3C//DTD HTML 4.01 Transitional//EN">
<HTML>
<HEAD>
<%@ taglib uri="http://jakarta.apache.org/taglibs/utility" prefix="util" %>
<%@ taglib uri="http://jakarta.apache.org/taglibs/datetime-1.0" prefix="dt" %>
<%@ page
language="java"
contentType="text/html; charset=ISO-8859-1"
pageEncoding="ISO-8859-1"
%>
<META http-equiv="Content-Type" content="text/html; charset=ISO-8859-1">
<META name="GENERATOR" content="IBM WebSphere Studio">
<META http-equiv="Content-Style-Type" content="text/css">
<LINK href="../theme/Master.css" rel="stylesheet" type="text/css">
<TITLE>UsingTL.jsp</TITLE>
</HEAD>
<BODY>
<P>Place UsingTL.jsp's content here.</P>
</BODY>
</HTML>

Design | Source | Preview
```

Figure 14.6: Tag library tag inserted in JSP.

To use a custom tag from one of the defined libraries, you start by entering the prefix of the library, followed by a colon and then the name of the custom tag. For example, to display the current date on the page, using the *utility* library as defined in Figure 14.6, you would enter

```
<util:Date/>
```

If you don't know, or remember, the exact name of a custom tag, you can use the **JSP →
Insert Custom** menu item. It's best to do this from the Design view of the JSP editor, as shown in Figure 14.7. That way you can place the tag precisely where you want it shown on the page. The result of inserting the Date tag is shown in Figure 14.8. Switching to the Source view (Figure 14.9) reveals the code that was inserted into the JSP page.

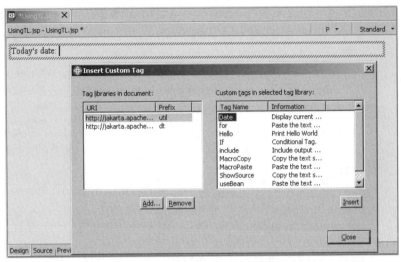

Figure 14.7: Adding a custom tag to the JSP page through Design view.

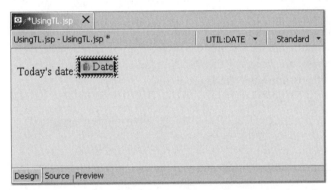

Figure 14.8: Visual indication that the custom tag has been inserted.

```
<!DOCTYPE HTML PUBLIC "-//W3C//DTD HTML 4.01 Transitional//EN">

<HTML>
<HEAD>
<%@ taglib uri="http://jakarta.apache.org/taglibs/utility" prefix="util" %>
<%@ taglib uri="http://jakarta.apache.org/taglibs/datetime-1.0" prefix="dt" %>
<%@ page
language="java"
contentType="text/html; charset=ISO-8859-1"
pageEncoding="ISO-8859-1"
%>
<META http-equiv="Content-Type" content="text/html; charset=ISO-8859-1">
<META name="GENERATOR" content="IBM WebSphere Studio">
<META http-equiv="Content-Style-Type" content="text/css">
<LINK href="../theme/Master.css" rel="stylesheet" type="text/css">
<TITLE>UsingTL.jsp</TITLE>
</HEAD>
<BODY>
<P>Today's date: <util:Date /></P>
</BODY>
</HTML>
```

Figure 14.9: Code inserted by adding a custom tag to a JSP page.

Creating your own custom action tags

It is beyond the scope of this book to go into a detailed explanation of how to create your own custom tag libraries. Creating tag libraries is not a difficult task for a Java programmer to perform. There are numerous resources available through books and the Internet from which you can learn how to code your own tag libraries. A good place to start is the JSP 1.2 Specification and tutorials, available from *java.sun.com/products/jsp/*.

Creating your own custom action tags involves two tasks: developing the tag handler (the code that performs the operation) and declaring the tag in the tag library descriptor (TLD) file.

Tag handlers usually implement the Tag or BodyTag interface. These interfaces can be used to turn an existing class into a tag handler. In most cases, however, you will create tag handlers from scratch. In those cases you should start by extending the TagSupport or BodyTagSupport base class. Both of these classes are contained in the javax.servlet.jsp.tagext package.

In the simplest tag handlers, which extend the TagSupport class, you need only develop the implementation of the doStartTag(), doEndTag(), and set*XXX*() methods (Figure 14.10). The first two methods are called when the tag's begin tag and end tag, respectively, are encountered in the JSP code. The set*XXX*() methods (where *XXX* represents the name of an attribute) are called by the Web Container before the doStartTag() method is called, to initialize any attributes the tag requires.

```
public class MyTag extends TagSupport {

    private String anAttribute;

    public int doStartTag() throws JspException {
       ...
    }
    public int doEndTag() throws JspException {
       ...
    }
    public void setAnAttribute(String attr){
       this.anAttribute = attr;
    }

}
```

Figure 14.10: Code for tag handler class.

The doStartTag() and doEndTag() methods are declared to return int values. These values are predefined in the interface and cause the tag body to be skipped, evaluated, or re-evaluated. Other return values signal whether processing should continue on the page or stop.

The coverage of tag libraries in this chapter is by no means complete, but it is adequate for you to become aware that tag libraries exist and get an idea of their usage and purpose. You are encouraged to further investigate and learn more about creating your own tags and simplifying your JSP pages through the use of tag libraries.

Exercise

In this exercise you will use the JSTL tag libraries to "clean up" one of the JSP pages that you worked with earlier in the book. As you will see, the tag library version will appear much cleaner and will contain no JSP scripting elements, such as JSP scriptlets or expressions.

Start by loading the Chapter-14 workspace into WebSphere Studio. Wait till the workspace is loaded and initialized.

1. Copy the InvoiceManagement.jsp file to the PartnerWeb/Web Content/jsp folder under the new name of TLInvoiceManagement.jsp.

   a. Select **InvoiceManagement.jsp**. From its context menu click **Copy**.

   b. Select the **jsp** folder. From its context menu click **Paste**.

   c. On the Name Conflict dialog (Figure 14.11), change the name of the file to **TLInvoiceManagement.jsp** ("TL" because it uses tag libraries).

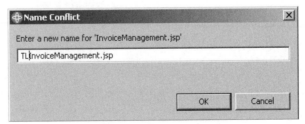

Figure 14.11: Renaming while pasting InvoiceManagement.jsp.

   d. Click **OK**.

2. Open the TLInvoiceManagement.jsp file on the JSP (Page Designer) editor and switch to the Design view. Several areas in this view indicate that the JSP page contains scripting elements; some of these areas are circled in Figure 14.12.

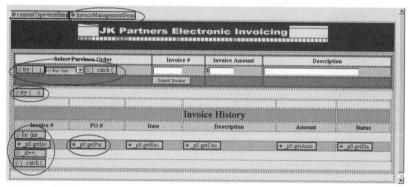

Figure 14.12: Invoice management.jsp in design view of editor.

3. Switch to the Source view and locate the following code lines:

```
<jsp:useBean id="InvoiceManagementBean"
class="com.ibm.wscg.view.InvoiceManagementBean" scope="request" />
```

This tag is used to locate and load the InvoiceManagementBean from the request scope. This bean was placed in the request by the InvoiceManagement servlet. The bean contains information regarding invoices for the currently logged-in partner. The ID used by the servlet to place the bean in the request is *InvoiceManagement.*

4. In this exercise you use the JST core library's EL version, which does not require the use of a <jsp:useBean> tag to locate and use scoped variables. Delete the line(s) containing the whole tag from <jsp:useBean through />. Save the file. You will get some errors in the Tasks view; ignore them until finished.

5. Locate the code that populates the SELECT (drop-down list) widget on the upper left corner of the page. The code is similar to the snippet shown in Figure 14.13. In this code you see how the InvoiceManagementBean is used to populate the OPTION elements of the SELECT widget. There are combinations of scriptlets, JSP expressions, and HTML lines to serve this purpose. While this is a workable solution, it requires that the person assembling the page have Java and JSP scripting language knowledge. You will now replace this code and build the same functional capability using core JSTL custom actions.

```
<%
try {
  java.lang.String[] _a0 = InvoiceManagementBean.getPOs();
  java.lang.String _p0 = _a0[0]; // throws an exception if empty.
  %>
<SELECT name="PO">
<%
for (int _i0 = 0; ; ) { %>
  <OPTION value="
<%= _p0 %>"><%= _p0 %>
  </OPTION>
<%
  _i0++;
  try {
    _p0 = _a0[_i0];
  }
    catch (java.lang.ArrayIndexOutOfBoundsException _e0) {
      break;
  }
} %>
  </SELECT>
<%
}
catch (java.lang.ArrayIndexOutOfBoundsException _e0) {
}
%>
```

Figure 14.13: JSP code using scripting elements to populate a selection list.

6. Delete all the JSP scripting code from this section of the page. You can do this several different ways:

a. From the Source view, carefully select the scripting code and delete it (only from the section of the page dealing with the SELECT widget). Leave the HTML code in place.

b. From the Design view, select and delete the three scripting markers around the drop-down list. This can be tricky, because selecting *only* the scriptlet part inside the SELECT widget is not easy.

c. Another approach is to select the SELECT widget, expand it in the Outline view of the Web perspective, and remove the scripting elements (scriptlets and expressions) using the Outline view widget context menus. This is the most precise way to achieve the task.

7. Verify that you have deleted only the JSP scripting elements of this section of the page. The code in the Source view, for that row of the table, should look like the code in Figure 14.14.

```
<TR bgcolor="#cccccc">
   <TD bgcolor="#cccccc">
      <SELECT name="PO">
         <OPTION> </OPTION>
      </SELECT>
   </TD>
   <TD><INPUT size="12" type="text" maxlength="12" name="invoice"></TD>
   <TD>$<INPUT size="10" type="text" maxlength="10" name="amount"></TD>
   <TD><INPUT size="40" type="text" maxlength="80" name="description"></TD>
</TR>
```

Figure 14.14: Code for table row after scripting elements have been removed.

8. Before you can start using any of the tag libraries in JSP pages, the JAR files containing the libraries need to be added to the project, and the deployment descriptor for the Web project (web.xml) needs to be altered to indicate which tag libraries will be used in the project. These steps are usually performed when the Web project is first created, but they can be added afterward as well, as follows.

   a. Open the **Properties** dialog for the PartnerWeb project; select **Web**, and select **Include the JSP Standard Tag library**, as shown in Figure 14.15. Click **OK**.

   b. Now that the Web project "knows" that you intend to use a tag library, the next step is to indicate that the TLInvoiceManagement.jsp file will use the JSPT core library. Ensure that you are editing TLInvoiceManagement.jsp, switch to the Source view, and place the cursor near the top of the file inside the <HEAD> tag. Make sure that you are in a blank line. Select **JSP** → **Insert Custom** from the main menu.

   c. Since no tag libraries are yet in use in this JSP file, the lists on the Insert Custom Tag dialog (Figure 14.16) are empty. From this dialog you can select which libraries will be used in the JSP being edited. Click **Add**.

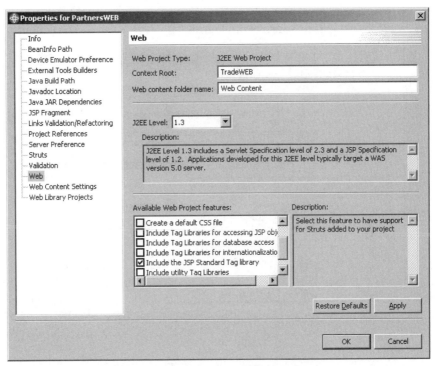

Figure 14.15: Adding JSTL core tag library to Web project.

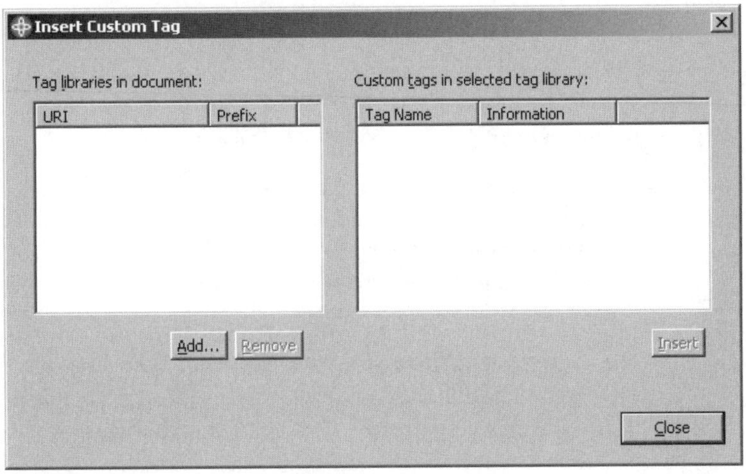

Figure 14.16: Adding a tag library to a JSP file.

d. As you can see in Figure 14.17, in the Select a Tag Library dialog you can pick from a variety of libraries.

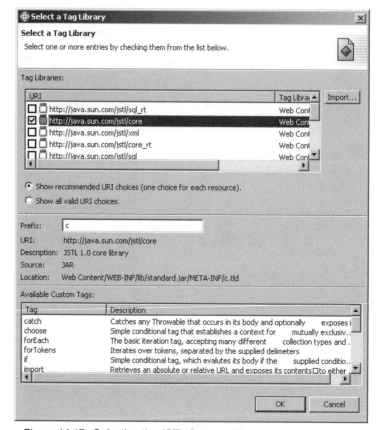

Figure 14.17: Selecting the JSTL Core tag library.

Note: Only the tag libraries defined at the Web project level are available to use in JSP pages belonging to that Web project. If the tag library you are looking for is not in the list, then the library is not known at the Web project level.

e. Select **http://java.sun.com/jstl/core**. Take a look at the suggested Prefix and at the Custom tags available on this library. This information, displayed on the dialog, is very useful to help you ensure that you are selecting the right library. For example, in the JSP page you are modifying, the forEach custom action is needed.

f. Click **OK**.

g. After you click **OK**, a JSP directive is inserted at the current cursor position on the JSP page.

```
<%@taglib uri="http://java.sun.com/jstl/core" prefix="c"%>
```

9. Now that you have picked the library you need, it is time to pick one or more custom tags to insert into the JSP page. However, if you did that now, the code would be inserted at the current cursor position, which may not be exactly where you want it.

a. Click **Close** to return to the Source view of the JSP file.

b. Locate the section of the page where the SELECT widget is defined. Manually format the existing code so that it looks like the snippet in Figure 14.18.

```
<TD bgcolor="#cccccc">
    <SELECT name="PO">

        <OPTION> </OPTION>
    </SELECT>
</TD>
```

Figure 14.18: Stub of SELECT widget.

Note: The purpose of this section of the JSP page is to initialize the SELECT widget with a list of purchase orders for the currently logged-in partner. By the time this page is displayed, the model layer of the application has already performed the appropriate query on the database and has placed information regarding the purchase orders in a String array called POs in the InvoiceManagementBean. This bean has been placed in the request scope so that it can be accessed by the JSP page. If you need a refresher, you may want to look at this JavaBean, which can be found in the Java Source folder under the com.ibm.wscg.view package.

---

c. Place the cursor where the custom tag needs to be inserted: in the blank line between SELECT and OPTION.

d. From the main menu, select **JSP → Insert Custom** to bring up the Insert Custom Tag dialog (Figure 14.19).

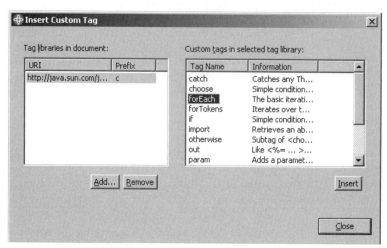

Figure 14.19: Inserting a custom tag in a JSP page.

e. Since you need to construct a loop, the forEach custom tag is appropriate for the task. Select it from the list and click **Insert**. Click **Close**. The code for the section of the page you are working with should look like the snippet in Figure 14.20.

```
<TD bgcolor="#cccccc">
    <SELECT name="PO">
        <c:forEach></c:forEach>
        <OPTION value=""></OPTION>
    </SELECT>
</TD>
```

Figure 14.20: Inserted forEach custom tag.

Note: The prefix c, identifying the Core tag library, is used before the name of the custom action tag. As you remember, the prefix was defined when the taglib page directive was added at the top of the page.

f. The forEach tag creates a loop that iterates through the POs array. The body of the tag is executed each time through the loop with a different element of the array. Each time, you need to enter that element of the array into the corresponding one of the OPTION attributes that make up the SELECT widget. Clearly the OPTION attribute of the SELECT needs to be inside the loop. Put a line break between the <c:forEach> and </c:forEach> tags and place OPTION inside the body, as follows.

```
<SELECT name="PO">
    <c:forEach>
        <OPTION></OPTION>
    </c:forEach>
</SELECT>
```

g. The next step is to define the parameters with which the loop operates. The tag library requires that both the looping parameter (items), and the name of the variable used to address the looping parameter (var) be defined. In the case of this JSP page, the looping parameter is the array of POs in the InvoiceManagementBean. Complete the definition of the forEach action tag, as follows:

```
<SELECT name="PO">
    <c:forEach var="IMBPOs" items="${requestScope.InvoiceManagementBean.POs}">
        <OPTION> </OPTION>
    </c:forEach>
</SELECT>
```

The declaration, items="${requestScope.InvoiceManagementBean.POs}", indicates that the loop parameter can be found in the bean located in the request scope, under the ID of InvoiceManagementBean, and the attribute where the values to be iterated are found is POs. The declaration var=IMBPOs indicates that inside the loop, the loop parameter is known as *IMBPOs*, this is an arbitrary name.

h. Now that le loop is defined, all you need to do is add each element of the array to the OPTION attribute of the SELECT widget. This is very simple to do. You use another custom action of the same library: out, as follows:

```
<SELECT name="PO">
    <c:forEach var="IMBPOs" items="${requestScope.InvoiceManagementBean.POs}">
        <OPTION> <c:out value="${IMBPOs}" /> </OPTION>
    </c:forEach>
</SELECT>
```

i. Save the TLInvoiceManagement.jsp file.

10. In a similar fashion, replace the loop coded by the scriptlets and JSP expressions, which builds the Invoice History table. Also replace the enclosing try/catch block.

a. Before the table, delete the following scriplet:

```
<%
try {
  com.ibm.wscg.model.Invoice[] _a0 = InvoiceManagementBean.getInvoices();
  com.ibm.wscg.model.Invoice _p0 = _a0[0]; // throws an exception if
empty. %>
```

Locate and very carefully remove the next set of scriptlets and JSP expressions, used to populate the Invoice History table. Only remove code in <%...%>, and <%=...%>. After removal, only the HTML code for the table should remain and look similar to the snippet listed in Figures 14.21a and 14.21b.

```
<TABLE width="100%">
  <TBODY>
    <TR>
      <TD></TD>
      <TD></TD>
      <TD></TD>
      <TD></TD>
      <TD></TD>
      <TD></TD>
    </TR>
    <TR bgcolor="#e99d49">
      <TD></TD>
      <TD></TD>
      <TD></TD>
      <TD><H2>Invoice History</H2></TD>
      <TD></TD>
      <TD></TD>
    </TR>
    <TR bgcolor="#7dffbe">
      <TH>Invoice #</TH>
      <TH>PO #</TH>
      <TH>Date</TH>
      <TH>Description</TH>
      <TH>Amount</TH>
      <TH>Status</TH>
    </TR>
```

Figure 14.21a: Bare table with all scripting elements removed.

```
<TR bgcolor="#b3b3ff">
    <TD></TD>
    <TD></TD>
    <TD></TD>
    <TD></TD>
    <TD></TD>
    <TD></TD>
  </TR>
 </TBODY>
</TABLE>
```

Figure 14.21b: Bare table with all scripting elements removed.

b. The last row of the table, after the table headings, is where the loop to populate the table is required. Start by enclosing the table row definition (with all the columns) in a forEach loop.

Since these rows will contain invoice information, and this information is also contained in the InvoiceManagementBean, defining the loop parameter is fairly easy. By looking at the bean itself you know that invoice information is available in the bean as an array of Invoice objects, called invoice. Call the variable in the loop **IMBInv**. Concentrating on the last row of the table only, the code now looks like the snippet listed in Figure 14.22.

```
<c:forEach var="IMBInv"
      items="${requestScope.InvoiceManagementBean.invoices}">
   <TR bgcolor="#b3b3ff">
     <TD></TD>
     <TD></TD>
     <TD></TD>
     <TD></TD>
     <TD></TD>
     <TD></TD>
   </TR>
</c:forEach>
```

Figure 14.22: Retrieving invoices to populate table.

c. The last step, before you can declare the page completed, is to enter the values from the Invoice object into each of the columns, of the repeating rows, of the table. Once again, you use the out custom action tag to access the attributes of the Invoice objects in the elements of the invoice array (Figure 14.23).

```
<c:forEach var="IMBInv"
     items="${requestScope.InvoiceManagementBean.invoices}">
   <TR bgcolor="#b3b3ff">
      <TD><c:out value="${IMBInv.invoiceNumber}" /></TD>
      <TD><c:out value="${IMBInv.purchaseOrder}" /></TD>
      <TD><c:out value="${IMBInv.receivedDate}" /></TD>
      <TD><c:out value="${IMBInv.description}" /></TD>
      <TD><c:out value="${IMBInv.amount}" /></TD>
      <TD><c:out value="${IMBInv.statusCode}" /></TD>
   </TR>
</c:forEach>
```

Figure 14.23: Filling in the table columns with attributes of retrieved invoice.

d. After the table, delete the catch block represented by the following scriptlet:

```
<%
}
catch (java.lang.ArrayIndexOutOfBoundsException _e0) {
} %>
```

e. Save the file. There should be no errors reported in the Tasks view.

11. Before you can test the new JSP page, you need to change the line of code on the InvoiceManagement servlet that transfers control the page. Currently the code will forward to the InvoiceManagement.jsp file. You need to change that line so that it forwards to the TLInvoiceManagement.jsp file instead.

a. Open **InvoiceManagementServlet.java**, found in the com.ibm.wscg.servlet package.

b. Locate the following line of code:

```
getServletContext().getRequestDispatcher("/jsp/InvoiceManagement.jsp").
   forward(request, response);
```

    c. Change it to

```
getServletContext().getRequestDispatcher("/jsp/TLInvoiceManagement.jsp").
    forward(request, response);
```

    d. Save the file.

12. Now it is time to test your work.

    a. Select the PartnersWeb Web project, and from its context menu select **Run on Server**.

    b. After the server starts, login to the system. You can use one of your IDs you created previously, or use one of the predefined IDs, for example **jones** with a password of **password**.

    c. After login completes, click **Review and Submit Invoices**. This will call the new JSP page.

    d. Verify that the page displays correctly.

    e. Open both InvoiceManagement.jsp and TLInvoiceManagement.jsp and compare the sources of both files. Decide for yourself which JSP looks cleaner.

This was a simple example of how to use JSP tag libraries. As with any other library, be it a JSP tag library, a Java Framework, or just the standard Java language libraries, becoming proficient and confident requires practice. We believe that the more you use JSP tag libraries in your projects, the more you will like them and the more productive you will become.

Test yourself

Key terms

custom actions

tag library

JSTL

Review questions

1. What is the main motivation behind JSP tag libraries?

2. What is JSTL?

3. How do you indicate that the JSTL core tag library will be used in a JSP?

4. What are the four major areas of functionality in JSTL?

5. What are the two versions of each of the libraries in JSTL?

6. What are the steps involved in creating your own tag library?

7. Which of the following tag libraries are available with WebSphere Studio?
   a. Mail
   b. Input/Ouput
   c. Response Object
   d. Application Object

8. Where can you add a tag library definition to a Web project in WebSphere Studio?
   a. Project properties under Web Properties
   b. During the Create New Project wizard
   c. Tag menu
   d. Outline view

9. A custom tag handler usually implements which interface?
   a. Tag
   b. Taghandle
   c. BodyTag
   d. SampleTag

Accessing databases with JDBC

Topics covered

- ❖ *JDBC 2.0 API*
- ❖ *Error processing*
- ❖ *Transaction control*
- ❖ *Basic broker/mapping architecture*
- ❖ *The Data perspective*

Certification objectives

- ❖ *Run/operate server*
- ❖ *Create connection and load catalog into a project*
- ❖ *Create schema and generate DDL*

Java Database Connectivity (JDBC) provides Java programmers with a consistent mechanism for accessing relational databases. JDBC isolates programmers from the nuances between different implementations of database managers. In this chapter we explore how to access databases using JDBC by covering the basics of using the JDBC API.

This chapter is not meant to be an all-inclusive source for JDBC or for Structured Query Language (SQL) information. Much to the contrary, it is meant to give you a basic understanding of JDBC. To get more complete details of JDBC you should consult the JDBC 2.0 specifications and corresponding Javadoc. There are many good books dedicated to the subject, and there are many online resources for learning it. The same thing can be said for SQL. You will see simple SQL statements throughout this book, and in most cases they are self-explanatory. SQL documentation frequently ships with the database manager of your choice, and it can also be found online.

The JDBC 2.0 API

WebSphere Studio and WebSphere Application Server V5 both support JDBC 2.0. The JDBC 2.0 API can be found in two packages:

- java.sql, the JDBC 2.0 Core API

- javax.sql, the JDBC 2.0 Standard Extension API

JDBC 2.0 Core API

The JDBC 2.0 Core API provides a collection of classes and interfaces used to perform basic database operations. Table 15.1 lists the packages that make up the core API. These packages, and the types they contain, deal with managing JDBC drivers, providing connections, handling results, and defining new data types.

Table 15.1: JDBC 2.0 Core API packages.

java.sql.Array	java.sql.Ref
java.sql.BatchUpdateException	java.sql.ResultSet
java.sql.Blob	java.sql.ResultSetMetaData
java.sql.CallableStatement	java.sql.SQLData
java.sql.Clob	java.sql.SQLException
java.sql.Connection	java.sql.SQLInput
java.sql.DatabaseMetaData	java.sql.SQLOutput
java.sql.DataTruncation	java.sql.SQLWarning
java.sql.Date	java.sql.Statement
java.sql.Driver	java.sql.Struct
java.sql.DriverManager	java.sql.Time
java.sql.DriverPropertyInfo	java.sql.Timestamp
java.sql.PreparedStatement	java.sql.Types

Using JDBC 2.0 Core API fundamentals

You can perform all basic database operations by interacting with the types in JDBC Core API packages. Figure 15.1 shows the interactions between the types to obtain a connection from the driver manager and to use the connection to create a statement, execute the statement, and manipulate the results.

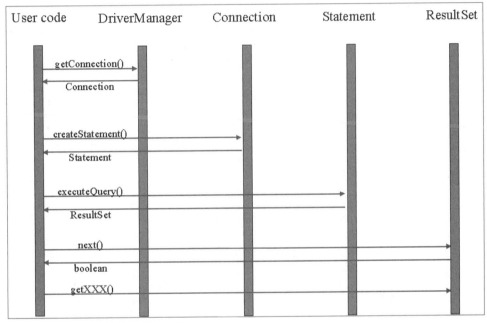

Figure 15.1: JDBC class interaction.

The listing in Figures 15.2a and 15.2b show a generic code snippet that illustrates one possibility on how to code the actions represented in Figure 15.1.

```
...
//Somewhere in the initialization code for the class...
Class.forName("com.ibm.db2j.jdbc.DB2jDriver");
...
//Later when needed
// Get connection from DriverManager
Connection con = DriverManager.getConnection(
                    "jdbc:db2j:c:\\wscg\\database");
//Create statement
Statement stmt = con.createStatement();
// Execute the SQL query
```

Figure 15.2a: Possible coding for JDBC class interactions.

```
ResultSet rs = stmt.executeQuery("SELECT * FROM PURCHASEORDER");
// Iterate through the result set
while (rs.next()) {
    // Extract column data from data at current cursor position
    String ponumber = rs.getString(1);
    String customer = rs.getString(2);
    System.out.println("Found PO: " + ponumber + " for " + customer);
}
conn.close();
...
```

Figure 15.2b: Possible coding for JDBC class interactions.

Let's briefly run through the code:

1. The appropriate JDBC driver is loaded. This should happen only once in the application. The code can be in the class's constructor, main() method, or static initializer. In the code example in Figure 15.2 we are using the Cloudscape database driver.

2. Get a connection from the driver manager, using a string representing the URL for the database. A valid user ID and password are required for some databases' connections. The URL's format will change depending on the driver you use. Consult the database's documentation for the proper URL format for the database and driver you are using.

3. Ask the connection to create a statement.

> **Note:** You could have also used the Connection's methods prepareStatement() and prepareCall() to use a prepared statement or a call to a database stored procedure, respectively. The syntax for these methods is a bit different in that the actual SQL statement is one of the arguments to the method.
>
> Prepared statements should be used when the same SQL statement will be repeated several times in a row, as in a loop. PreparedStatements run more efficiently than Statements.
>
> Callable statements are, in many cases, the most efficient, because they are actually executed by the database engine and can be optimized for the best performance.

4. Use the statement object instance to execute the query. The actual SQL statement is passed as a parameter.

5. Executing the query returns a result set encapsulating the rows of the database that match the selection criteria. (For some queries the executeQuery() method

returns an integer, indicating the number of rows in the database that were affected, rather than a result set. For example, an Update operation returns the number of rows, or records, that were changed.)

6. The returned result set has a *cursor* that enables it to be iterated. At first, the result set cursor is pointing to an imaginary row located just before the first returned row. The next() method moves the cursor to the first row, returning true if there is a next row, false if there are no more rows.

7. In the while loop, you extract column data from the current row. There are a number of get*XXX*() methods for the different data types a column can contain: getString(), getInt, getFloat(), and so forth. You must use the right method, which implies that you must know the structure of the database. The parameter passed to these methods is the column number. This is a one-based number (i.e., the first column is column 1). You may also pass a string representing the column's name.

8. The connection is closed when it is no longer needed.

JDBC 2.0 Standard Extension API

The JDBC 2.0 Standard Extension API provides packages that, as the name implies, extend the Core API. Table 15.2 lists the packages that make up the Standard Extension API.

Table 15.2: JDBC 2.0 Standard Extension API packages.

javax.sql.ConnectionEvent	javax.sql.RowSetImpl
javax.sql.ConnectionEventListener	javax.sql.RowSetMetaData
javax.sql.ConnectionPoolDataSource	javax.sql.RowSetMetaDataImpl
javax.sql.CursorMovedEvent	javax.sql.RowSetUpdatedEvent
javax.sql.CursorMovedListener	javax.sql.RowSetUpdatedListener
javax.sql.DataSource	javax.sql.XAConnection
javax.sql.PooledConnection	javax.sql.XADataSource
javax.sql.RowSet	

Data sources and connection pools

One of the functions of the extensions is to provide access to a managed, and more efficient, type of connection through the use of data sources and connection pooling. In this environment, connections are shared from a pool of connections. Creating and destroying a database connection is a very time-consuming operation, and it is especially inefficient when, in most cases, the connection is used only for a short period of time. It makes sense to have a pool of live connections that are managed and shared. The connection pool manager can optimize the number of connections available at any one time depending on workload.

To take advantage of connection pooling, only minor differences need to be made to the code snippet in Figure 15.2. The main change is the way the connection is obtained. Instead of loading a JDBC driver and asking the driver for a connection, you find a data source and then get a managed connection from it. From then on the connection is used normally.

There are some things to consider before you can use a managed connection. Some infrastructure elements must be in place, mainly a JNDI (Java Naming and Directory Interface) server and a server that will manage the data sources and pooled connections. If you run your Web applications in the WebSphere Studio test server or WebSphere Application Server, you have all the infrastructure pieces you need already in place.

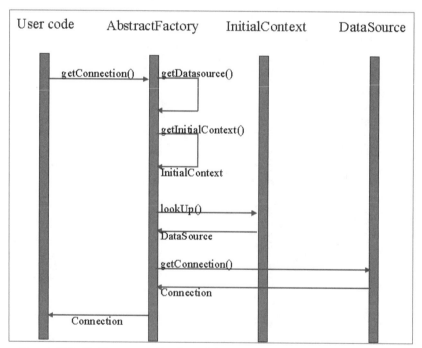

Figure 15.3: Getting connection from data source.

The diagram in Figure 15.3 illustrates the call sequence, which in our example is encapsulated in an AbstractPersistenceFactory, as described later in this chapter in the "Basic broker/mapping architecture" section.

Figure 15.4 contains a listing of the code from our example application that illustrates how to use JNDI and data sources to get a managed connection.

```java
public class AbstractPersistenceFactory implements Serializable {

    private static InitialContext context = null;
    private final static String datasourceName = "jdbc/partnerds";
    private static DataSource ds;

    protected static InitialContext getInitialContext() {
        if (context == null) {
            try {
                context = new InitialContext();
            } catch (NamingException ne) {
                System.out.println("ERROR: Can't access JNDI namespace");
            }
        }
        return context;
    }

    protected static DataSource getDataSource() throws NamingException {
        if (ds == null) {
            InitialContext context = getInitialContext();
            ds = (DataSource) context.lookup(datasourceName);
        }
        return ds;
    }

    protected Connection getConnection() {
        try {
            DataSource ds = getDataSource();
            if (ds != null)
                return ds.getConnection("userid", "PASSWORD");
        } catch (NamingException ne) {
            return null;
        } catch (SQLException se) {
            return null;
        }
        return null;
    }
}
```

Figure 15.4: Code to use managed connections.

The lookup operation is done using JNDI. To oversimplify it, JNDI is a directory lookup mechanism in which you supply a name and you get an object in return. Names are registered with JNDI by configuration on the server. The names are bound to the JNDI server when the application server initializes.

In the example in Figure 15.4, the lookup occurs on the JNDI name *jdbc/partnerds*, which is associated with a DataSource configured to access the database. If the lookup is successful, an object, cast to the type DataSource, is returned. If the lookup fails, a NamingException is thrown.

Note that once the connection is obtained, it is treated just like a connection given by the driver manager in the previous example.

In addition to querying databases, JDBC can be used to perform all other types of database operations, for example:

- Creating databases and tables

- Inserting, updating, and deleting records

- Executing Stored Procedures

Extra credits: Look up the Javadoc for the java.sql and javax.sql packages and further investigate the types that make up these packages. Pay special attention to the Statement, PreparedStatement, CallableStatement, and ResultSet interfaces.

TYPE mappings

Database records contain data stored using SQL data types. Java programs use Java language data types. When data is exchanged between Java programs and databases, some form of data type conversion must occur. Here are some examples of SQL data types:

- INTEGER

- VARCHAR

- CHAR

- BLOB

- CLOB

- TIMESTAMP

Some of these data types have obvious conversions into Java types; for example, the INTEGER type appears to be compatible to the Java int type.

The JDBC driver performs some basic conversion when retrieving data from the result set by using the getXXX() methods.However, in some cases you may need to establish your own mapping depending on the content of the column.

Often, boolean data is stored in a SQL CHAR type. There is no direct mapping between a Java boolean type and the SQL CHAR type. One approach is to use the getString() method of the result set and examine the returned value. Using the returned value, you set the boolean value appropriately. For example, values of "Y", "y", "T", "t", or "1" would be equivalent to true, "N", "n", "F", "f", or "0" to false.

Table 15.3 lists the standard type mappings performed by the JDBC driver when you use the get*XXX*()result set methods:

Table 15.3: Standard type conversions.

Java method	SQL Type
getInt()	INTEGER
getLong()	BIGINT
getFloat()	REAL
getDouble()	FLOAT
getBignum()	DECIMAL
getBoolean()	BIT
getString()	VARCHAR
getString()	CHAR
getDate()	DATE
getTime()	TIME
getTimeStamp()	TIMESTAMP
getObject()	(cast to proper type)

Error processing

Most JDBC operations are designed to throw an exception when some operation does not complete as expected. The top-level exception is SQLException. The SQLWarning exception extends SQLException. Further, the DataTruncation exception extends SQLWarning.

An SQLException provides information about itself through the following methods:

- The getMessage() method returns a string that describes the error

- The getSQLState() method returns an "SQLstate" string, which follows either the XOPEN SQLstate conventions or the SQL 99 specifications (see the appropriate spec).

- The getErrorCode() method returns an integer error code (ordinarily the error code returned by the underlying software provided by the database vendor).

- The getNextException() method returns a link to the next Exception, which can be used to provide additional error information.

Programs should check for these exceptions and act appropriately if an exception is encountered. Depending on the driver used, the message of the exception should provide relevant information, such as the SQL error number, that can be analyzed and used for recovery purposes if appropriate.

The SQLWarning is an exception that provides information on database access warnings. A warning is silently linked to a Connection, ResultSet, or Statement object within whose method the warning arose. The term *silent* means that SQL warnings are not thrown; you must explicitly query the Connection, ResultSet, or Statement object instances to see whether a warning occurred. All of these classes have a getWarnings() method for this purpose.

The DataTruncation warning object is a special warning that reports that data has been lost, either on a read operation or on a write operation.

Transaction control

A *unit of work* (UoW) is a series of operations that must all succeed or all fail as a unit. The typical example is the transfer of funds between two bank accounts, consisting of a withdrawal from one account and a deposit to the other. Both the withdrawal and the deposit must succeed for the unit of work to be correctly performed. If one operation succeeds but the other fails, the customer will be left with an incorrect balance on one account or the other. *Transactions* are a way to represent and manage such units of work. A transaction manager ensures that either all the operations in a unit of work complete successfully or the unit of work, as a whole, is considered a failure. Failure of a transaction causes each of the components of the unit of work to be *rolled back,* or put back to its original state.

The Connection interface provides four methods that control how transactions are committed:

- getAutoCommit()
- setAutoCommit()
- commit()
- rollback()

As the application proceeds executing SQL statements, and depending on the state of AutoCommit, the transactions may or may not be being written to the actual database as they execute. If AutoCommit is true, then, at the end of every successful SQL statement, the transaction is written out. If AutoCommit is false, then the transactions can either be committed or rolled back at a later time.

In the scenario for the account transfer, let's suppose that the withdrawal operation succeed and the deposit operation fails. The SQL statement that sets the balance for the deposit account will throw an SQLException. In the catch block, you should call Connection.rollback(). This will have the effect of undoing the withdrawal of funds, returning both accounts to their initial balances.

In general it is good practice to run with AutoCommit set to false and commit the unit of work only after all of the operations execute without error.

Basic broker/mapping architecture

It is very easy to fall into poor programming practices for the sake of completing a project on time, thinking, "as long as it works, it's OK." Often we don't think about good layering practices in our applications. Layering greatly improves the reliability, scalability, and maintainability of our code.

Coding a data access layer makes good sense. This layer is frequently called a *database broker*. In the sample application with this book, we use the "factory" approach to database brokers. The AbstractPersistenceFactory class provides the basic services that all factories need, and factories for specific kinds of objects extend this class. As was shown in Figure 15.4, the abstract factory exposes only one method to the specific factories: getConnection(). Internally there are two protected methods: getInitialContext() and getDataSource().

Our example uses two specific factories: InvoiceFactory and PartnerFactory, which, as seen in Figure 15.5, both extend AbstractPersistenceFactory. They provide specific methods dealing with retrieving and inserting invoices and partners from the respective database tables. These classes could be expanded to provide other services as well, such as updating existing records or creating reports.

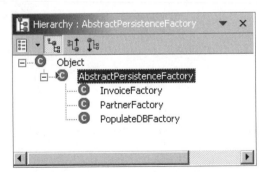

Figure 15.5: Abstract persistence factory hierarchy.

In the following exercise you will follow the path taken by the application to create a new vendor record in the database. We will concentrate on the data broker part of the code.

The Data perspective

The Data perspective in WebSphere Studio can be used to work with databases without leaving the tool. Database administrators can use this perspective to create, alter, view, and remove databases.

As a Java developer you can use the Data perspective to connect to an existing database, examine its schemas and contents, and perhaps even modify the existing tables or create new ones. If you work for a larger company, be aware that "playing" with existing databases is usually forbidden and that databases should not be altered by "mere mortals"— that is the realm of the Database Administrator. However, there is nothing wrong with examining a database and querying the contents of its tables as long as you do nothing that can change the database structure.

Note: Creating a connection to a database is equivalent to cataloging a database, it allows you to examine the contents and structure of the database and its components.

The Data perspective is opened the same way as any other perspective. From the main menu you select **Window → Open perspective → Other → Data**, or use the Open a Perspective icon and select **Data** from the Select Perspective list, as shown in Figure 15.6.

The Data perspective is made up of three new views:

- Data Definition

- DB Servers

- DB Output

The Data Definition view is used to display database-related information. The DB Servers view allows you create and work with database connections on one or more database servers. You will need to

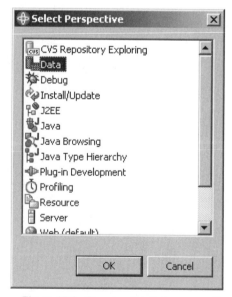

Figure 15.6: Opening the Data perspective.

create a new database connection before you can access a database within WebSphere Studio. Finally, the DB Output view displays the results of executing a query, or command.

Even though these next few paragraphs are not formally part of the end-of-chapter exercise, you are encouraged to follow along so that you get acquainted with the Data perspective.

You may start with any of the completed exercise workspaces from the previous chapters, or you may load the Chapter-15 startup workspace, which you will use as the starting point for the exercise later in this chapter.

    1. After WebSphere Studio starts with a workspace for the Partner application loaded, switch to the Data perspective (Figure 15.7) as previously described.

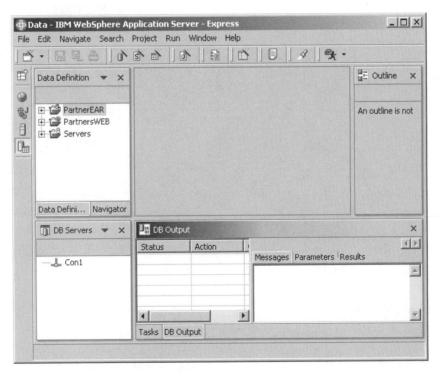

Figure 15.7: The Data perspective.

2. Create a new connection to the Partners database.

   a. From the context menu of **Con1** in the DB Servers view, select **New Connection**.

   b. Complete the New Connection wizard as shown in Figure 15.8.

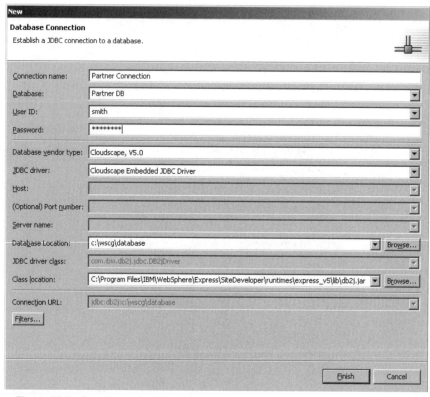

Figure 15.8: Creating a new database connection.

   c. The Connection name and database name can be anything you like when connecting to a Cloudscape database server. Depending on the type of database, and how its been setup, you might need to supply a valid User ID and Password; we used **smith/password** in this example.

   d. Cloudscape databases exist as files on the file system. The location of this particular database is **C:\WSCG\database**.

   e. For the parameter requiring the location of the driver class, enter **C:\Program Files\IBM\WebSphere\Express\SiteDeveloper\runtimes\express_v5\lib\db 2j.jar**, or, better still, click **Browse** and navigate to the proper file. This is the location of all runtime libraries for WebSphere Studio; **db2j.jar** contains the Cloudscape database drivers.

f. Click **Finish**. The information in the wizard is verified, and if the information is correct, a connection is established with the database manager and the database is opened.

Note: Cloudscape databases are not to be used in a production environment. They can accept only a single connection at a time, so when multiple users attempt to connect, only one will be successful. These are nice, small, and very good test databases to be used during development. Having said that, do not attempt to create a connection when the Partner application is up and running; you will not be able to connect. Remember, only one connection at a time. By the same token, make sure to disconnect any open database connection in the Data perspective before running the application, or the application will not run.

---

3. Once the connection is established, the DB Servers view allows you to explore the connection. As you can see in Figure 15.9, there are three tables in the database. APP is the name of the database *schema*. Schemas are used to further qualify the name of tables in a database. The three tables are INVOICE, PURCHASEORDER and VENDOR.

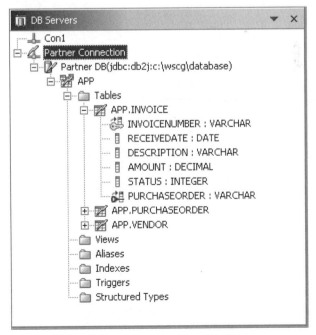

Figure 15.9: DB Servers view after connection.

4. One of the most interesting things you can do from the DB Servers view is to display the contents of a table. This can be done without writing any code. Pick any of the three tables, and from its context menu, select **Sample contents**. The table appears in the DB Output view, as shown in Figure 15.10.

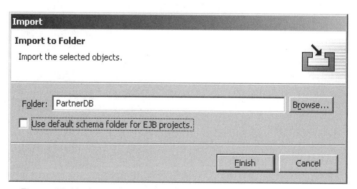

	DB Output				✕
Status	Action	Sample contents			◀▶
✓ Success	Execute	Messages Parameters Results			
		USERNAME	PASSWORD	VENDORNA...	EMAIL
		jones	password	Jones Land...	info@jonesland...
		smith	password	Smith Cater...	ap@smth-cateri...
		Shadow	dog	Puppies Inc.	shad@pups.com

Figure 15.10: DB Output view.

5. Before you can perform any changes to the database, you need to create a folder to hold these changes. Select the connection, and from its context menu select **Import to Folder**. In the Import dialog (Figure 15.11), enter **PartnerDB** as the Folder name. Make sure you uncheck the **Use default schema folder for EJB projects** check box, since we have no EJBs in this project.

Import

Import to Folder
Import the selected objects.

Folder: PartnerDB   Browse...

☐ Use default schema folder for EJB projects.

Finish   Cancel

Figure 15.11: Importing connection to folder.

6. A new folder is created in the Data Definition view. From this view you can alter the database by adding new schema definitions, creating tables under the existing schemas, altering existing tables, and so forth.

> **Note:** Feel free to explore and discover. If by chance you damage this database, you can always reload it from the \WSGC\database directory on the CD-ROM that came with the book.

7. Although in this case you are on your own, in general you are advised, as stated before, not to alter anything unless you know what you are doing and have the permission of the Database Administrator. You can, however, make changes but not export them directly to the database server. Instead, after making the changes in the Data Definition view, you can generate *DDL* (Data Definition Language), a file that can be imported into the database using utilities to make permanent changes. Usually you would give this DDL file to the Database Administrator, who would know what to do with it to incorporate your changes.

8. As an experiment, create a DDL file that represents the database as it currently exists.

   a. From the Data Definition view select the PartnerDB folder, and from its context menu select **Generate DDL**.

   b. On the **Generate** dialog accept the defaults as shown in Figure 15.12.

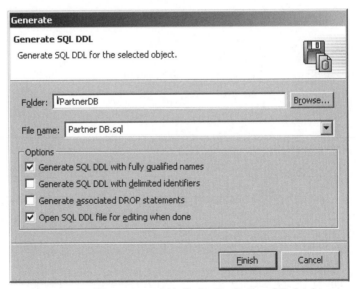

Figure 15.12: Generating a DLL file for the Partner DB database.

   c. Click **Finish**. The database definition is generated in the DDL file, and the file is opened on the Editor view. As you can see in Figure 15.13, this file fully defines the database and is in a format (DDL) suitable to be imported into a database server.

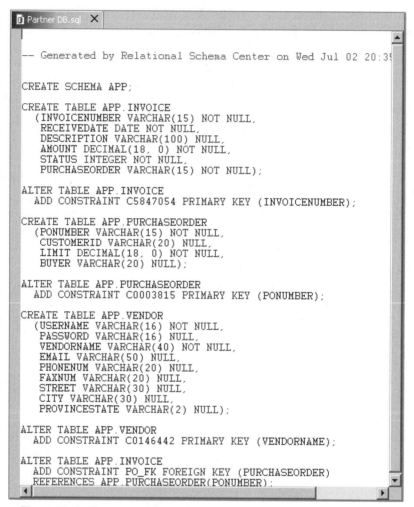

Figure 15.13: Generated DDL file.

The Data perspective is very powerful, and you will find many uses for it as you become more and more familiar with capabilities of WebSphere Studio. It sure is convenient to be able to use this perspective to work with databases within WebSphere Studio.

Exercise

In this exercise you will use the debugger to "walk" through the code executed to create, or register, a new vendor. You will be able to "see" the enterprise application use JDBC and the data broker to insert a new record into the database. At the end of the exercise you will understand how you can use and expand this architecture and add other database-related functions to the application.

By the time you do this exercise, you should be familiar with operating in the WebSphere Studio development environment. Therefore, instructions on performing this lab will be short and to the point. If you find that you cannot perform a task, please revisit the chapter where the task was originally explained.

1. Start WebSphere Studio and load the startup workspace for chapter 15 workspace from C:\WSCG\Workspaces\Startup\Chapter-15 .

2. From the Java perspective, expand the **com.ibm.wscg.mapping** package.

3. Open the **AbstractPersistenceFactory** class in the Java editor. Examine all three methods, listed in Figure 15.14a and 15.14b.

   - getConnection()
   - getInitialContext()
   - getDataSource()

```java
public class AbstractPersistenceFactory implements Serializable {

    private static InitialContext context = null;
    private final static String datasourceName = "jdbc/partnerds";
    private static DataSource ds;

    protected static InitialContext getInitialContext() {
        if (context == null) {
            try {
                context = new InitialContext();
            } catch (NamingException ne) {
                System.out.println("ERROR: Can't access JNDI namespace");
            }
        }
        return context;
    }
}
```

Figure 15.14a: AbstractPersistenceFactory class methods.

```
protected static DataSource getDataSource() throws NamingException {
    if (ds == null) {
        InitialContext context = getInitialContext();
        ds = (DataSource) context.lookup(datasourceName);
    }
    return ds;
}

protected Connection getConnection() {
    try {
        DataSource ds = getDataSource();
        if (ds != null)
            return ds.getConnection("userid", "PASSWORD");
    } catch (NamingException ne) {
        return null;
    } catch (SQLException se) {
        return null;
    }
    return null;
}
}
```

Figure 15.14b: AbstractPersistenceFactory class methods.

The getConnection() method is called by the application to get a managed connection to the database. The getConnection() method internally uses the other two methods to get the JNDI InitialContext so that a lookup can be executed to find the DataSource. Once the DataSource is returned by the lookup operation, it is used to retrieve a connection, which is passed back to the application.

4. Open the **RegistrationServlet** class and place a breakpoint on the first line of code in the doPost() method. This is the servlet called when registering a new vendor. The application will suspend here when you click Register later on the exercise.

5. Run the PartnerWeb application. Start in debug mode.
   a. Open the Server perspective.
   b. Select the PartnersWEB folder. From its context menu select **Debug on Server**.

c. Wait until the server starts and the welcome page (Figure 15.15) is displayed.

d. Click **Register (add new vendor).**

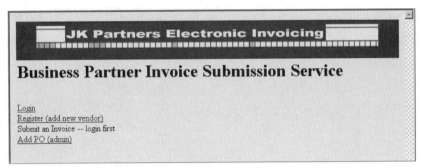

Figure 15.15: Adding a new vendor.

6. When the Step-by-Step Debug dialog comes up, select **Skip** and **Disable step-by-step mode**, as shown in Figure 15.16. Click **OK.**

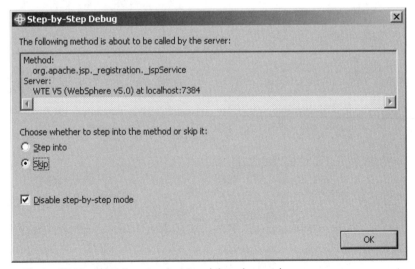

Figure 15.16: Disabling step-by-step debugging mode.

7. The Vendor Registration page appears. Fill in the page as shown in Figure 15.17, or use your own data. The password we used is **dog**.

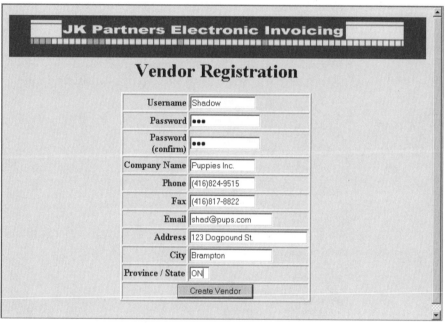

Figure 15.17: Entering vendor registration data.

8. Click **Create Vendor.**

9. Execution suspends at the Registration servlet. Examine the code in the **doPost()** method, listed in Figure 15.18.

```
Protected void doPost(HttpServletRequest request,
                      HttpServletResponse response)
                      throws ServletException, IOException {
  RegistrationFormBean regBean = new RegistrationFormBean();
  Partner partner = regBean.getPartner(request);

  PartnerFactory factory = new PartnerFactory();
  factory.insertPartner(partner);

  getServletContext().getRequestDispatcher(
    "/jsp/ack_insert.jsp").forward(request, response);

}
```

Figure 15.18: doPost() method of new vendor registration servlet.

a. The first line creates a RegistrationFormBean. This bean has one method, getPartner(), which extracts the contents from the HTML form, creates a Partner object instance, and initializes it.

b. Next, a PartnerFactory object instance is created. This object is the database broker that handles all database-related operations involving partners.

c. The broker is called to insert a partner on the database table using the insertPartner() method. The Partner object created by the form bean is passed as a parameter.

d. Lastly, a JSP page is dispatched to acknowledge that the partner was inserted.

e. Step into the code to see how these actions are executed.

Note: Make sure you are careful and step into the insertPartner() method.

---

10. Let's examine the insertPartner() method, listed in Figure 15.19.

```java
public void insertPartner(Partner partner) {
    Connection conn = null;
    PreparedStatement ps = null;
    try {
        conn = getConnection();
        ps = conn.prepareStatement(insertVendorString);
        ps.setString(1, partner.getUsername());
        ps.setString(2, partner.getPassword());
        ps.setString(3, partner.getVendorname());
        ps.setString(4, partner.getEmail());
        ps.setString(5, partner.getPhonenum());
        ps.setString(6, partner.getFaxnum());
        ps.setString(7, partner.getStreet());
        ps.setString(8, partner.getCity());
        ps.setString(9, partner.getProvincestate());
        int rows = ps.executeUpdate();
    } catch (SQLException se) {
        System.out.println("ERROR inserting invoice" + se);
    } finally {
        try {
            ps.close();
            conn.close();
        } catch (SQLException se2) {
        }
    }
}
```

Figure 15.19: insertPartner() method.

a. A Connection object and a PreparedStatement object are declared and initialized to null.

b. A managed connection is obtained from the superclass, AbstractPersistenceFactory.

c. The connection is used to initialize the prepared statement. Notice that the insertVendorString string is used as a parameter to the method call. This string is declared on the PartnerFactory class and represents the SQL statement that will be executed.

```
protected String insertVendorString =
"INSERT INTO VENDOR (USERNAME, PASSWORD, VENDORNAME, EMAIL, PHONENUM,
FAXNUM, STREET, CITY, PROVINCESTATE)" +
"VALUES (?,?,?,?,?,?,?,?,?)";
```

d. The insertVendor string looks straightforward. The INSERT INTO VENDOR part defines the action and table. You will be inserting a record into the VENDOR table.

e. The next group of names in the parentheses are the names of the columns in the table.

f. The only thing that looks odd is the series of question marks after VALUES. Each question mark represents a place holder for a value for each of the columns. Note that there are nine columns and nine question marks. Runtime data must be used to insert the proper data into the proper columns just before the prepared statement is executed.

Note: One or more of the question marks could be replaced in the string by a constant value of the right type. If so, that value will be inserted in *every* record (database table row) created using the prepared statement.

---

g. In the code recapitulated in Figure 15.20, the runtime data to replace the question marks in the VALUE part of the prepared statement is extracted from partner, the Partner object instance that was passed to the method call. There are a number of set*XXX*() methods for inserting different data types; these are complementary to the get*XXX*() methods for extracting column data from the result set.

```
ps.setString(1, partner.getUsername());
ps.setString(2, partner.getPassword());
ps.setString(3, partner.getVendorname());
ps.setString(4, partner.getEmail());
ps.setString(5, partner.getPhonenum());
ps.setString(6, partner.getFaxnum());
ps.setString(7, partner.getStreet());
ps.setString(8, partner.getCity());
ps.setString(9, partner.getProvincestate());
```

Figure 15.20: Setting the column values in the prepared statement.

h. Note that a column number is used to address each column. You could also use column names instead of column numbers.

i. The following Java statement executes the prepared SQL statement. The executeUpdate() method is used for INSERT, DELETE, and UPDATE database operations.

```
int rows = ps.executeUpdate();
```

j. The finally clause, recapitulated in Figure 15.21, is used to ensure that both the prepared statement and the connection are closed, regardless of success or failure.

```
finally {
        try {
            ps.close();
            conn.close();
        } catch (SQLException se2) {
}
```

Figure 15.21: finally clause in insertPartner() method.

11. Single-step through the code in this method and feel free to examine any variables that might be of interest to you, to verify that the actual data entered on the form is really being used.

12. At the end of the method, click **Resume** to continue executing the rest of the code to completion.

13. A page indicating that the new vendor was added is displayed (Figure 15.22).

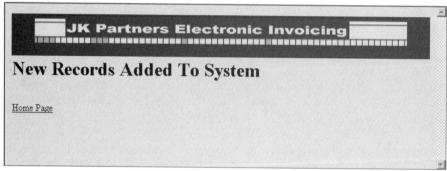

Figure 15.22: New Records Added page.

14. Click **Home Page** to return to the welcome page.

15. Login to the application using the new vendor you just registered. If you entered the vendor data as shown in Figure 15.17, use **Shadow** for the user id and **dog** for the password (Figure 15.23).

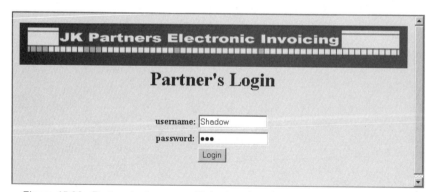

Figure 15.23: Partner login page, with login values for the new vendor.

16. The Welcome page appears as shown in Figure 15.24, indicating a successful login.

Figure 15.24: Successful login as new vendor.

17. Stop the server; remove any breakpoints you have set.

This concludes this exercise.

Test yourself

Key terms

JDBC	*cursor*
JDBC Driver	*data broker*
driver manager	*JNDI*
connection	*InitialContext*
statement	*DataSource*
result set	

Review questions

1. Which are the two packages containing the JDBC APIs?

2. What's the difference between the packages containing the JDBC APIs?

3. When should JDBC drivers be loaded?

4. What is the format of the URL required to obtain a database connection?

5. Name at least two advantages of using a DataSource connection versus a regular connection obtained directly from the JDBC Driver.

6. Why is it considered better to abstract the database layer of an application?

7. What must be done when a connection is no longer needed?

8. The DataTruncationException extends
   a. SQLException
   b. SQLData
   c. SQLWarning
   d. SQLError

9. Which of the following is not a transaction control method in JDBC?
   a. getAutoCommit()
   b. createTransaction()
   c. commit()
   d. rollback()

10. In JDBC which object is used to execute a query?
    a. statement
    b. query
    c. ResultSet
    d. connection

16

Deploying applications

Topics covered

- ❖ *What deployment is*
- ❖ *Remote server deployment from WebSphere Studio*
- ❖ *Command line server administration*
- ❖ *Classpath, classloaders, and module dependencies*

Certification objectives

- ❖ *Understand classpath and module dependencies*
- ❖ *Export J2EE applications*

In this chapter we will explore how to deploy and run Web applications outside the WebSphere Studio test environment. We will look at deploying to the WebSphere Application Server - Express runtime environment, as well as discuss the differences when dealing with the more standard WebSphere Application Server (non-Express) environment.

What deployment is

As a developer of Web applications you spend most of your time working in WebSphere Studio. This work involves creating the various files that make up the application, setting up a test environment, and running and debugging the application until you are satisfied that you have completed your part.

The next step is, usually, to integrate your work with that of others and deploy the completed application to a test server, where it will be exercised in an environment more like real life.

We will not deal with the integration of work from several developers in this book. We will instead assume that you are the sole developer of the application and are at the point of turning the application over to be deployed.

Before deployment of an application can take place, a step known as *assembling* the application needs to be performed. Assembly involves packaging the application into one or more files. Typically, an Enterprise Application Archive (EAR) file is delivered to the deployer to install on an application server. The EAR file contains a combination of Web Archive (WAR), utility, and EJB JAR files packaged as a self-contained Enterprise Application.

Both WebSphere Studio and the Application Assembly Tool (AAT) can be used to combine the different files that make up the application into the EAR file. They can also be used to configure many aspects concerning runtime resources and other settings required to make the application work and perform in the production environment.

Deploying an application involves taking the EAR file and installing it on the application server.

Application servers that are compliant with the J2EE specification can handle EAR files to manipulate, adjust, and install them in a test or production environment.

Often it is necessary to adjust the files, given by the developer, to the runtime environment. Resources and naming of components are usually different in the development environment and must be made to match the production environment.

Exporting an EAR file out of WebSphere Studio is a very simple task. Just select **File → Export** and make the proper choices in the Export wizard (Figure 16.1).

As you are about to see, exporting the WAR or EAR files is not necessary when using WebSphere Studio to publish to a remote server.

We will now examine how to install, or deploy, an Enterprise Application into WebSphere Application Server - Express and show you how you can run the application without using WebSphere Studio's test environment.

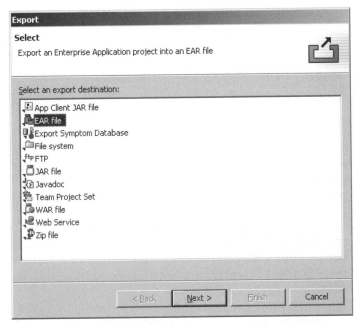

Figure 16.1: File Export dialog.

Remote server deployment from WebSphere Studio

WebSphere Application Server - Express includes a fully functional application server capable of supporting J2EE Web applications, which contain HTML pages, JSP pages, and servlets. These applications can run stand-alone without having WebSphere Studio running.

There are, however, some restrictions when using WebSphere Application Server - Express. The three main differences between the application server included with WebSphere Application Server - Express and the other editions of WebSphere Application Server are as follows:

- Configuration of the server is done using WebSphere Studio.

- EAR or WAR files containing the application do not need to be explicitly exported out of WebSphere Studio for installation on the server.

- Installation and configuration of the Web application is done using WebSphere Studio.

These restrictions exist because there is no administrative console application supplied with WebSphere Application Server - Express. In the non-Express editions of WebSphere Application Server, both server configuration and Web application installation and configuration are performed using the administrative console, which is an Enterprise Application running on the application server.

Command line server administration

As just mentioned, there is no server administration application installed on the WebSphere Application Server - Express.

It is not exactly true, however, that all configuration and installation tasks must be performed through WebSphere Studio. A command line interface tool known as *wsadmin* is provided with all editions of WebSphere Application Server. This tool can be used to perform administrative functions, including installing and removing applications.

Whether you use the Server Configuration pages in WebSphere Studio or the *wsadmin* command line interface, configuration changes result in the alteration of one or more XML files, as shown in Figure 16.2. These XML files are accessed through a set of management beans (MBeans), which expose administrative objects of the server. The Java Management Extensions (JMX) Architecture is used to implement this consistent approach to manipulating server properties using these two different methods.

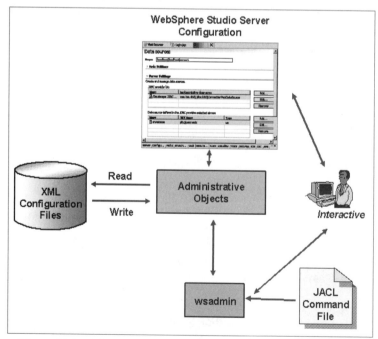

Figure 16.2: Administering the Application Server.

We will not go into detail on the usage of *wsadmin*. It is considered an expert-level tool, which requires you to know which administrative objects are available, which methods they expose, and what parameters they accept. There is very good coverage of using *wsadmin* in the product's help files.

The *wsadmin* command line tool allows you to work within two modes:

■ Interactive

■ Using scripts

To use the tool *interactively*, you start *wsadmin* from a command line prompt. The batch file that starts the tool can be found in the *bin* directory where the application server is installed. After a startup sequence, you are presented with the *wsadmin* prompt, at which point you can start entering commands.

You can also use script files, which allow you to use Jacl (Java Application Control language) to group a series of commands and add logical components to the script. Jacl is a Java implementation of Tcl (Tool Control Language).

If you wish to learn more about *wsadmin*, Jacl, or administrating WebSphere Application Server - Express from the command line using *wsadmin*, please see the product's documentation.

Classpath, classloaders, and module dependencies

The ability for an application to run depends on the ability of the Java virtual machine (JVM) to find and load the classes that the application modules need. The first time a class is required by the application, the compiled (bytecode) file that defines the class must be found and loaded into the virtual machine. This is the job of the classloader. These binary representations of classes can be found in different types of files: .class, .jar, .war files all contain the compiled class files.

One of the main concerns when deploying an application is to make sure that all the classes and property files needed by an application can be found by the classloader. J2EE makes this task a bit easier by providing for packaging applications into EAR files. However, there are other types of files that contain classes that are not part of the application's EAR file. These files are mainly library and utility JAR files that serve more than one particular application.

To be more specific, the JVM's classpath definition determines where in the file system the classloader will look for the classes that are needed by the application.

In WebSphere Studio the classpath is defined on the Path tab of the Server Configuration editor. There are two areas where you can specify the classpath. One is used for WebSphere-specific extensions. In this classpath you should point to classes that are used by

WebSphere as a whole rather than any particular application, such as the J2EE runtime libraries. The other area is used for application modules. These are libraries used by EJBs and Web modules. Note that in most cases you do not enter anything special in the areas of the Path tabs, because the defaults and EAR file structure usually provide you with all the path information required. Dependency JAR files can also be defined in this classpath.

Classloaders in WebSphere

The behavior of the classloaders can be, to a certain extent, defined through the Configuration and Applications tabs of the Server Configuration editor.

The Configuration tab lets you configure what the application classloader policy is. The choices are SINGLE and MULTIPLE. When the application classloader policy is set to SINGLE, a single application classloader loads all EJB modules, dependency JAR files, and shared libraries in the system. When the application classloader policy is set to MULTIPLE, each application receives its own classloader, which is used for loading only that application's EJB modules, dependency JAR files, and shared libraries.

On the Applications tab of the Server Configuration editor you can define the Classloader mode and the WAR classloader policy. When multiple classloaders are involved in a virtual machine, there is a parent/child relationship between them, forming a chain of classloaders that is accessed in sequence until the class is found or an exception is thrown. When a new classloader is added, it becomes the child of the previous classloader. Depending on the circumstances, you may want to start the search for a class using the Parent or Child classloader first. Remember that the first class found on the classpath is loaded and the search ends, so reversing the search order may find a different class in the classpath. The search order is controlled by the Classloader mode setting, which can be PARENT_FIRST or PARENT_LAST.

The value of the WAR classloader policy setting, MODULE or APPLICATION, determines which classloader loads each application's Web modules. If the WAR module's classloader policy is set to APPLICATION, the application's loader loads the WAR module's classes. If the WAR classloader policy is set to MODULE, then each WAR module receives its own classloader.

You can learn more about classloaders in the product's documentation or online help.

Module dependencies and utility JAR files

In more complex applications you may have code that is shared among multiple WAR projects, such as utility classes and model objects. Repeating the classes in each of the modules that require them is not a good solution, as you now have to maintain multiple copies of the same class and you increase the size of the application by having more than one class performing the same function. The solution to this problem is to place these common classes in a separate Java project, containing all the necessary common classes. At deployment time these classes will be contained in what is commonly called a utility JAR file.

The WAR modules that need this utility JAR file are said to be dependent, or have a dependency, on the Java project.

The dependency occurs both at build time, when the compiler needs to be able to resolve references to all classes, and also at runtime, when the JVM needs to be able to find the class files to satisfy the classloader.

While you are working in WebSphere Studio, your Web modules can refer to other projects in the workspace to satisfy their build time requirements. To set these dependent folders, you open the **Properties** of the Web project, select **Java Build Path**, then click the **Projects** tab. There you see the applicable projects that can be added.

To resolve runtime references, you include the utility JAR file, containing the classes in the common Java project, in the EAR file that packages the application. To configure this, you work with the Enterprise Application's deployment descriptor. Open the application.xml file in the deployment descriptor editor. You can most easily do this from the J2EE perspective's J2EE Hierarchy view by expanding the Enterprise Applications folder and then double-clicking the enterprise application that needs to include the utility JAR file.

Once the file is opened in the deployment descriptor editor, select the **Module** tab and click **Add** below the Project Utility JARs. This causes the Add Utility JAR dialog to open, where you choose from a list of Java projects in the workspace. When you export the EAR file for the application in preparation for deployment, a JAR file containing all the classes in the selected Java folder will be created and included. The classes in the JAR file are accessible to the other modules in the EAR file.

Although the application in this book does not use any utility JARs, you will find that, as soon as you start developing more complex applications with multiple Web modules and perhaps EJBs, you will need to start creating these utility JAR files to share classes among the modules of the application.

Exercises

In the following exercises you create a remote server and configuration, install the application on the remote server, and test the application. These steps are performed inside WebSphere Studio. After verifying that the application runs inside WebSphere Studio, you shut down WebSphere Studio, start the stand-alone server, and test the application outside the WebSphere Studio development environment.

Creating a remote server and server configuration

So far, in the examples for this book, you have been running and testing the exercises in the WebSphere Test Environment provided by WebSphere Studio. If you want the application to be available without WebSphere Studio running you need to install and configure it in a remote server.

Don't let the word *remote* worry you too much. In this case, it just means that the server is not running in WebSphere Studio. The remote server could be running on same machine as WebSphere Studio or be installed on another machine. It could even be an Apache Tomcat server (not part of the WebSphere Application Server - Express installation).

Creating a remote server and server configuration is similar to creating a WebSphere Test Environment server and configuration. There are however, additional definitions that describe the location of the server (its IP address) and the method used to deploy the files that make up the application.

1. Start WebSphere Studio using the completed working solution of the application from the previous chapter, or load the chapter 16 startup workspace from **C:\WSCG\Workspaces\Startup\Chapter-16**.

2. Switch to the Server perspective.

3. Create a new server and server configuration.

   a. On the Server perspective and select **New → Server and Server Configuration** from the **Servers** context menu in the Server Configuration view (Figure 16.3).

Figure 16.3: Adding a server and server configuration.

4. In the Create a New Server and Server Configuration wizard (Figure 16.4), name the new server **Standalone Server**. Select **Express Remote Server** from the Server type list, and click **Next**.

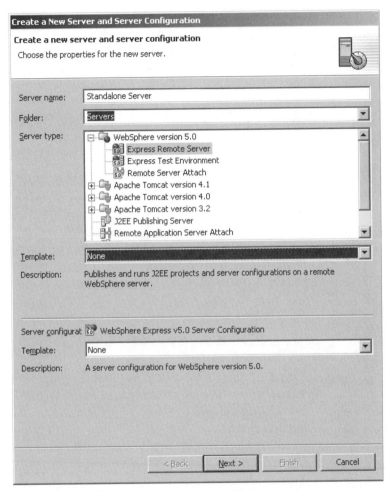

Figure 16.4: Selecting server name and type.

5. The next step is to define the IP address or URL defining the location where the remote server is located. We'll assume the server will be located on the same machine. Enter **127.0.01** for the Host address as shown in Figure 16.5. You could also enter **localhost**. Click **Next**.

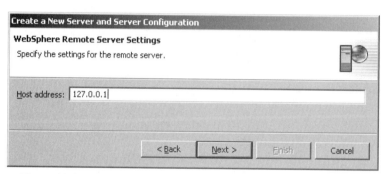

Figure 16.5: Defining the host address.

6. In order for WebSphere Studio to be able to deploy, or copy, the files that make up the application to the remote server, you need to provide the installation directory for the remote server.

a. Enter **C:\Program Files\IBM\WebSphere\Express\AppServer** in the WebSphere installation directory field on the WebSphere Remote Server Settings page, shown in Figure 16.6. (This setting assumes that you have installed WebSphere Application Server - Express to the default installation directory, adjust the path accordingly if you didn't.)

b. Check the **Use default WebSphere deployment directory** check box. Click **Next**.

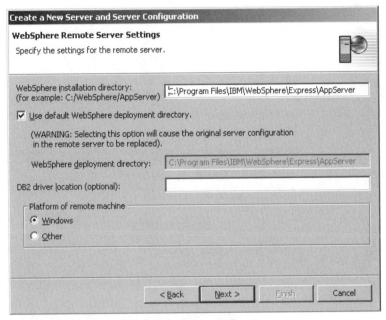

Figure 16.6: Selecting the deployment directory.

7. Now that WebSphere Studio knows where the deployment directory is located, you need to define how to copy the files necessary for deployment to that directory.

a. On the Create or Select a Remote File Transfer Instance page (Figure 16.7), the choices for the file transfer mechanism are Copy (to copy files to a local or shared remote directory using the operating system copying capability) or FTP (which you need to use if you are deploying to a system that has no compatible shared file system, such as from Windows to UNIX).

b. The "remote" server is on your local machine, so select **Copy file transfer mechanism**. Click **Next**.

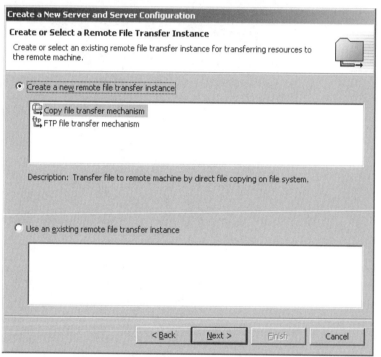

Figure 16.7: Selecting file transfer mechanism.

8. On the Create a New Server and Server Configuration page of this dialog (Figure 16.8), you define where the target directory is located, as seen from the local machine.

a. Since our server is located on the same machine as WebSphere Studio, a local directory name can be entered here. Enter **C:\Program Files\IBM\ WebSphere\Express\AppServer** in the Remote target directory field. Click **Next**.

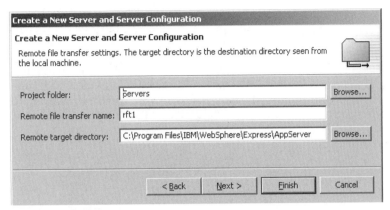

Figure 16.8: Selecting remote target directory.

9. On the WebSphere Server Configuration Settings page, the last page of the Create a New Server and Server Configuration wizard (Figure 16.9), you can select the port on which the embedded HTTP server will listen.

a. The default is 7080; this is fine at this time. Click **Finish**.

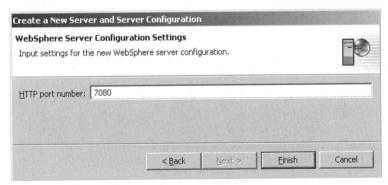

Figure 16.9: Selecting HTTP port number.

Note: If you don't plan to have another HTTP server in the topology of your installation, you could change the port number here to the standard HTTP port, 80.

Creating the data source

Now that the remote server and server configuration have been created, it is time to configure the server so that the resources needed for the application are available. In the case of the Partner application, the only required resource is the datasource.

1. Create a Cloudscape data source. These steps are exactly the same as the ones you performed earlier (Chapter 10) when you defined the data source for the WebSphere Test Environment.

   a. From the Server Configuration view, select the new server, **Standalone Server**. From its context menu select **Open**. You can also double click **Standalone Server** and achieve the same effect, which is to open the Server Configuration editor.

   b. Select the **Data source** tab of the Server Configuration editor.

   c. A JDBC provider for the Cloudscape database JDBC driver already exists and is properly configured. Make sure it is selected.

   Note: You may delete the data source definitions that already exist on this page, they are used with some of the examples included with WebSphere Studio and are not needed on the stand-alone server.

   ---

   d. Add a new data source by clicking the **Add** button to the right of "Data source defined in JDBC provider selected above".

   e. On the first page of the Create a Data Source wizard (Figure 16.10), select **Version 5_0 data source**. Click **Next**.

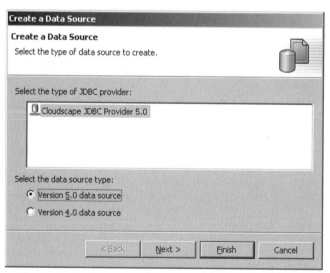

Figure 16.10: Selecting data source provider and version.

f. On the next page of the wizard you define the settings for the new data source. Complete the dialog by filling in the Name (**PartnerDS**), the JNDI name (**jdbc/partnerds**), and Description (**Data source for Partner application**) as shown in Figure 16.11. The Name and JNDI name parameters are mandatory and must be unique for each server.

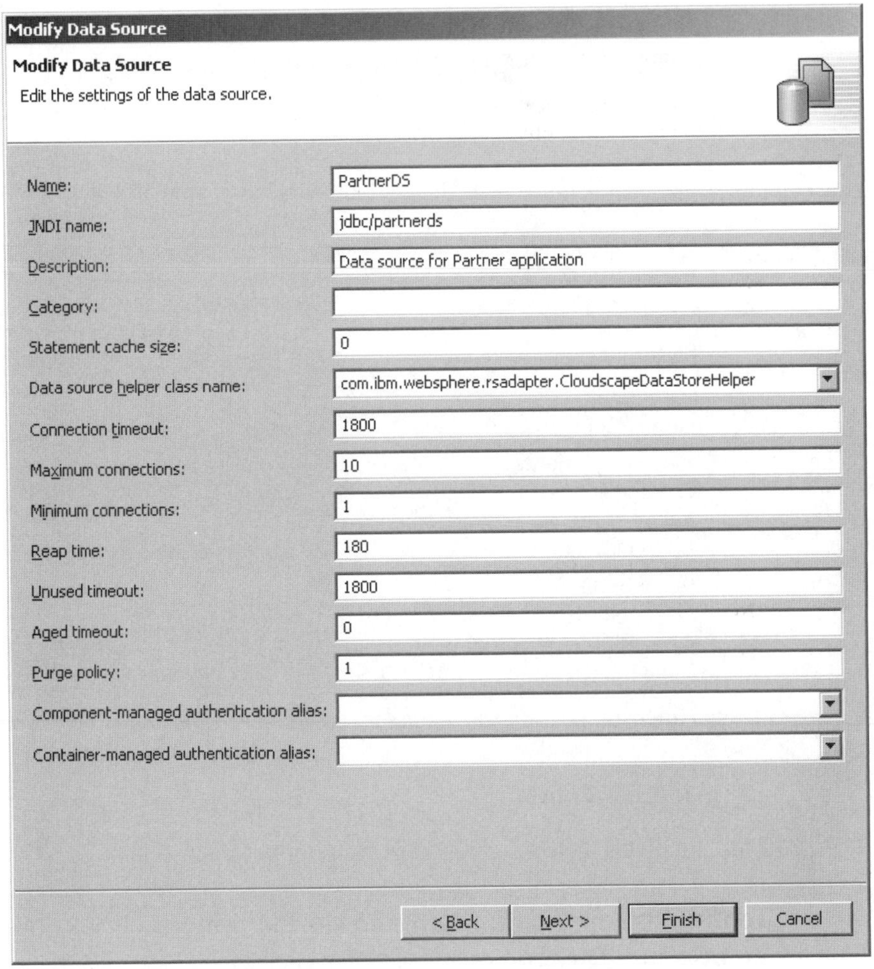

Figure 16.11: Defining data source name and JNDI name.

g. Click **Next**.

h. Finally, on the Modify Resource Properties page (Figure 16.12), you must define the location of the database name. Cloudscape stores its database components on the file system, so the database name refers to the directory where the database files are stored. (In other databases, such as DB2, the database name is just that: a name.) Select **databaseName** on the **Resource Properties** list and enter **c:/wscg/database** in the **Value** field.

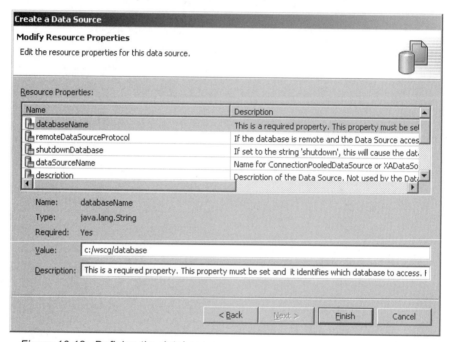

Figure 16.12: Defining the database name.

i. Click **Finish**.

This completes the configuration of the remote server.

Testing the application running on the remote server in WebSphere Studio

The next step is to make sure that the application runs on the remote server. The first test will be performed while you are still in WebSphere Studio. That way, if there are problems, they can be addressed quickly. Note that at this point, debugging an application on the remote server is no different from debugging in the WebSphere Test Environment.

Because you have been running the Partner application in the WebSphere Test Environment, there is an association between the test server, WTE V5, and the Enterprise Application.

1. Before a project can be associated with a server, the Enterprise Application, containing the project, must be added to the server configuration.

   a. From the Server Configuration view, select the **Standalone Server** and from its context menu select **Add** → **PartnerEAR** (Figure 16.13).

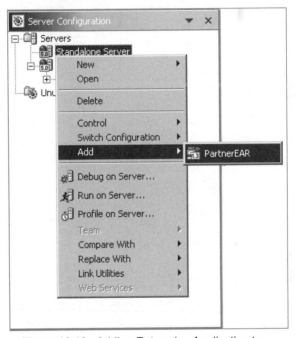

Figure 16.13: Adding Enterprise Application to server.

2. Set the server preference of the PartnerWEB project so that it runs always on the new Standalone server.

   a. Select the PartnersWEB project.

   b. From its context menu select **Properties**.

c. In the Properties dialog (Figure 16.14), click **Server Preference**.

d. Select **Always run on the following server:**

e. Select **Standalone Server** from the servers list.

f. Click **OK**.

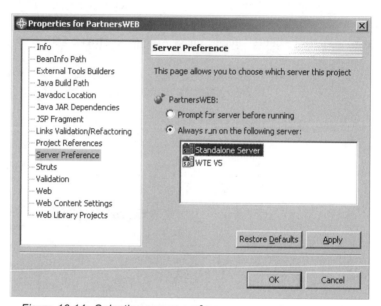

Figure 16.14: Selecting server preference.

Note: If you need to have the ability to run on either server, you should select the **Prompt for server before running** option instead of Always run on the following server. This option will present you with a list of servers for you to pick from and run the application in.

3. Run the PartnerWEB project on the Standalone server.

a. Select PartnerWEB from Navigator view. From its context menu select **Run on Server**, as shown in Figure 16.15.

Figure 16.15: Running application on server.

Note: Just before the server starts, the application is published (deployed) to the remote server.

b. Once the server starts, it should display the home page of the application in the Web Browser view (Figure 16.16).

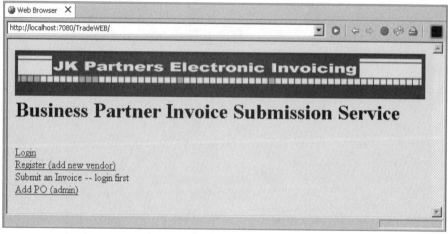

Figure 16.16: Application's home page.

c. Proceed to test the application as you have in the past. Make sure you can log in and exercise the other functions provided.

4. Stop the remote server.

5. Close WebSphere Studio.

Starting the remote server outside WebSphere Studio

The first time you selected the PartnerWEB project and clicked Run on Server, the application was published, or deployed, to the WebSphere Application Server - Express server you configured as the remote server.

Publishing involves creating the appropriate J2EE directory structure and copying to the server the files that make up the application.

Take a minute to examine the directory structure and become familiar with the files the publishing process copied to the server. As you can see in Figure 16.17, the EAR file containing the Enterprise Application has been expanded under the InstalledApps/ DefaultNode directory.

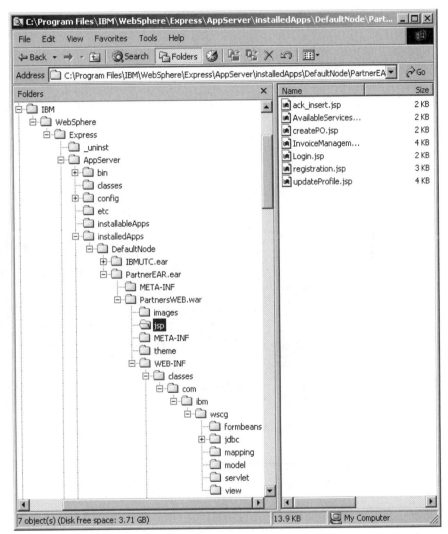

Figure 16.17: Directory structure of Standalone server showing the deployed application.

Before the application can be run, you'll need to start the server.

1. Start the Standalone server.

   a. Open a command prompt window.

   b. Change directory to **C:\Program Files\IBM\WebSphere\Express\App Server\bin**.

   c. Type **startserver server1** at the command prompt. The first part of the command, *startserver*, is the name of a batch file that sets up the correct operating environment for WebSphere Application Server and then starts the server. The second part of the command, *server1*, is the name of the server to be started; *server1* happens to be the default name of the server that is installed.

d. Wait until the *startserver* command completes and you get an indication that the server has started successfully. The message "Server server1 open for e-business" followed by a process number, as in Figure 16.18, gives you a positive indication that all is well and ready for you to access the application.

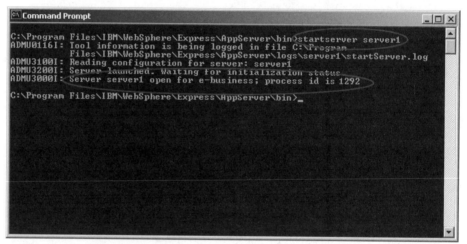

Figure 16.18: Starting the Standalone server.

e. Verify the process ID in a file named server1.pid, located in the C:\Program Files\IBM\WebSphere\Express\AppServer\logs\server1 directory. In this same directory you can look at the various log files produced by the server as it starts up and also during runtime. For example, the SystemOut.log file will contain any output produced by the application server and user applications that have System.out.println() statements. If the server fails to start, looking at the logs can provide you with information to fix the problem.

Testing the application running on the remote server

To test the Partner application, open a Web browser, and enter **http://localhost:7080/ TradeWEB/** on the address line. The home page of the application should come up on the browser. From then on, test the application as you have already done several times in other chapters of the book.

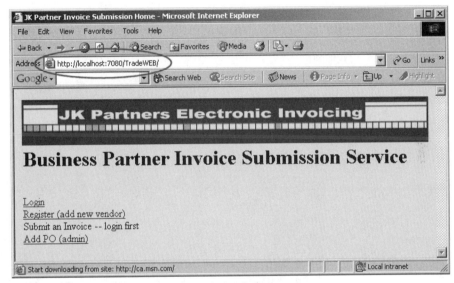

Figure 16.19: Application running on stand-alone server.

If the application does not come up, here are some things to check:

- Has the server started?

- Is the URL correct?

- Are there any errors in the logs?

Test yourself

Key terms

deployment

remote server

wsadmin

Review questions

1. What types of files are exported in preparing an application to be deployed?

2. True or False: A remote server must be located on a different machine than where WebSphere Studio is installed.

3. Where can output produced by an application using System.out.println() statements be found on a remote server?

4. WebSphere Application Server - Express supports J2EE applications that contain:
   a. HTML pages
   b. EJBs
   c. JSP pages
   d. servlets

5. The command line administration tool provided with WebSphere Application Server Express is
   a. admin
   b. wadmin
   c. wsadmin
   d. studio

6. Which of the following can be deployed to an application server?
   a. EAR
   b. WAR + EJB JARs
   c. JavaScript objects
   d. CSS

7. Exporting EAR and WAR files out of WebSphere Studio can be done by selecting _____.

8. Configuration changes made through the command line administration tool result in changes in one or more _____ files.

9. Configuration of WebSphere Application Server - Express is done using _____

10. The two modes in which you are can use the command line administration tool are _____ and _____.

Appendix A—End-of-chapter questions with answers

Chapter 1: Scope and coverage of the Certification Guide

This chapter contains no key terms or review questions.

Chapter 2: System requirements and installation

This chapter contains no key terms or review questions.

Chapter 3: Overview of Eclipse, Studio Workbench, and WebSphere Studio

Key terms

open source	Software whose source code is made available for use or modification as users or other developers see fit.
Eclipse Platform	An open extensible IDE that provides building blocks and a foundation for constructing and running integrated software development tools.
Eclipse Workbench	The user interface (UI) component of the Eclipse Platform.
plug-ins	A program that can easily be installed and used as part of Eclipse to enhance the core functionality.

perspective	A collection of related views that make performing a particular task easier.
views	Visual components within the Workbench, typically used to navigate a hierarchy of information, open an editor, or display properties for the active editor.
editor	A component of Eclipse that allows editing, modifying, and debugging a certain type of component in the finished application, such as a Java project.
Java virtual machine (JVM)	A program for a particular computer's processor that interprets compiled Java binary code so that that computer can execute a Java program's instructions.
J2EE	J2EE (Java 2 Platform, Enterprise Edition) is a Java platform designed for the mainframe-scale computing typical of large enterprises.

Review questions

1. What is the Eclipse?

"Eclipse" refers in general to the ongoing efforts on the part of the Eclipse Consortium, comprising numerous leaders in the software industry, to develop an open-source, extensible integrated development environment for a wide variety of software projects. The Eclipse Consortium's work comprises four projects: the Eclipse Project, the Eclipse Tools Project, the Eclipse Technology Project, and the Eclipse Web Tools Platform Project.

2. What is the Eclipse Project?

The Eclipse Project is the Eclipse Consortium's project for developing a robust, full-featured, commercial-quality, open-source industry platform for the development of highly integrated software tools.

3. What are the three main subprojects of the Eclipse Project?

The Eclipse Project is composed of three subprojects:
a. Platform
b. Java Development Tools (JDT)
c. Plug-in Development Environment (PDE)

4. What is the Eclipse Platform? What are its main features?

The Eclipse Platform is an "open extensible IDE for anything and yet nothing in particular." The Eclipse Platform provides building blocks and a foundation for constructing and running integrated software development tools. The Eclipse Platform allows tool builders working independently to develop tools that integrate with other builders' tools so seamlessly that one can't tell where one tool ends and another starts.

5. What is the Eclipse Workbench?

The Eclipse Workbench is an integration framework provided by Eclipse, on top of which more sophisticated and specialized tools can be built. It is provided free of charge.

6. What are plug-ins? How do they make Eclipse a great IDE?

Plug-ins are programs that can be easily installed and used to extend the functionality of Eclipse.

7. List a few features provided by the Java editor.

a. Keyword and syntax coloring

b. Context-specific code assist

c. Method-level edit

d. Code formatting

8. How do I find out about future releases of the Eclipse Platform and IBM WebSphere Studio?

The following sites provide information about Eclipse and IBM WebSphere Studio:

a. *www.eclipse.org* (The Eclipse Consortium)

b. *http://www-3.ibm.com/software/awdtools/studiositedev/* (IBM's site for WebSphere Studio)

9. What is a perspective a collection of?

a. Views

b. Editors

c. Outline

d. Tools

Chapter 4: Developing a simple Java application

Key terms

Java perspective	The perspective in WebSphere Studio that enables quick development of Java-based applications.
Java projects	A file organization structure supported by WebSphere Studio that helps keep related packages and their classes in one logical place.
Web application	An interactive application that can be accessed using a Web browser through a corporate intranet or through the Internet. Web applications can perform complex business processes on either the client or the server.
Enterprise Application	A large, complex distributed business application software package designed to meet a certain need of an entire firm and to be operated on a variety of platforms across corporate networks, intranets, and the Internet. The J2EE platform supports Enterprise Applications that are component-oriented and expandable according to the demands on performance and services..
J2EE (Java 2 Enterprise Edition)	A version of the Java platform designed for the mainframe-scale computing typical of large enterprises.
JAR (Java archive)	A file that contains a collection of Java classes gathered into a single file and compressed.
Task view	A component of the Java perspective in WebSphere Studio that displays errors and tasks to be completed on the current Java file.
source control	A technique used by developers to make sure that a file's source does not get changed improperly.
Debug perspective	A perspective in WebSphere Studio that enables the developer to debug applications.
JRE (Java Runtime Environment)	Software that provides the minimum requirements for executing a Java application. The JRE consists of the Java virtual machine, core classes, and supporting files.
editors	Visual components within the Eclipse Workbench typically used to edit or browse a resource.

Outline view

A view in WebSphere Studio that enables the developer to view various components of the Java file currently being edited.

code assist

A feature of WebSphere Studio that provides assistance to the developer in writing Java code. Code assist is provided through templates.

templates

A feature of WebSphere Studio that replaces certain predefined keywords with complete Java constructs.

filters

A feature of the outline view in WebSphere Studio that allows developers to view selectively components of the Java file currently opened in the editor.

Javadoc

The tool from Sun Microsystems for generating API documentation in HTML format from documentation comments in source code.

Package Explorer

A component of the Java Perspective of WebSphere Studio that displays all packages existing under each project.

Review questions

1. How does WebSphere Studio support role-based development?

   WebSphere supports role-based development through the use of perspectives. A perspective combines a number of panes, views, and editors to facilitate development in a particular role.

2. How do you view the list of available perspectives?

   You can view the list of perspectives by selecting the following menu option: Window → Open Perspective → Other

3. What is a Java project, and how do you create one in WebSphere Studio?

   Java projects are organizational artifacts used to keep packages and their related classes in one logical place. There is no equivalent Java construct for a Java project outside of WebSphere Studio.

   There are two ways to create a project in WebSphere Studio:
   a. Select the menu option File → New → Project
   b. Select the "Creating a Java project" toolbar icon.

4. What are the various components of the Java perspective?

The Java perspective is made up of different views and editors, including the following:

a. Editor view

b. Outline view

c. Package Explorer

d. Hierarchy navigator

e. Task view

f. Console view

5. What is code assist, and how can you activate it in the editor?

Code assist is a feature of the Java editor in WebSphere that assists the developer in writing Java programs. Code assist completes entering lines of code for you based on what you have already typed on a particular line. You can manually activate code assist by pressing Ctrl+Space. Code assist can insert other Java constructs by using the templates provided by WebSphere Studio. Settings for code assist can be found by selecting Window → Preference → Java → Editor → Code Assist.

6. What is the Outline view?

The Outline view displays an organized component view of the file opened in the editor view. The Outline view will display different things depending on the file type. If a Java file is open, the Outline view displays the package and import statements, type definitions, global variable types, and methods. The Outline view has different icons that indicate different components of a Java file.

7. How do you compile a program in WebSphere Studio?

In WebSphere Studio the Java compiler is tied to the editor. A Java file is compiled whenever it is saved. Saving can occur when you select File → Save from the main menu or press the Ctrl+S key combination.

8. Briefly describe the source control available in WebSphere Studio.

WebSphere Studio provides simple source control via a mechanism called the Local History. The Workbench features Compare with, Replace with, and Restore from Local History functions. These features can be selected from the context menu of any Java file (right-click on the class to view context menu). The Compare and Replace functions allow you to see the differences and, in the case of Replace, to regress to a different version of the file.

The Restore from Local History function allows you to recover an element of a file you previously deleted.

9. How do you execute a simple Java program (non-Web-based) in WebSphere Studio?

To execute a Java program, select the Java file in the Package Explorer and click the Run icon.

10. How are errors handled in WebSphere Studio?

Errors are tracked by WebSphere when you save the file. An entry for each error is created in the Tasks view. Double-clicking on the task opens the appropriate editor and positions the cursor at the error. Errors are also indicated in the Package Explorer and the outline views with red circles containing a white X. The marker bar of the editor view also displays icons based on the situation.

Chapter 5: Debugging techniques

Key terms

tracing	The technique used by developers to track the sequence of execution in an application.
breakpoint	A forced stop in execution placed at a certain point of a program to facilitate debugging.
debugger	The component of WebSphere Studio that debugs the program and provides access to various components of the program.
Debug perspective	A perspective in WebSphere Studio that enables the developer to debug applications.
process	An instance of a program running in a computer. In WebSphere Studio each executing program has a few processes associated with it.
thread	One sequence of execution in a program.
step filtering	A feature of WebSphere Studio that allows the developer to selectively filter the classes to step into.
Variables view	A view in the Debug perspective that provides access to variables and their values.
Expressions view	The view in which variables being inspected are displayed.

Display view	A view in the Debug perspective that provides the developer with a way to evaluate any valid Java expression.
Scrapbook	A special type of file a developer can create in WebSphere Studio for trying new code and testing it before including it in a class.
conditional breakpoint	A breakpoint that stops execution only if a set condition is met rather than every time a line is encountered.
Java Exception breakpoint	A breakpoint that stops execution only when a Java exception is thrown.
watchpoint	A forced stop in execution that occurs when a specified variable is accessed or modified.
method breakpoints	Breakpoints that are triggered when the method they apply to is reached.

Review questions

1. Why and when to debug?

   Debugging is used to determine logic errors made by the developer that are not caught by the compiler. It also helps you understand the flow of a program written by other developers.

2. What are some traditional techniques of debugging?

   One traditional debugging technique is using print statements to display variable value and status information on the screen. In Java the methods that can be used are System.out.println and System.out.print().

3. How do you debug a program in WebSphere Studio? What is the goal behind debugging?

   WebSphere Studio has an excellent debugger built in. You can debug a program by clicking on the Debug icon, which will start the debugger in the Debug perspective.

   The goal is to set breakpoints in the code where you suspect a problem is being caused, or just before it. Once the breakpoint is reached, single-step and examine variable values as the program executes under the control of the debugger, fix the error, and test again.

4. How do you set a breakpoint in the Java editor?

   There are primarily two ways:
   a. Double-click to toggle between setting and resetting a breakpoint.
   b. Select Add Breakpoint from the context menu.

5. What operations can you perform on breakpoints?

   ◆ **Enable**
   ◆ **Disable**
   ◆ **Remove**
   ◆ **Remove All**
   ◆ **Go To File**

6. What are the three controls available to the developer while single-stepping through the Java program?

   a. Step Into
   b. Step Over
   c. Step Return

7. What is step filtering? How can I set up step filtering?

   Step filtering is a way to avoid stepping into methods for which you have no source.

   You can set up step filtering by selecting Window → Preferences → Java → Debug → Step Filtering.

8. How can you view the value of variables in the Debug perspective?

   There are two primary ways to view variable values:
   a. Hover over the variable in the Editor view.
   b. Use the Variables view, which is stacked along with the Breakpoint view.

9. What is the Display view?

   The Display view provides you with a way to evaluate any valid Java expression. Code executed in the Display view runs in the context of the current stack frame.

10. Name two techniques for controlling breakpoints.

    a. Hit count
    b. Conditions

Chapter 6: Essential HTTP and HTML

Key terms

HTML (HyperText Markup Language)	The set of markup symbols or codes inserted in a file intended for display on a World Wide Web browser page.
HTTP (HyperText Transfer Protocol)	The set of rules for exchanging files (text, graphic images, sound, video, and other multimedia files) on the World Wide Web.
HTTPS	A Web protocol, developed by Netscape and built into its browser, that encrypts and decrypts user page requests as well as the pages that are returned by the Web server.
SSL (Secure Sockets Layer)	A protocol for managing the security of a message transmission on the Internet.
URL (Uniform Resource Locator)	A text string that identifies the location of a file on the Web.
servlet	A class written in the Java programming language and executed on a server. A servlet is typically accessed through an HTTP request and outputs an HTTP response.
CSS (Cascading Style Sheets)	Files that contain visual formatting properties for one or more HTML files.
Page Designer	*A* component of WebSphere Studio that allows you to work with HTML files, JSP files, and embedded JavaScript.
HTTP response	The message sent back from the server to the client that has sent an HTTP request.
JSP (JavaServer Pages)	Technology that provides a simplified, fast way to create Web pages that display dynamically generated content.
Web server	A software program dedicated to retrieving and sending Web pages upon request.
DTD (Document Type Definition)	A file that defines the structural rules of a type of document in HTML and XML. These rules include a complete list of allowable elements and attributes, special character entities, and rules for external files as well as the hierarchical structure of all elements.

| JavaScript | An interpreted programming or script language that is used to perform client-side processing in Web applications. |
| Web perspective | The perspective that combines views and editors that assist in Web application development. |

Review questions

1. Explain the request/response mechanism of HTTP.

   In HTTP, the client makes a request to the server, and the server receives the request, determines whether and how it can be fulfilled, and creates an appropriate response, which is sent back to the client.

2. What is a URL? Give an example of a URL and name its five distinct parts.

   A URL (Uniform Resource Locator) is the address of a file (resource) accessible on the Internet. An example of a URL is *http://www.ibm.com:8080/index.html?action=open.*

   This URL has five distinct parts:

   a. Protocol: *http*

   b. Target server: *www.ibm.com*

   c. Port number (optional): *8080*

   d. Desired document: *index.html*

   e. Query string (optional):

3. What are the contents of the request header?

   Request headers are made up of a field name and its associated value. Some common header fields are User-agent, Referer, and From.

4. What are the contents of the HTTP response?

   The response is made up of several components:

   a. Status line

   b. Headers

   c. Message body

5. Explain the flow of request/response using the HTTP GET method.

   The flow of request/response using the GET method includes the following steps:

   a. A client requests a page by entering a URL in a browser. This generates a GET request.

   b. The request header is built by the browser and sent to the Web server.

   c. The Web server examines the request and determines whether it can satisfy request.

   d. The Web server then creates a response and includes the document in the body of the response.

   e. The response is then sent back to the client.

6. How is the HTML document returned to the client?

   The HTML document requested by the client is contained in the message body of the response.

7. What tools can be used to design and develop HTML pages?

   Since HTML documents are text documents, any text editor can be used. There are also specialized WYSIWYG (what you see is what you get) editors, such as WebSphere Studio, that simplify the design of HTML documents.

8. How can you add JavaScript or JSP code snippets to your HTML document?

   You can add JavaScript or JSP code snippets to your HTML document using the library view in WebSphere Studio's Web perspective.

9. What view can I use to modify properties of a table?

   The Attributes view can be used to modify HTML tag properties.

10. How can you view the Cascading Style Sheets (CSS) available?

   You can view the style sheets available by selecting the Style sheet option in the Gallery view.

Chapter 7: Introduction to servlets

Key terms

servlet	A a server-side Java component that executes within a J2EE Web Container.
J2EE	Java 2, Enterprise Edition, is a version of the Java platform designed for the mainframe-scale computing typical of large enterprises.
Web Archive (WAR) file	A Java archive (JAR) file containing all of the files in a Web application.
WebSphere Application Server	A high-performance and extremely scalable transaction engine for dynamic e-business applications.
Enterprise Archive (EAR) file	A JAR file that contains all the Web modules that collectively perform as a single entity in a J2EE Enterprise Application.
Application Deployment Descriptor	A configuration file that is used to describe the contents of a Web archive file and provide information on how the application should be deployed.
EJB (Enterprise JavaBean)	A JavaBean that runs inside an EJB server and is used to implement the business logic in enterprise applications.
lifecycle	The sequence of stages that a servlet goes through from initialization to execution to removal.

Review questions

1. When is a servlet object created?

   It is created either at server startup (if preload is selected) or upon first request.

2. What is the sequence for initialization of a servlet?

   Create servlet, create ServletConfig object, invoke init method.

3. What is the role of the methods doGet() and doPost() defined in javax.servlet.http.HttpServlet?

   These are specialized service handlers that get called only when the incoming request *method* matches, e.g., if the request method is POST; then doPost() gets called to handle the request.

4. Where will you find the web.xml file within a .war file?

The web.xml file is located in the WEB-INF folder.

5. What does a URL mapping for a servlet accomplish?

A servlet's URL mapping establishes a way to address or invoke the servlet from a browser. There may be more than one URL mapping for a given servlet.

6. Where are initialization parameters for servlets defined?

Initialization parameters are defined in the Web deployment descriptor using the <init-param>, <param-name>, <param-value> tags.

7. In what method does a servlet typically read and process initialization parameters?

Initialization parameter are typically read and processed in the init() method.

8. What does the getWriter() method on the javax.servlet.http.HttpServlet do?

The getWriter() method returns a PrintWriter accessing the HTTP response stream (body).

9. What is the default behavior of doGet() for a servlet?

For each of the HttpServlet's do*XXX*() methods, the default behavior is to return an error status code indicating that this resource does not handle the particular *method*. So doGet() would say that GET is not supported on this resource.

10. What is the easiest way to test a servlet within WebSphere Studio?

Select the servlet from the J2EE Navigator view; then, from the context menu, select Run on Server or Debug on Server.

Chapter 8: Handling HTTP requests

Key terms

HTTP headers	Parts of an HTTP request sent from the client that provide information to the server through fields.
form bean	A special type of value bean that transmits form parameter data.
value bean	An object that is used to communicate data between application layers.
JavaScript	A scripting language used in Web site development to perform client-side processing.

Review questions

1. Under what circumstances will a servlet receive an IllegalStateException when accessing a method of the HttpServletRequest interface?

   If a servlet is currently processing input in any one of the two modes (stream- and form-based parameters) and an attempt is made to request an object in the other mode, the servlet will receive an IllegalStateException error.

2. What method should you use to retrieve HTTP cookies delivered by the browser?

   Answer: getCookies().

3. JavaScript should be used to apply business rules to input values. True or false?

   False. JavaScript should be used only to perform simple validation.

4. The TCP/IP monitor server can be used to observe both the HTTP request stream and the response stream. True or false?

   True.

5. A form bean is used to encapsulate an HTML form layout. True or false?

   False.

6. Explain what the Extract Method refactoring tool accomplishes.

   The Extract Method refactoring tool extracts code from a program and converts it into a method.

7. Why do you want to create a JavaBean that encapsulates request parameter values?

   You want to use a JavaBean to encapsulate request values for the following reasons:

   a. These beans can be then passed on to other business objects.

   b. It is easy to create a factory class to map the input parameters to a bean.

8. Under what circumstances would you want or need to access the request stream as either a ServletInputStream or a BufferedReader?

   When the HTTP request needs to be processed as a binary or character stream.

9. Why do some values of the HttpServletRequest object not show up immediately in the Variables view of the debugger?

   It is due to a feature called "lazy instantiation" in WebSphere Studio.

10. List what the getParameterValues() method returns.

    ◆ **An enumeration of the values of the named request parameter**

    ◆ **A map of parameters of this request**

    ◆ **An enumeration of all header names**

    ◆ **A port number**

Chapter 9: Case study

This chapter contains no key terms and no review questions.

Chapter 10: Application state with servlets

Key terms

HttpSession	A Java class that is used to maintain application state on the server side. The HttpSession object is provided by the HttpSession API.
HTTP cookie	A small text file that is stored on the client to store state information.
application state	Information about the current status of the application.
thread-safe	Capable of being called from multiple programming threads without causing unwanted interaction between the threads.

Review questions

1. When using HttpSessions, where is the application state (session) stored? On the browser or Application Server?

   When HttpSessions are used, the application state is stored on the Application Server.

2. Why can't application state be stored directly within the servlets themselves?

   Servlets are multi-threaded. As such, servlets need to be written in a thread-safe manner, and the most basic approach to enforce thread safety is to make the servlets stateless.

3. The HttpSession object manages a collection of _____ pairs.

   Answer: name, value

4. For the WebSphere Web Container, the session ID is identified by the cookie or parameter name of _____.

   Answer: JSESSIONID

5. When working with HttpSessions, be sure that all objects on the session are _____.

   Answer: Serializable

6. Which of the following is (are) true regarding servlets?
   a. They are multi-threaded.
   b. They are stateless.
   c. They are stateful.
   d. They are read-write.

   Answer: a and b

7. What are the different ways to maintain state in a Web application?
   a. Cookies
   b. Hidden form fields
   c. HttpSessions
   d. Application Server console

   Answer: a, b, and c

8. Which of the following HttpSession methods do *not* manipulate individual state?
   a. Object getAttribute(String)
   b. Enumeration getAttributesNames()
   c. HttpSession getSession()
   d. Void setAttribute(String)

   Answer: c

9. The creation and management of session objects is provided by the
   a. WebSphere Studio
   b. Servlet
   c. Web Container
   d. JSP

   Answer: c

10. Which of the following methods can be used to invalidate sessions?
    a. invalidate()
    b. cleanSession()
    c. setMaxInactiveInterval()
    d. cleanup()

    Answer: a and c

Chapter 11: Model-View-Controller basics

Key terms

Model-View-Controller	The name of a methodology or design pattern for successfully and efficiently relating the user interface to underlying data models.
application layers	The different components of an application that perform different tasks as part of the MVC architecture.
Domain object	An objects that is used to store information coming from a client.
form bean	A bean that is used to manage input form parameters.
value bean	An object that provides the raw data for display.
state marker	An object that represents a logical application state.

Review questions

1. What is the difference between using the HttpServletRequest object as a scope for sharing object references between two servlets and using the HttpSession object for the same purpose?

   The main difference of using the HttpSession as a scope object for managing shared object references is the default lifetime of the corresponding reference. If data is needed only to complete the current HTTP request, any object reference to that data, if stored on the HttpSession, will remain available until that reference is explicitly removed from the session.

2. The RequestDispatcher interface supports what two mechanisms for delegation to other Web resources?

   Answer: include() and forward()

3. What is the role of the controller application layer?

   The controller layer consists of components that
   a. interpret an incoming request,
   b. extract any input parameters, and
   c. select and delegate appropriate components to carry out the operation.

4. What is the role of the model application layer?

   The model layer contains the business logic components of the application.

5. What is the role of the view application layer?

   The view layer consists of user interface components.

6. The _____ layer encapsulates your business logic components.

   Answer: model

7. The _____ acts as a traffic cop.

   Answer: controller

8. The state of an application can be interrogated by retrieving data from _____.

   Answer: HttpSession

9. The objects that provide the raw display data are called _____.

   Answer: value beans

10. A RequestDispatcher is obtained from a _____ object.

    Answer: ServletContext

Chapter 12: Introduction to JavaServer Pages

Key terms

JavaServer Pages	A server-side scripting technology designed to provide the ease of development of Web pages along with the flexibility and expressiveness of servlets.
XML	A markup language that was designed to describe data and focus on what data is.
scriptlets	A scripting element of a JSP page that allows insertion of Java code fragments into the JSP source.
expressions	A scripting element that is used to display content to the output stream.
page compilation	The process of converting a JSP page to a servlet.

Review questions

1. What is JavaServer Pages technology?

   JavaServer Pages is a server-side scripting technology designed to provide the ease of development (via Web page design tools) of Web pages along with the flexibility and expressiveness of servlets.

2. List the three categories of tags in JSP.

   Answer: directives, scripting elements, and actions

3. What are the three directives in the JSP 1.2 Specification? Provide an example of a JSP directive.

   The three directives are *include, taglib,* and *page*. An example of a directive: <%@ include file="hello.html" %>

4. Explain the use of the page directive. List a few attributes of the page directive.

   The page directive has a large number of attributes that provide direction to the translator about various characteristics to be associated with the generated class. Some attributes are language, extends, and import.

5. List three flavors of scripting elements.

    ◆ **Declarations**

    ◆ **Scriptlets**

    ◆ **Expressions**

6. How do you publish a JSP file in WebSphere Studio?

    Selecting the JSP file in either the J2EE Navigator or Navigator view and then selecting either Run on Server or Debug on Server will publish the enclosing Web project to its associated test server, start the server if necessary in the corresponding mode (debug or not), and finally issue the URL to a Web browser.

7. What is the syntax for using a scriptlet in a JSP file?

    The syntax for writing a scriptlet in JSP is *<% some Java code %>*

8. What is page compilation?

    JSP is really just an alternative source model for building servlets. The runtime manifestation of a JSP is a servlet. Page compilation is the process by which this servlet is automatically generated.

9. Which of the following scripting elements is used to define class-level members?
    a. Scriptlets
    b. Expressions
    c. Declarations
    d. Actions

    Answer: c

10. Which of the following does the <jsp:useBean> action tag allow?
    a. Runtime inclusion of a resource available in the same Web component into the current response stream
    b. Association of an instance of a Java object defined within a given scope and available with a given ID, with a declared scripting variable
    c. Initialization of a bean
    d. Obtaining a value from a bean

    Answer: b

Chapter 13: Considerations for building robust Web applications

Key terms

error page	A page that is executed in your application to display details about exceptions that occurred in your application.
Exceptions	An event that occurs during the execution of a program that disrupts the normal flow of instructions.
Struts	A framework for developing robust Web applications using standard technologies such as servlets, JavaBeans, and XML.
log4j	A package provided by the Apache Jakarta Project to facilitate logging in your Web applications.

Review questions

1. What are the basic elements of a Web application?

   The basic elements of a Web application are controller, application state, user input, application response, and application behavior.

2. A controller component in a Web application is implemented using which Java technology?

   Answer: Servlet

3. What are the exception design issues facing developers of Web applications?

   Some design issues are
   a. How to handle an improperly configured environment
   b. Bad or incomplete input data
   c. Inappropriate state transition
   d. Model failures or exceptions

4. What are the different levels at which input validation can take place?

   Input validation can take place at
   a. browser level
   b. FormBean level

5. How is a data validation exception handled?

   A data validation exception is usually handled by redisplaying the input page pre-populated with the data previously entered and an additional error message indicating the problem.

6. What is the base class in the servlet API for exception handling?

   Answer: ServletException

7. What are the two design patterns that facilitate precondition checking?

   Answer: state pattern and action pattern

8. Business rules validation should only be performed in the _____ layer.

   Answer: model

9. The _____ provides the most robust way to handle both expected and unexpected errors within your applications.

   Answer: Java Exception mechanism

10. The application-specific errors that your application's model layer will generate will need to be handled by your _____.

    Answer: controller

Chapter 14: JSP tag libraries

Key terms

custom actions	Java classes that perform particular business operations and are declared in tag libraries so that they can be invoked from JSP pages in the same way as the tags built into JSP. Also known as custom tags, custom actions, extend JavaServer Pages' ability to divide development responsibilities between back-end business component developers and front-end presentation designers. Custom tags enable component developers to encapsulate complex business functionality into XML-like tags that are as simple to use for a page designer as HTML's BODY tag.

tag library	A collection of custom tags. JSP tag libraries define declarative, modular functionality that can be reused by any JSP page. Tag libraries reduce the necessity to embed large amounts of Java code in JSP pages by moving the functionality provided by the tags into tag implementation classes.
JSTL	The JSP Standard Tag Library. JSTL encapsulates, as simple tags, core functionality common to many Web applications. JSTL has support for common structural tasks such as iteration and conditionals, tags for manipulating XML documents, internationalization tags, and SQL tags.

Review questions

1. What is the main motivation behind JSP tag libraries?

   The main motivation was to provide Web designers the ability to include dynamic content in their JSPs without requiring knowledge of Java.

2. What is JSTL?

   JSTL is the JavaServer Pages Standard Tag Library. JSTL provides functionality for most actions required by the Page Designer role.

3. How do you indicate that the JSTL core tag library will be used in a JSP?

   Syntax: <%@ taglib uri="http://java.sun.com/jstl/core" prefix="c" %>

4. What are the four major areas of functionality in JSTL?

   The four major areas are
   a. General Purpose
   b. Internationalization
   c. Relational database access
   d. XML-processing actions

5. What are the two versions of each of the libraries in JSTL?

   There are two versions of each of the libraries in JSTL:
   a. An Expression Language (EL)
   b. Run time version (RT)

6. What are the steps involved in creating your own tag library?

Creating your own custom action tags involves
a. developing the tag handler (the code that performs the operation), and
b. declaring the tag in the tag library descriptor (TLD file).

7. Which of the following tag libraries are available with WebSphere Studio?
   a. Mail
   b. Input/Ouput
   c. Response Object
   d. Application Object

   Answer: a, c, and d

8. Where can you add a tag library definition to a Web project in WebSphere Studio?
   a. Project properties under Web Properties
   b. During the Create New Project wizard
   c. Tag menu
   d. Outline view

   Answer: b

9. A custom tag handler usually implements which interface?
   a. Tag
   b. Taghandle
   c. BodyTag
   d. SampleTag

   Answer: a or c

Chapter 15: Accessing databases with JDBC

Key terms

JDBC	Java Database Connectivity, an application program interface (API) specification for connecting programs written in Java to the data in commonly used databases.
JDBC Driver	A piece of software provided by database (DB) vendors to interact with their databases. DB-neutral drivers are also available.

driver manager	A class that is part of the java.sql package that is used to create and manage database connections.
connection	A connection object is used to store a connection (session) with a specific database. SQL statements are executed and results are returned within the context of a connection.
statement	The object used for executing a static SQL statement and returning the results it produces.
ResultSet	An object that contains a table of data representing a database result set, which is usually generated by executing a statement that queries the database.
cursor	A mechanism used to navigate through records returned by an SQL query.
data broker	The layer in the application that provides functionality for database access.
JNDI	The Java Naming and Directory Interface (JNDI) is a standard extension to the Java platform, providing Java technology-enabled applications with a unified interface to multiple naming and directory services in the enterprise.
InitialContext	A class that is the starting context for performing naming operations.
DataSource	An object that represents a physical data source and serves as a factory for connections to it.

Review questions

1. Which are the two packages containing the JDBC APIs?

   Answer: java.sql (Core API) and javax.sql (Extension API)

2. What's the difference between the packages containing the JDBC APIs?

   The Core JDBC 2.0 API allows you to perform basic database operations. The extension API extends the Core API and provides advanced functionality such as connection pooling.

3. When should JDBC drivers be loaded?

   Loading JDBC drivers should be the first step you perform when trying to interact with databases (constructors or static initializers).

4. What is the format of the URL required to obtain a database connection?

   The URL format is dependent on the driver being used. In most cases it will be a String that is a combination of database name, user ID, and password.

5. Name at least two advantages of using a DataSource connection versus a regular connection obtained directly from the JDBC Driver.

   a. It minimizes connection overhead.

   b. It spreads connection cost out over repeated uses.

6. Why is it considered better to abstract the database layer of an application?

   It is considered better to abstract the database layer because layering greatly improves reliability, scalability, and maintainability of code.

7. What must be done when a connection is no longer needed?

   A connection must be closed when it is no longer needed.

8. The DataTruncation Exception extends
   a. SQLException
   b. SQLData
   c. SQLWarning
   d. SQLError

   Answer: c

9. Which of the following is not a transaction control method in JDBC?
   a. getAutoCommit()
   b. createTransaction()
   c. commit()
   d. rollback()

   Answer: b

10. In JDBC which object is used to execute a query?
    a. Statement
    b. query
    c. ResultSet
    d. connection

    Answer: a

Chapter 16: Deploying applications

Key terms

deployment	The task of transferring a development application onto an application server for production.
remote server	An application server that is not physically located on the same machine is known as remote server.
wsadmin	A command line tool that can be used to administer WebSphere Application Server.

Review questions

1. What types of files are exported in preparing an application to be deployed?

   Answer: Enterprise Archive (EAR) files, which can contain a combination of Web Archive (WAR), EJB JAR, and application client and utility JAR files

2. True or False: A server running WebSphere Application Server must be located on a different machine than where WebSphere Studio is installed.

   Answer: False

3. Where can output produced by an application using System.out.println() statements be found on a remote server?

   It can be found in the SystemOut.log file.

4. WebSphere Application Server - Express supports J2EE applications that contain
   a. HTML pages
   b. EJBs
   c. JSP pages
   d. servlets

   Answer: a, c, and d

5. The command line administration tool provided with WebSphere Application Server Express is
   a. admin
   b. wadmin
   c. wsadmin
   d. studio

   Answer: c

6. Which of the following can be deployed to an application server?

   a. EAR

   b. WAR + EJB JARs

   c. JavaScript objects

   d. CSS

   Answer: a and b

7. EAR and WAR files can be exported out of WebSphere Studio by selecting _____.

   Answer: File → Export

8. Configuration changes made by the command line administration tool result in changes in one or more _____ files.

   Answer: XML

9. Configuration of WebSphere Application Server - Express is done using _____

   Answer: WebSphere Studio

10. The two modes in which you can use the command line administration tool are _____ and _____.

    Answer: Interactive and using scripts

Index

A

Action pattern, 299
Actions, 264–265
Apache Struts framework, 295
Application Assembly Tool (AAT)
  function of, 356
Application state
  action pattern, 299
  controller layer and, 248
  interrogation of, 249
  managing in Web applications, 228–229
  session lifetime and, 234–235
  state marker, 249
  state pattern, 299
  using HttpSession interface, 229–233
  writing stateless servlets, 228

B

Breakpoints
  conditional, 98–101
  line, 79–82
  Method, 105–**106**
  setting in JavaServer Pages, **275–276**
  single-stepping and, 87
  using Breakpoints view, **81**–82
  Watchpoints, 104–105

C

Callable statements, 330
Cascading Style Sheet (CSS), 151–152

C (continued)

Certification test objectives, 6–7
Classloaders, 359
  configuring policies, 360
Classpaths, 359–360
Cloudscape, 217
Conditional breakpoints
  enabling hit count, 98–**99**
  Java Exception, 101–104
  setting the logic condition, **100**–101
Controller layer
  defined, 248
  form beans and, 248

D

Database brokers, 337
Data Definition Language (DDL) file
  creating, 343–344
  defined, 343
Data perspective
  Data Definition view, 338, 342
  DB Output view, 339
  DB Servers view, 338, 341, 342
  opening, 338
DataTruncation exceptions, 335, 336
DDL file. *See* Data Definition Language
  (DDL) file
Debugging practices
  changing variable values, 91
  checking variable values, 90 (*See also*
  Variables view)

Note: Boldface numbers indicate illustrations.

Debugging practices (*Continued*)
  displaying output in Console view, **77**
  evaluating a Java expression, **95**–96
  fixing code with hot code replace, 110–113
  implementing the toString() method, 77
  inspecting variables, 93–94
  Java Exception breakpoints, 101–104
  JavaServer Pages and, 274–276
  managing processes and threads, 89
  Method breakpoints, 105–**106**
  Scrapbook pages, 107–110
  setting hit count, 98–**99**
  setting line breakpoints, 79–82
  single-stepping through code, 87–88
  step filtering, 88–**89**
  using logic condition breakpoints,
    100–101
  using print statements, 76
  Watchpoints, 104–105
Debug perspective, 76
  Breakpoints view, **81**
  Debug view, **84**
  description of, 82–84
  Display view, **86**–87 (*See also* Display
    view)
  Editor view, **85**–86
  Outline view, **85**
  Pause function, 89
  removing views, 87
  Resume function, 89
  Run to Line action, 89–90
  Servers view, 84
  Terminate function, 89
Declarations
  defined for JavaServer Pages, 261–262
Deployment Descriptor Editor. *See* Web
    Deployment Descriptor editor
Display view, **86**–87
  evaluating a Java expression, **95**–96
Document Type Definition (DTD), 137
doGet() method, 178. *See also* GET method
doPost() method, 178. *See also* POST method

E

EAR files. *See* Enterprise archive (EAR)
    files
EAR project. *See* J2EE Enterprise Applica-
    tion project
Eclipse, 23–24
  architecture, **25**
  JDT and, 26–27 (*See also* Java Develop-
    ment Tools [JDT])
  Platform, 24–25
  Plug-in Development Environment (PDE),
    28
  products built on, 28
  tools built for, 32
  websites for, 32
  Workbench, 25–26
Enterprise archive (EAR) files
  contents of, 180
Error handling
  precondition check, 298
  validating data with JavaScript, 286,
    287–289
  validating FormBeans, 286–287
Explicit scripting objects, 262
Expressions, 263–**264**
Expressions view, 93–95

F

Form beans, 196. *See also* Forms, encapsu-
    lating data with JavaBeans
  creating, 214
  validating input data, 286–287,
    290–295
Forms
  encapsulating data with JavaBeans,
    196–201
  <FORM> tag, 140, 142
  validating input data with JavaScript,
    201–202, 286, **287**–289
  validating input data with servlets,
    290–294
  widgets for, 140

G

GET method, 129
  request and response interaction, **132**
Getters, 191
Go to File for Breakpoint button, 103

H

Hot code replace, 110–113
HTTP. *See* HyperText Transfer Protocol
  (HTTP)
HTTP requests, 189
  components of, 128
  debugging input streams, 194–195
  encapsulating with JavaBeans, 196–201
  GET method, 129
  headers, 129–130
  HttpServletRequest interface, 191–193,
    194
  message stream contents, 190–**191**
  POST method, 129
  reading input streams, 194
  server responses to GET, **132**
  server responses to POST, 132–**133**
  servlet controllers and, 248–249
  URLs and, 128
  validating with JavaScript, 201
HTTP responses
  components of, 130
  GET requests and, **132**
  headers, 131
  message body, 132
  POST requests and, 132–**133**
  status line, 130–131
HttpServletRequest interface, 191–193
  getters for, 192
  lazy instantiation, 194
  request scope and, 265
  sharing object references, 251
HttpSession interface, 229–233
  configuration settings for, 235
  controlling session size, 234
  determining session lifetime, 234

  disadvantage of using as scope object, 251
  invalidation of expected sessions, 235
  Serializable objects and, 235
  session persistence and, 235
  session scope and, 265
  storing application state, 234–235
HyperText Markup Language (HTML)
  description of, 133
  disadvantages of creating with text editors,
    133–134
  <FORM> tag, 140–142
  <LINK> tag, **152**
  using tags, 136–139
  using WebSphere Studio Page Designer
    (*See* Page Designer)
  website resource, 133
HyperText Transfer Protocol (HTTP)
  description of, 128
  GET method, 129
  HttpServletRequest interface, 191–193,
    194
  HttpSession interface, 229–233
  interaction of requests and responses,
    132–133
  POST method, 129
  producing response streams, 178
  requests (*See* HTTP requests)
  responses (*See* HTTP responses)
  Secure Sockets Layer (SSL) and, 128
  status line, 130–131
  website resource, 127

I

IBM Agent Controller, 14
IBM Certification tests
  website for, 2
IDE. *See* Integrated Development Environment (IDE)
Implicit scripting objects, 262
include directive, 260
Initialization parameters
  accessing in servlets, **185**

Note: Boldface numbers indicate illustrations.

Initialization parameters (*Continued*)
  displaying, 186
  setting in servlets, 183–**184**
Integrated Development Environment
      (IDE), 2

J

Jacl. *See* Java Application Control language
      (Jacl)
Jakarta tag libraries, 303
JAR files. *See* Java Archive files
Java Application Control language (Jacl)
Java Archive (JAR) files
  utility JAR files, 361
JavaBeans
  encapsulating request parameters,
      196–201
  form beans and, 196
  value beans and, 196
Java Database Connectivity (JDBC)
  connecting to databases, 340–341
  connection pooling, 331–332
  controlling transactions, 336
  function of, 327
  managing with JNDI, 332, 333–334
  mapping data types, 334–335
  processing errors, 335–336
  using database brokers, 337
  version 2.0 Core API, 328–331
  version 2.0 Standard Extension API, 331
Java Development Tools (JDT)
  Core, 26
  Debug, 27
  user interface (UI), 26–27
Java editor
  displaying errors, **55–57**
  functions of editor view, 47–49
  functions of outline view, 51–**54**
  using code assist, **49–51**
Java Exception breakpoints, 101–104
  Caught option, 103
  Uncaught option, 103

Java Exception mechanism, 296
Java Management Extensions (JMX) Archi-
      tecture, 358
Java Naming and Directory Interface
      (JNDI), 332, 333–334
Java perspective, 30, **31**, 64
  creating Scrapbook pages, **107**–110
  using, **41**–42
Java Platform 2, Enterprise Edition. *See*
      J2EE
Java programs
  changing variable values, 91
  checking variable values, 90 (*See also*
      Variables view)
  compatibility with SQL, 334–335
  debugging, 77–79
  debugging with Scrapbook pages,
      107, 110
  evaluating a Java expression, **95**–96
  inspecting variables, 93–94
  Method breakpoints and, 105–**106**
  running in WebSphere Studio, 62–64
  setting conditional breakpoints, 98–101
  setting line breakpoints in, 79–82
  step filtering, 88–**89**
  stepping through, 87–88
  using hot code replace, 110–113
  using Java Exception breakpoints,
      101–104
Java projects
  compiler and, 54
  creating packages, 42–**43**
  creating types, 44
  creating with WebSphere Studio,
      38–40
  error messages, **55–57**
  New Java Class wizard, **44**–46
  New Java Interface wizard, **46**–47
  using Java editor (*See* Java editor)
  using Java perspective, **41**–42
JavaScript, validating form data with,
      201–202, 286, **287**–289

JavaServer Pages (JSPs)
  actions, 264–265
  building in Page Designer,
    271–273
  building servlets, 258
  compilation validator, 274
  creating, **266–271**
  declarations, 261–262
  debugging, 275–276
  directive syntax, 259
  document structure, **258**
  editing in Page Designer, 274
  explicit scripting objects, 262
  expressions, 263–**264**
  function of, 258
  implicit scripting objects, 262
  include directive, 260
  _jspService() method, 259
  <jsp:useBean> tag, 265
  page compilation, 258–259
  page directive, 260
  scriptlets, **263**
  taglib directive, 260
  tag libraries (*See* JSP tag libraries)
  typeSpec attribute set, 265–266
  URL Mappings for, 182–183
  Web components of, 182
Java virtual machine (JVM)
  classloaders and, 359
  classpaths and, 359–360
  JDT Debug and, 27
JDBC. *See* Java Database Connectivity
    (JDBC)
JDT. *See* Java Development Tools
    (JDT)
JMX Architecture. *See* Java Management
    Extensions (JMX) Architecture
JNDI. *See* Java Naming and Directory
    Interface (JNDI)
JSP. *See* JavaServer Pages (JSPs)
_jspService() method, 259
  explicit scripting objects, 262

  implicit scripting objects, 262
JSP Standard Tag Library (JSTL),
    303
  defining in JSP pages, 304
  expression language (EL) versions,
    304
  runtime (RT) versions, 305
  website for, 305
JSP tag libraries
  creating custom action tags, 312
  creating custom tag libraries, 312
  defining, 306–308
  Jakarta tag libraries, 303
  reasons for using, 302
  selecting, **309**
  standard tag library (JSTL), 303–305
  <taglib> element and, 308
  using custom tags, 310
<jsp:useBean> tag, 265, 266, 277
JSTL. *See* JSP Standard Tag Library
    (JSTL)
J2EE
  Web applications and, 3–4
J2EE Enterprise Application project
  associating with a Web project,
    167–169
  modules of, 180
  packaging for, 179–180
JVM. *See* Java virtual machine (JVM)

L
Line breakpoints, 79–82
<LINK> tag, **152**

M
Management beans (MBeans), 358
Mapper classes, 219
Method breakpoints, 105–**106**
Model layer
  defined, 248
  domain objects and, 248
  validating business rules in, 295

Model-View-Controller (MVC) design
   principle, 285
   controller layer, 248, 285–286
   model layer, 248, 295
   view layer, 247, 285–286

N

New Java Class wizard, **44**–46
New Java Interface wizard, **46**–47
New JSP File wizard, **266–271**
New Servlet wizard, **170–172**

P

Package Explorer, 41–42
   comparing to Outline view, 53
   error indication, **56**
   running Java programs, 62
Page compilation, 258–259
page directive
   attributes of, 260–261
Page Designer
   Attributes view, **147**
   building JSP pages, 271–273
   Cascading Style Sheets and,
     151–152
   changing style sheets, 161–162
   Colors view, 150–**151**
   Design view, 135, **136**
   editing JSP pages, 274
   formatting a table, 160–161
   functions of, 143
   Gallery view, 145
   inserting a heading, 159–160
   inserting a link, **160**
   inserting scriptlets, 272–273
   Library view, **145**–146
   Links view, **148**
   Outline view, **147**
   Preview view, **135**
   Source view, 135
   Styles view, **150**
   Thumbnail view, 145, 148–**149**

Pause function, 89
POST method, 129
   request and response interaction,
     132–**133**
Precondition check, 298
Prepared statements, 330

R

RequestDispatcher interface, 250
Resume function, 89
Run to Line action, 89–90

S

Schemas, 341
Scrapbook pages, 107–110
Scriptlets, **263**
   inserting with Page Designer, 272–273
Secure Sockets Layer (SSL), 128
ServletContext interface, 250
Servlets
   accessing initialization parameters, **185**
   acting as controllers for HTTP requests,
     248–249
   catching exceptions, 296
   creating, **170–172**
   defined, 165
   determining lifecycles of, 173–174
   HTTP response streams and, 178
   JavaServer Pages and, 258
   lifecycle of, 166–167
   overriding methods, **173–174**
   passing object references between, 251
   populating FormBeans, 290
   RequestDispatcher interface, 250
   ServletContext interface, 250
   setting initialization parameters, 183–**184**
   testing lifecycles of, 174–178
   URL Mappings for, 182–183
   using HttpSession interface with, 230–233
   validating form data, 292–294
   Web components of, 182
   writing thread-safe servlets, 228

ServletException class, 296
SessionContext interface, 265
Show Breakpoints Supported by Selected
    Target button, 103
Silent warnings, 336
SQL. *See* Structured Query Language (SQL)
SQLException, 335
SQLWarning exceptions, 335, 336
SSL. *See* Secure Sockets Layer (SSL), 128
State marker
    defined, 249
State pattern, 299
Structured Query Language (SQL)
    callable statements, 330
    compatibility with Java, 334–335
    prepared statements, 330

T
Tag handlers, 312
Tag library descriptor (TLD) file, 312
taglib directive, 260
Tcl. *See* Tool Control Language (Tcl)
TCP/IP monitoring server
    setting up, 211
Terminate function, 89
Tool Control Language (Tcl)
Transactions
    controlling with JDBC, 336–337
    defined, 336
typeSpec attribute set, 265–266

U
Unit of work (UoW), 336
Universal Resource Locator (URL), 128
URL. *See* Universal Resource Locator
    (URL)
Utility JAR files, 361

V
Value beans, 196, 219, 249
    class diagrams for, **220**
Variables view

changing variable values, 91
checking variable values, 90
displaying information, 92–93
inspecting variables, 94
View layer, 247

W
WAR files. *See* Web archive (WAR) files
Watchpoints, 104–105
Web applications
    assembling, 356
    defined, 3
    deploying, 356
    layers of, 247–248
    managing application state, 228–233
    resolving runtime references, 361
Web archive (WAR) files
    dependence on utility JAR files, 361
    determining classloader policy settings,
        360
    contents of, 180
Web Container
    function of, 166
Web Deployment Descriptor editor
    Environment tab, 186
    Filters tab, 186
    Listeners tab, 186
    Overview tab, **181**
    Pages tab, 186
    Parameters tab, 186
    References tab, 186
    Security tab, 186
    setting error pages, **297**
    Source tab, 181
Web projects
    associating with Enterprise Application
        project, 167–169
    creating a J2EE project, 167–170
    creating a static project, 153–**154**
WebSphere Application Server
    configuring classloader policies, 360
    differences from Express edition, 357–358

Note: Boldface numbers indicate illustrations.

WebSphere Application Server (*Continued*)
  wsadmin command line interface tool,
    358–359
WebSphere Application Server – Express
  adding data sources, **368–370**
  adding Enterprise Applications, 371
  configuring classloader policies, 360
  configuring the test environment,
    238–241
  creating remote server configurations,
    362–367
  creating the Test Environment Server,
    237–**238**
  installing, 11–12
  Linux versions supporting, 11
  restrictions of, 357–358
  running launchpad.exe, 12
  starting remote servers, 375–376
  starting the test environment, 241–242
  system requirements, 10–11
  testing applications on remote
    servers, 377
  using Installer, **15–22**
  verifying Agent Controller installation, 14
  verifying Application Server
    installation, 14
  verifying installation of directories, 13
  verifying Site Developer installation, 14
  Windows versions supporting, 11
  wsadmin command line interface tool,
    358–359
WebSphere Studio
  Application Developer, 29
  Application Developer, Integration Edi-
    tion, 29
  Asset Analyzer, 29
  Cascading Style Sheet (CSS) editor,
    151–152
  connecting to databases, 340–341
  creating HTML pages, **157–158**
  creating Java classes, **44**–46
  creating Java interfaces, **46**–47

creating JSP pages, **266–271**
creating J2EE Web projects (*See* Web
  projects: creating a J2EE project)
creating servlets, **170–172**
creating shortcuts to, 65–66
creating static Web projects (*See* Web
  projects: creating a static project)
creating Java projects, **38–40** (*See also*
  Java projects)
Data perspective, 338–**339** (*See also* Data
  perspective)
debugging (*See* Debug perspective)
defining tag libraries, 306–308
Device Developer, 28
differences between editions, 29
displaying errors in Java projects, 55–57
Enterprise Developer, 29
exporting a Java Archive file, 70–72
functions of Local History, 57–62
Homepage Builder, 28
HTML editor (*See* Page Designer)
Integrated Development Environment
  (IDE), 2
Java editor (*See* Java editor)
Java perspective, **41**–42
JSP Compilation validator, 274
methods for starting, 67
perspectives, 30–32
product editions, 2
role-based development, 30
running Java programs in, 62–64
Server perspective, 175
Site Developer, 29
Web perspective, **144**
Workbench (*See* WebSphere Workbench)
working with perspectives, 36–38
WebSphere Workbench
  compare function, 57, **59**–60
  configuring Local History, 61–**62**
  Eclipse and, 2
  replace function, 57, 59–**60**
  restore function, 57, 60–**61**

web.xml file
  editors for opening,
    180–181
  functions of, 180
  location of, 180
  specifying Web components with,
    182

Wizards,
  New Java Class, **44**–46
  New Java Interface, **46**–47
  New JSP File, **266–271**
  New Servlet, **170–172**
wsadmin command line interface tool,
  358–359

Note: Boldface numbers indicate illustrations.